Moon in Full

A MODERN-DAY COMING-OF-AGE STORY

Marpheen Chann

ISLANDPORT PRESS

ISLANDPORT PRESS

Islandport Press
P.O. Box 10
Yarmouth, Maine 04096
www.islandportpress.com
info@islandportpress.com

All photographs, unless otherwise noted, courtesy of Marpheen Chann
Author cover image by Dave Dostie

Print ISBN: 978-1-952143-35-9
Ebook ISBN: 978-1-952143-54-0
Library of Congress Control Number: 2021946866

Printed in the United States of America

Dean L. Lunt, Editor-in-Chief | Publisher
Genevieve A. Morgan, Senior Editor
Piper K. Wilber, Assistant Editor
Trevor Roberson, Book Designer

Moon in Full

A MODERN-DAY COMING-OF-AGE STORY

Also from Islandport Press

Dear Maine
Morgan Rielly and Reza Jalali

Take it Easy: Portland in the 1970s
John Duncan

The Ghosts of Walter Crockett
W. Edward Crockett

Whatever It Takes
May Davidson

Shoutin' into the Fog
Thomas Hanna

Hauling by Hand
Dean Lawrence Lunt

Available at www.islandportpress.com

To my nieces, nephews, and future generations;
To my birth mother and grandmother, who through
the pains of childbirth, genocide, trauma, and immigration,
made my story possible.

CONTENTS

● ◐ ◑ ◔ ○ ○

PROLOGUE

How did a boy born into a Cambodian refugee family, who was put in foster care, then adopted by a white, working-class evangelical family in rural Maine, get to this point—an out-and-proud, gay public figure in Maine?

I found myself thinking these thoughts as I lay in bed at two a.m. on Tuesday, June 8, 2021.

I had just tweeted and posted about winning the first at-large seat to the Portland Charter Commission after, finally, getting the election results from the city clerk's office. It was not only Election Day, but also my thirtieth birthday. I lay there, my body and back aching from months and months of campaigning, dropping my phone on my nightstand beside me, a wave of gratitude and optimism sweeping over me. Grateful for my family, friends, mentors, and people I have met throughout my thirty years on Earth.

I thought the same when, later that month, I walked past a pride flag hanging on the Governor's Mansion, the Blaine House, on my way to a Pride celebration hosted by EqualityMaine and Gov. Janet Mills in Augusta.

I was filled with gratitude for the village of people, throughout the years, who have helped me, loved me, and encouraged me to shoot for the moon. To dream big. To do hard things.

My life—the trials and tribulations of domestic violence, hunger, foster care, and navigating a complex and intersectional identity, among other things—is a tribute, a testament, not only to the possibility and power of an individual to overcome, but also to a community, like the one I've found in Maine, to come together and cheer for one of their own.

My last name is Chann. In Cambodian, this means "moon," or "moonlight." As I think back on these last three decades, I understand that the title of this book may seem premature. I know that in the fullness of time, there will still be a lot to learn and many challenges ahead, but this stopping point feels full enough right now for me to tell my story as I have lived it so far.

This book, my memoir, I dedicate to Maine, and to all the people I've encountered along the way, both named and unnamed.

I hope that in these pages you will find an opportunity to step into another's shoes. My shoes. To gain an understanding from my lived experiences—all the messiness of life and love, with all of my mistakes, triumphs, and lessons learned.

I hope you will walk away knowing that, like the moon, as you pass through all the phases of life, you are still on your way to becoming fully you.

—Marpheen Chann
Portland, Maine
March 2022

PART ONE

California, 1991

● ◗ ◖ ○ ○

I was born on June 8, 1991, at Dameron Hospital in Stockton, California, to an eighteen-year-old Cambodian refugee. Her name was Mum Chum. I don't have many photos from that time, but I imagine she had the same round face and full cheeks characteristic of many Cambodians. I imagine her eyes, big and dark brown, sheltered by black brows that arched in almost perfect crescents. I imagine her hair, thick and wavy, higher up on the peak above her forehead than it was on most people. But probably what I imagine most are her lips, large and a deep pinkish-brown.

She passed down most of her looks to me, save her eyes. The thick and wavy hair I'd grow up with and fuss over, her cheeks and round face, and her lips. I have big lips. I've always been proud of these lips. Many times, when I look in the mirror, I can almost see her face staring back at me.

My eyes and eyebrows and ears, though, I got from my dad, who wasn't in the picture much at all. He was a short man who, at the time, was probably already balding. He was part Cambodian and part Vietnamese. His eyes, unlike my mom's, were smaller and more almond-shaped. His eyebrows were on the thicker side and peaked a little as they headed toward the temples, before dropping off. His ears were long, resembling the ears of the people painted in the Buddha posters.

But when I look in the mirror, I don't see much of him. Probably because I don't have much memory or visual reference to go by.

I didn't learn until later in life that when I was born, my mother, who was just a teenager at the time, left me in the care of a Cambodian pastor and his family in San Diego. She had just been admitted into a mental hospital, but instead of leaving me with my maternal grandmother, their relationship shaped by the trauma they shared, I was left with Khandarith and Leap Hay, my godparents. My mother didn't exactly have the most pristine and peaceful life. With her childhood stripped from her during the Cambodian genocide, how could she be expected to raise children herself?

Most, if not all, of what I have learned about the Cambodian genocide has been through books like *First They Killed My Father* by Cambodian American author Loung Ung, the Netflix adaptation, and a lot of academic research and online articles. Survivors of the Cambodian genocide talk very little about that period and avoid answering questions from their grandchildren, often by changing the subject.

As many as two million Cambodians were systematically murdered by Pol Pot and the Khmer Rouge between April 1975 and January 1979. In just four years, one-quarter of Cambodia's population was wiped out through executions, forced labor, and starvation. To help put this in perspective, Maine's population is just under one and a half million people.

What hit home for me was that the Khmer Rouge persecuted and killed anyone who was believed to be an intellectual. This included doctors, lawyers, teachers, people who wore glasses, those who spoke foreign languages, and ethnic minorities. In other words, they would have killed me!

They based this on the idea that Cambodia had been corrupted by the influence of Vietnam and the capitalist West, and used American bombing campaigns in Cambodia during the Vietnam War effectively to drive home this point. Those who supported their idea of a self-sufficient Cambodia and agrarian society were considered "pure people," while those they murdered and persecuted were considered "impure."

But what they did went beyond just the murder of those who disagreed with them. They were intentional in tearing apart the very fabric of Cambodian society and culture. Many of their policies, like re-education schools and forced communal living, were designed to not only spread propaganda, but tear apart and destroy Cambodian ideas, values, and family structures. Families were forced to turn on each other, creating a legacy of mistrust and trauma that lives on to this very day.

My maternal grandmother talks very little about her experience living, if you can call it that, during this period. I always considered her short, because all of her sons were on the taller side. Despite this, I always knew her to be strong and fierce, the matriarch. The survivor. Her sons learned to both fear and love her despite her size. If they misbehaved, they were sure to feel the sting of a lightning-fast slap or a flick of a stick or her sandal. But even that didn't compare to her sharp tongue when she spoke angrily in Khmer. I have personally witnessed grown-ass men twice her size shrink and curl into prostrated balls before her as she humiliated them in Khmer.

Pardon my French, but she was the kind of woman who was not going to take shit from anyone—especially her husband or sons.

The little that she's said about the Khmer Rouge tells me just how much it still hurts, and how horrific and traumatic this period was for her and her fellow countrymen and -women. Before the

Khmer Rouge, she was a businesswoman, a member of one of the groups the Khmer Rouge did not like. When she was forcibly removed and relocated to the countryside, she would have been killed had it not been for a Khmer Rouge soldier or supervisor who vouched for her, saying she was not a business owner and that she was not Vietnamese (my family does have some Vietnamese blood, although not much).

Was I surprised to learn that my birth mother would leave me with a family at a Cambodian church? Yes and no. I was surprised the first time I heard about it. But not surprised that she felt there was no other choice.

I had grown accustomed to her being on the run. When I was a child, I didn't know the details of her past—but I saw it in the way she always tried to run from it. I could see it in the way, during the early years, that she would sometimes disappear and I would end up, again, with the pastor of that Cambodian church and his family (whom I now consider my godparents). I could see it in the desperate way she would try to find refuge in the men who exploited her fragile and broken heart. I could see it in the way she submitted to the authority of these men and stayed even when they beat and abused her.

That's the thing about untreated trauma: You get trapped in it, because it's all you know. To step outside of it can be just as scary and uncertain as the trauma itself.

There was one man she was married to for a short time, my sister Tanya's father, who lived in the state of Washington. We lived in a single-story house where you'd walk in to a combined living room and kitchen. To the right you'd enter a very, very small hallway the size of a closet. The bathroom was dead ahead, and to either side were bedrooms. Toward the back of the house was my bedroom, which was covered wall to wall with Buddha paintings and posters of all varieties, it seemed, pale blue and green. Most likely they thought it wouldn't bother me, more of a blessing really, but I'd wake up at night and be a little terrified of those eyes that seemed to stare at me.

Theravada Buddhism plays a large role in Cambodian culture, to the point where a large portion of the Khmer language is devoted to how to properly address and converse with monks. It also influences almost every part of Cambodian life, whether it's public life, education, economics, sports, or art. In short, Theravada Buddhists follow the teachings of the Buddha closely, and the belief that humans are in a constant cycle of reincarnation until they reach nirvana, or "Enlightenment." One reaches this point by accumulating merit through donations of money, food, goods, or labor to the temples. Many boys and young men spend short periods of time as monks.

The various poses and styles of paintings of the Buddha are less the creative license of the artist and more the depiction of the Buddha's journey to Enlightenment. The most familiar depiction of the Buddha is called *Vitkak*, or "contemplating" or "concentrating." This shows the Buddha sitting cross-legged with one palm on top of the other, facing upward. This is the Buddha in the state of contemplating, trying to understand and alleviate the suffering of all living things. The other stances and poses seen in paintings and statues depict the Buddha in other stages along the path to Enlightenment, including one where the Buddha has the right hand turned inward (or downward), in order to tap into the Earth's power to repel temptation. In another pose the Buddha is smiling and reclining on his right side. This depicts the Buddha at the end of his journey to Enlightenment, when he leaves behind his physical body. This conveys the idea that death is natural, or akin to sleep, and that the Buddha accepted this and was unafraid.

As a young child, I didn't know any of this. Religion and its meaning were foreign to me. For my mom and stepdad at the time, plastering the walls with Buddha paintings was to provide a bubble of Buddhas to keep me safe from the evils of the world.

Tanya's dad wasn't physically abusive that I can remember. But he was emotionally abusive and controlling of my mother. I was afraid of him because he always seemed angry, and made me feel as if I was a burden. His father, who was a grandfather of sorts for me during that time, tried to compensate. I was four when I did something that made Tanya's dad extremely angry, to the point where he actually hit me. Not hard, but he hit me nonetheless. The grandfather was irate and yelled at him, I remember, before taking my hand and giving me a warm bath. He sat beside the bathtub helping me wash and talking softly to me, washing away the pain and shock.

Afterward, I remember the grandfather taking me for a walk to the neighborhood video store, where we browsed and browsed. I'm not sure exactly what movie or show we rented, but I remember sitting on the couch watching it with him. I felt safe and cared for and loved, by a man who wasn't even my real grandfather. This is the kind of love that I think we all long for beyond the love of our own mothers, fathers, sisters, and brothers. The kind of love a human being has for another, expressed through not only sympathy but also time and the act of being present.

While time has been reduced, at least in the West, to a commodity or currency, when it comes to life and love, I think that is where we find its true meaning. Not in how it is spent, but in how it is shared. Time, love, and life create value greater than money and finite materials. It creates memories and emotions that are shared and passed down through generations. In putting that memory and experience in writing, in this book, I am doing just that. Sharing the love a human being showed to me with you, my readers.

My mom became pregnant with my sister Tanya during this time, and over the months I watched as her belly bloomed with life and became rounder and rounder. She had formed friendships with women in the area, and she'd visit them from time to time. There was laughter and lots of cooking, the smells of homemade Cambodian dishes like *prahok*, a salty fish paste made from fermented mudfish, or *kuy teav*, Cambodian noodle soup with beef or pork stock, rice vermicelli, bean sprouts, green onions, and your choice of meat. My favorite is *lok lak*, made with lettuce, tomato, and cucumber topped with slices of marinated beef, stir-fried in a savory brown sauce that includes American ketchup and onions. Some, like my grandmother, added eggs (in her case, sliced, hard-boiled eggs) as a topping. What makes this dish all come together is the dipping sauce made from a mixture of lime juice, ground pepper, garlic, and fish sauce, creating a combination of sweet, sour, and savory in one bite. Absolutely irresistible, in my opinion—the kind of dish that is etched forever in your taste-bud memory banks.

Cambodian food often includes the staples of fish sauce, oyster sauce, and soy sauce that never fail to permeate every living space with their pungent but mouthwatering aromas. Most, if not all, Cambodian cooking involves garlic. And lots of it.

Because Cambodia is a culture and society reliant on its rivers and the ocean, much of Cambodian food involves fish and a lot of vegetables and herbs like ginger, Thai basil, cilantro, lime, and green onion. And don't forget the red Thai chili peppers. They're hard to forget, as a kid, when you're touching them and eating them and all of a sudden you touch your face or, like lots of kids do, pick your nose or scratch your butt. I can't quite explain the feeling, but I'm sure many are familiar with it. As a kid, it felt like torture and like it lasted forever. The adults would tell you to stop rubbing your face and crying, but all that made you want to do was rub your face some more, which then just made you cry more.

Sometime later, my sister Tanya's dad and my mom separated. Why, I'm not entirely sure. But then my mother met another man who would make our lives a living hell for the next few years. How she met him is still a mystery to me, or maybe it's simply lost in the fog of memories from that time. When I asked a relative recently, all he said was: "That man was from hell." I mentally nodded in agreement, because most of my memories of Mr. Dith, the father of my two youngest siblings, throb like scars that remind me of the fear and isolation we experienced for years.

When we were in California, I vividly remember the home we lived in because of its similarity to a prison, even though this was most likely typical of homes in the San Diego area. It was sandwiched between two streets. There was a dusty, reddish dirt driveway with what seemed like a long, black iron gate that stretched across it like a reminder that we were trapped—I can't remember whether it slid open and closed or if it parted in the middle. There was a concrete path leading from the driveway to the doorstep and to another, smaller gated entrance that led to the street on the other side. Fencing surrounded the property.

I remember the fence and gates because they reinforced Mr. Dith's wish that my mom and me and Tanya not leave the premises. My mom always had this agitated feeling about her when she wanted to go visit another Cambodian family down the street, as if he could come around the corner at any moment. She'd gather us up, me and Tanya, and hurry us out the door, closing it behind her quietly as if he might somehow be secretly listening. When she'd usher us out the smaller gate, she'd look both ways frantically, her eyes darting back and forth, before grabbing our hands and veering left toward her friends.

Isolation is a powerful, dangerous, and harmful tool. We see it used in prisons, through solitary confinement, in torture, and even in schools. It is used by domestic abusers, and is listed on the Power and Control Wheel, developed by the Domestic Abuse Intervention Programs in Duluth, Minnesota. Isolation in this context is weaponized to control a partner—it controls who they see and talk to, what they read, and where they go and limits access to the outside world. From my experience, in what I observed with my mom and in my friends' relationships, the justifications always tend to be the same: "I'm doing this because I love you;" "This is for the best;" "Your friends and family just don't understand what we have;" or "I love you more than anyone, and I know what's best." That's only a short list, but it also combines with the other spokes on the Power and Control Wheel diagram.

The effect of all of this is that it boxes victims and survivors in, cutting them off from the world around them, one by one closing the exits in what quickly becomes a prison. All of it is done to create a torture chamber to keep the partner, and any children, locked away, silenced, and feeling as if they are unable to call for help. While we may think technology makes it easier to reach out, abusers are paranoid in many ways and will track phones, screen calls and texts, steal passwords and usernames for social media and e-mail accounts, and punish a partner if they don't have access to something.

This was very much what my mom and my siblings and I experienced.

Living there, or living with that man in general—all of the memories associated with him—all of it is clouded in that sort of hazy, halfhearted, and forced forgetfulness that accompanies both the direct and vicarious trauma of your mother being emotionally controlled and abused.

Memory is like that. It's a fickle thing, but necessarily so. Otherwise our brains would go *SPLAT!* Going back and remembering these moments, especially the stressful ones, is like sitting in front of your computer and selecting the "restore to a previous version" option. You stare and stare at the rotating digital circle as it winds around and around and around, a microcosmic reductive example of our existence.

We have to be careful with memory, too. Because to survive

and move on, our brains necessarily compress both good and bad memories to save space for living—for new memories. Traumatic memories, especially, can be dangerous. Like malware and viruses that bog down and slow your computer, unaddressed trauma impacts nearly every aspect of your life: the way you love, the way you think, and the way you respond to stress.

I learned early on, through child therapy sessions, literature, and mistakes I made, that it's important to express emotions in a healthy way, to process your thoughts and feelings and memories in a way that informs the present. In other words, the best way forward is to contemplate your past, feel the emotions those thoughts engender, and then integrate those memories and emotions and learn from them. There isn't much you can do to change your past. You can, however, find ways to change your present.

Although I've never kept a consistent journal, writing has become one important tool, along with playing and listening to music, reading and writing poetry, and enjoying nature.

Something else that I am grateful for is the ability to find the good in an otherwise dark time.

One memory that sticks out from my time in San Diego, in that prison of my mother's situation (and thereby, my situation), was my friendship with a boy from down the street. Like most deep friendships I've had in my life, I can scarcely recall how we met—only that we became good friends. He was a lifeline. A distraction. A reprieve from the otherwise lonely existence that my mom, my sister, and I had at the time.

At first, my friend and I hung out just by talking to each other through the wrought-iron fence. Eventually, however, I got my mom to let me out sometimes, usually when she herself was walking down to see her friends. My friend and I would play on the sidewalk, sometimes venturing onto the road, which wasn't terribly busy.

Soon, though, our little kingdom on the sidewalk became

too small, and our little-boy imaginations wanted, needed, to expand. Sometimes, my mom would take me and my friend to a store nearby; oddly, all I can remember was that it had really colorful clothing and accessories.

In the store my friend and I, like most children, would run in and out among the clothes, most likely raising the ire of the owners. As a result, I'd get a soft smack on the tush from my mom. We became so familiar with the store that we'd often venture there ourselves; I'd say that over time, we grew on the owners.

Our world probably didn't extend much beyond a one-block radius, but for two little boys around the age of four, it felt like an entire universe. Like little boys and girls often do, we ran around like little mayors. We'd entertain passersby with our stick fights, hosing-downs, and the occasional gooey gum off the hot, sunbaked tarmac that would either stick to the bottom of our thrift-store shoes or find its way into our mouths. Kids—am I right?

This was a different time for America, I think. The time before true-crime television poisoned the minds of helicopter moms and dads, who became afraid that their kids would get snatched up if they were left alone for just a single second. It was a time of peace in America during the beginning of the Clinton presidency, the years when America was dancing to "Macarena" or swooning to "I Swear" by All-4-One. It was the 1990s, after all.

America was entering a post-Cold War period, sandwiched between two defining eras. The Berlin Wall had fallen and the dust had settled from the Persian Gulf War. It was before the dot-com bubble and the 9/11 attacks and the general unease that would settle throughout the country. America was changing in other ways. Refugees from Asia and other parts of the world were arriving in the United States in droves, fleeing the proxy wars waged by the Capitalist West and the Communist East.

My mom was born in a small town called Pailin, just twenty

miles from the Thai border—the rough equivalent of a trip from Portland to Brunswick, or from Bangor to Ellsworth. Pailin was a Khmer Rouge stronghold and one of the first regions they took over because of the lucrative gem resources which they used to fund their offensives against the Khmer Republic.

My mom's time in Cambodia was short-lived. After the Vietnamese invasion and the fall of the Khmer Rouge in 1979, they were moved to the Khao-I-Dang refugee camp. There, my mom spent her formative years growing up in the shadow of the I Dang Mountain amid rows and rows of rectangular, thatched huts.

According to the United Nations, the Khao-I-Dang camp sheltered, at its peak, nearly 140,000 refugees. My family spent roughly ten years there until they were resettled in California sometime in the very late 1980s. I assume they were settled in the northern part, since I was born in Stockton, which is in San Joaquin County, slightly northeast of San Francisco.

My early childhood involved a lot of being passed back and forth between my mother, my maternal grandmother, and my godparents, depending on what condition my mother was in.

My godparents, Khandarith and Leap Hay, were a constant source of stability during my early years. My godfather was on the shorter side, with thick, black hair. He was a kind, quiet, and generous soul, most likely why he was also a pastor. His most notable feature was his lazy eye. My godmother was a big-boned woman with large, proportionate facial features. She was taller than my godfather and most other Cambodians. For some reason, my two godsisters remind me of the Cambodian version of Mary-Kate and Ashley Olsen.

I lived with my godparents off and on at their home near the corner of Orange Avenue and 5th Street in San Diego. When entering the apartment complex from 50th Street, you would walk up wide concrete stairs and pass through a metal gate and into a courtyard. You could see apartments built around the courtyard on two floors. My godfather was the property manager, so he had one of these apartments. If you swung a left and walked up the wooden stairs, the path led you to a wraparound balcony overlooking the grounds. It may sound grand, but knock the building materials and design down several pegs and you'll probably have the right image.

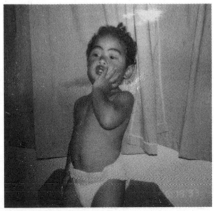

Even at two years old I loved playing dress up with my godsisters.

I'm pretty sure I thought of myself as a mini property manager at the time, most likely emulating my godfather as he went around and checked on the tenants. There were Cambodian families on the other side of the courtyard that we would always visit and have dinner with. Their girls were the same age as my godsisters, so naturally they were friends. As the baby of the group, I was their guinea pig for playing dress-up and their other little games. In fact, there's a photo of me striking a pose in my diapers with my hair bound in a knot, sporting blue eyeliner, bold, black eyebrows, and lipstick. If there were any signs that I would come out as gay later in life, that photo is surely one of them.

There was one particular tenant that I remember visiting often. She was a Black woman who lived on the first floor of the complex, toward the back. At first, I was scared of her because everyone said she was a witch, because she had a black cat. According to Cambodian superstition, when a person died, they had to guard the casket, because if a pregnant black cat landed on the casket, the deceased person would not be able to pass peacefully into the afterlife. Perhaps this is where the superstition of black cats stems from.

But much like cats, I was curious about this woman, despite what my godsisters and their friends said about her.

We officially met when I tried becoming friends with her cat while he was hanging outside. The little bugger ended up giving me a good scratch, and the woman ushered me inside her home to apply some first aid. That's when I decided she was okay and that we were friends. Even the cat warmed up to me, and from then on I'd visit and help her feed him (pretty sure it was a him) while making my rounds through the apartment complex.

Around this point, when I was four or five, my godparents decided that it was time for their family to move to Texas. I remember quite clearly being sat down and asked by my godfather to make a choice: Did I want to stay with my mother, who was following my grandmother to Maine, or did I want to go live with them in Texas? Even now, I remember being conscious of the choices I had been given, of the crossroads that I had reached. Even as a kid, I knew the difference between stability and safety and instability and hell.

I knew my godparents as if they had always been my real parents, and I loved them in that way. But I also knew and felt that way about my mother and my sister Tanya. I think only children who have grown up in situations like these, like living through their divorced parents' custody squabble, can know what that torn-between feeling is like. Agonizing.

I don't know why the decision was placed on my very small shoulders. I don't know why my godparents didn't just take me with them if they knew the situation was as bad as it was. In the end, I chose to stay with my mom. To stay in California. To stay in that dusty hell with the iron gates. And, I believe, to be there for my mom.

Questions revisit me every now and then, especially when I imagine how life might have been different if I had moved to Texas with them. In conversations with them later on, as an adult, my godfather made it clear to me that, as much as it had pained him to ask me to decide, he felt it was the right thing to do—to have me make the decision. It may appear that the crossroads was but a choice between stability and instability. But think again. Despite being four or five, I had some idea of the enormity of what lay before me. In however many minutes, hours, or even days I deliberated over what to do, I made a million decisions in my head and in my heart about my future.

Were they conscious and obvious thoughts? Absolutely not. But all the feelings I remember feeling then only happen when there are a million thoughts running through your head, a million split-second decisions being made. I remember feeling the dread that you feel when you are faced with the decision of whether or not to leave someone you love, whether it be a family member or a friend or a lover. I remember feeling, not necessarily *thinking* about, what life would be like living permanently apart from my birth mother. I remember feeling, not necessarily wondering, what it would be like to live with my godparents and not have to worry about the steady stream of awful men coming in and out of my life.

I am conscious now of the thoughts I must have had, knowing and remembering and conjuring up the feelings that I felt back then. Rationality had no meaning to me; it was pure gut reaction about who I wanted to be with, when, in fact, what I really wanted was to be with both.

But my attachment to my birth mother was still strong and compelling. I'd like to think that I felt a sense of duty to be there for my mother and my sister Tanya. And, honestly, I have always had that sense of duty, even to this day. My godparents told me that they always thought I was going to be a doctor, because when my godfather was sick, I tended to and cared for him and made sure he was okay.

I tell this part because I have paused many times to consider how big of a crossroads that was for my life and the path I ended up on. What if my godparents had made the decision for me? Don't we all wish it were that easy, sometimes? I would have been their only son. I would have received consistent care and lived a stable life. But how much of this is a longing for convenience fueled by regret? Decision-making can be painful, uncomfortable, time-consuming, and emotionally draining, especially for a small child.

Looking back now, I'm reminded of how we surrender much of our decision-making in the consumer-capitalist digital world. We outline our basic preferences, and from there we let the invisible hand—the convergence of hundreds of thousands of micro-forces—make decisions for us. What is available, our "supply of choices," is nothing more than those options presented to us.

Back then, I was presented with one of two options—not the life I now lead versus the other life that I didn't choose—but life *with* my mother or life *without* her. All I remember about the choice I made was how I felt: torn between two realities. Even now I can feel the faint tug-of-war and the fire of an upset stomach, unsure of what was being asked but aware of how consequential it could be.

These questions and memories return to me periodically, like a

Here I am, around age one, surrounded by my godfamily.

thorn in my side. But then I look back on my life and remember all the people I've met thus far, and, despite all of the trauma, I think of all the good memories I made growing up. Nostalgia replaces regret, and I begin to appreciate once again the path I've walked and who I've become.

It was in my childhood that I began to develop an independent spirit. I realized early on that the person I was closest to by the mere fact that she was my birth mother would not always be there for me. Although others tried to fill the gap over the years, when a child recognizes that his birth mother is incapable of providing stable and consistent care, it does something to him. You don't cease to love people who disappoint you (I never stopped loving my mother); you just love them differently. You adapt. It ultimately sinks in that they are incapable of caring for you in the way that they should, or in the way society expects they should, and you learn that the only way forward is to survive. To cope. To continue to hope.

In some ways, finding out that we were following my grand-mother and moving to Maine gave me new hope—a change of scenery … a new beginning.

The announcement was sudden. One day a U-Haul truck pulled into the dusty driveway and the queen-sized mattress was hoisted into the back. It was laid flat because my mom (who was pregnant), my sister, and I spent much of the trip sleeping on it during the drive cross-country. All I remember is the inside walls of the U-Haul, although a few stops were made along the way for bathroom breaks and some fresh air.

When the door was pulled up again, we found ourselves in Portland, Maine, in front of a blue apartment building where my grandmother and aunts and uncles came out to greet us.

Chestnut Street, Portland, Maine, 1997

● ◑ ◐ ◑ ○ ○

They make all sorts of candles and scents these days. If Portland were a candle, it would be a mixture of salt water and seaweed and probably a hint of tobacco.

The salt water and seaweed are obvious, given the city's coastal setting, but the tobacco might have you wondering. I suppose many cities have regulars who stand on street corners or out in front of shops, smoking cigarettes. Portland has its share, whether they're the fishermen who wake up at the crack of dawn hauling in the catch of the day on a cold winter morning, the businesswoman taking a drag out in front of the office after an ordeal with some sexist coworkers, or the hipster, flannel-wearing, man-bun-sporting, L.L.Bean-boots-with-strings-half-undone-wearing dude waiting for the Mumford & Sons show to start beneath the lights of the State Theatre marquee. If there was a good way to describe the smell of seagulls, I would probably throw that into the mix. It would be the perfect candle to accompany the city's motto, "Yes, life is good here."

Portland is a hidden gem, tucked away into the Northeast region of the United States and shielded by the islands of Casco Bay—Cushing Island, Peaks Island, Great Diamond Island, Chebeague Island, Long Island, and Cliff Island. Indeed, these islands were very much the protectors of the city in the days when tall ships sailed past the island forts with their imposing casements and cannon embrasures keeping watch over the waters. Later on during the world wars, battery forts were added to the mix, confirming once again the importance of protecting the largest port city in Maine.

There was one Civil War battle, the Battle of Portland Harbor, when Confederate Capt. Charles Read and his crew, in an attempt to evade the Union Navy, burned their own ship, commandeered a Maine fishing schooner, and entered Portland Harbor disguised as fishermen. They then captured another ship, the *Cushing*, and news began to spread of the incursion. Their plan was thwarted after a band of Union troops and volunteers, some led by Portland Mayor Jacob McLellan, pursued and captured the Confederate troops, who were then held as prisoners of war at Fort Preble in South Portland. That's about as exciting as the story of these forts gets.

The city itself sits on a large peninsula that looks like a boot in midstep, which I thought was peculiarly symbolic both of the history and contributions of Italian immigrants and Maine's motto, *Dirigo*, or "I lead."

From the peninsula, Portland spills out onto the mainland, due in large part to the state-sanctioned annexation of the town of Deering in 1899. It's a mixture of the brick facades of the Old Port and Commercial Street and the stately Victorian homes on the West End, blending into the Colonial style and mid-1900s single-family homes of the Deering (Deering Center, North Deering, East Deering), Riverton, and Stroudwater neighborhoods.

Portland is known as the Forest City, with its abundance of tree-covered parks, trails, waterways, and wetlands. Portland residents have a voracious appetite and taste for foods from around the world, reinforced by the city's significance as a port. Here you can find not only the iconic lobster roll or seafood dinner, but also sushi and authentic American Chinese, Thai, Vietnamese, Indian, Eritrean, and Hispanic restaurants.

The people here also love the arts. Despite being a smaller city, Portland boasts a symphony orchestra, several acting troupes and companies, several art galleries and countless artists. Along with the fishermen and waterfront and railroad workers who built Portland, from the 1800s to present day, I'd say that Portland was also built in large part by the artists who dared to depict the city's streets and people.

All of this comes together to create the quality of life that we so often boast about to other Mainers, and especially to those from out of state. That, along with the inclusive and welcoming schools and the low crime rate, has drawn many families here, including my grandmother's and other Cambodian families.

In the mid- to late 1990s, Cambodian students made up the majority of English Language Learners in the Portland Public Schools system. One of the people working in the schools was Pirun Sen, a Cambodian man who helped to facilitate the integration of many Cambodian refugee families in Maine. When I met Pirun years later, in my twenties, he remembered helping my grandmother and my family, connecting them to resources, food stamps, general assistance, and housing. My grandmother must have heard about the big Cambodian community here through word of mouth. The low crime rate, mentioned by relatives, was a big reason why she moved to Maine.

My sister Seyya was born shortly after we arrived in Maine, in 1997. Arriving in a new city and having a new baby sister were hopeful happenings. For the first year or so we lived with my grandmother, which fortunately helped with the situation with Mr. Dith, my mom's boyfriend. I say *fortunately* because if there was one person whom Mr. Dith feared, it was my grandmother. I learned at an early age to never underestimate a protective grandmother and her sandal—or her broom, from what I am told.

As I've mentioned, my grandmother was a small woman. Her face was slightly wrinkled, brown and leathery. But despite her size and appearance, she was the matriarch of the family, and wasn't afraid to chase my grandfather out of the house if he came home drunk. And she sure wasn't afraid to give Mr. Dith a smack with something if he stepped out of line.

My uncle Pheakdey reminded me of the time when my grandmother and Mr. Dith were fighting and she threatened to call the cops if he dared to hit her. His response? "Go ahead, call them." And so she did, and so they came. But what happened next is the part, in my mind, that is so very typical of domestic abuse situations: The cops came and talked to both my grandmother and Mr. Dith. My grandmother told them that he was getting violent again and went right back to sweeping the hallway as the police talked to Mr. Dith. He told the police that the older woman had struck him with her broom. The police arrested her and she spent the night in jail. My uncles had to scrape the money together to bail her out.

My grandmother was more of a mother to me than my own. Her two youngest children, Salut and Saly, were both younger than me—Salut by half a year, and Saly by a year and a half. Salut snickers when he reminds me that my grandmother used to breastfeed us both.

I remember my grandmother's two-bedroom apartment was in downtown Portland, across the street from Portland High School and just behind the Boys & Girls Club on Cumberland Avenue. It was here where I remember playing in the parking lot with my uncle Salut and my aunt Saly. I cut my foot on a rusty shaving knife, and the blood oozed and ran while we wrapped almost an entire roll of toilet paper around it, to help stop the bleeding. Good thing I had gotten my tetanus shot by then; otherwise I could've lost a foot to infection!

Around this time, my aunt Saly, who was four or five, announced she was "dating" two white boys in the same apartment complex. She recalls kissing one of the boys and then running around the corner to kiss another. My uncle Chinda, who was a senior at Portland High School, found out and gave her a spanking with a belt—one of those that were popular with teens back in the 1990s and early 2000s, the ones that were braided and worn with the end drawn up and tucked behind the belt and off to the side.

It was here that I had my first introduction to a Maine winter. When those first few flakes of snow began to fall, it was like magic. The bleak and gray barrenness of late fall was somehow transformed, brought to life in a way, as the world around me, the mud and dead grass, were washed in white. The trees surrendered their crowns of warmth and bright colors and now wore crowns of ice and crystal.

I clearly remember my youthful defiance toward donning warm clothes, running out in just a T-shirt and shorts to play in the snow, discovering how to make snow angels and snowmen. Our family, being from a tropical, humid climate in Cambodia and then living in the temperate weather of San Diego, was not prepared for a full-blown Maine winter.

Thankfully, there was a Salvation Army store down the street where we found old coats and jackets and other winter gear amid the musty hand-me-downs that hung from thin metal clothes racks. The ones that would let out a vicious *SCREEEEECH* when given a few spins by a young kid who knew exactly what his mother's reaction would be. My favorite part of the store, of course, was the toy section. Mostly it contained discarded toys for babies and toddlers, but occasionally I would find a neat action figure or some toy soldiers.

In fact, I don't remember ever going to a big superstore or the mall for anything brand-new. No Toys"R"Us. No shiny packages containing the latest and greatest from LEGO or Hasbro. My friends and relatives and I either got toys from Salvation Army or Goodwill, or we would use our imaginations.

I also remember the Ice Storm of 1998. Our family of twelve was crammed into the first- and third-floor apartments of that complex with only each other and a single space heater to keep warm. Not the fancy and sleek heaters they have today, but the old ones with the grills on the front and the elements that glowed a fierce orange in the dark. Hazards, if you ask me. We also had big Asian mink blankets, the ones with illustrations of ferocious tigers, dragons, and flowers in colors ranging from cherry blossom pink to light jade green.

My school photo from 1995.

I remember my first day of school at Baxter Elementary and how my grandmother got six-year-old me and five-year-old Salut butt-naked into a scalding hot bath to send me off to school squeaky clean.

Later, I attended Reiche Elementary, a school located in Portland's West End neighborhood. The most memorable physical features of the school, to my mind, were the big concrete ramps that we had to take sometimes to get to other parts of the building. Inside, you could see new concepts being implemented in terms of classroom and school design. In the wing that housed the classrooms, there was an open-air library in the center with colorful carpets and rows of books. Around the perimeter were classrooms separated by gray carpet cubicle walls, the spaces above them also open-air.

The school was very diverse, and I remember lots of multicultural events. In my day, the school hosted one where we put on an African play about a caterpillar in a hut. Guess who got to be the caterpillar? Yours truly. I still recall that night—the nervousness, especially, but also being in that little hut holding a microphone and the script, the stage lights peeking through the strands of fake paper straw that made up the door. They organized all the children to draw pictures for the multicultural calendar. I still have that calendar. I had drawn a straw hut sitting on stilts with a tiger lurking around outside.

To this day, Reiche is a school that prides itself on its multiculturalism. In fact, when I was googling photos to make sure my memory about the cubicle classrooms was correct, they had a news item celebrating one of their teachers becoming a US citizen.

It gives me a feeling of hope to know that schools like this exist across the United States. It was empowering then, and it's a powerful memory now, realizing that despite our diversity, we as one body celebrated the cultural and ethnic uniqueness of each person. That we were allowed to see each other fully, as our full selves. I wasn't asked to leave my Khmer heritage or language at the door. In fact, there was a Portland Public Schools banner hung up near the entrance with the word "welcome" written on it in multiple languages, including Khmer. There were also interpreters available, especially for issues involving parents and families.

While these may seem like small gestures, they signal, even to young children, that "we are trying." It speaks to the tremendous power of public education, of which I have been a strong proponent ever since I found my voice as an advocate, and serves as a powerful testament to the idea of America. A nation founded upon individual liberty—always in a struggle to define what that actually means—has pockets of hope where individuality is celebrated, yes, but that does not mean we are islands unto ourselves, living in silos or isolated in castles. Rather than walls meant to separate us, our individuality and our cultural beliefs, values, languages, religions, and so forth are contributions that we bring to the table. I think Reiche worked to make this vision a reality through their open-air concept and multicultural programming.

What peace we were able to enjoy during that time was provided by the hard work of my grandmother and two oldest uncles. While he was still in high school, my uncle Chinda started working at Barber Foods, where he works to this day. My grandmother barely spoke

English, so the only job she could land was working the graveyard shift collecting sea urchins, getting paid under the table. My uncle Sambo, who was either a freshman or sophomore at Portland High School at the time, also worked under the table doing the same.

Despite all of this, we were a large family, with the three of them working to support my alcoholic grandfather; my uncles, Pheakdey (in middle school at the time) and Salut; my aunt Saly; my mom; me; and, by 1998, my three younger siblings, Tanya, Seyya, and Brandon. Whenever I went to Shop 'n' Save (now Hannaford) with my grandmother, I'd often see the fancy-looking paper food stamps that she would use to buy groceries. I knew it wasn't money but I knew it kept us fed, and I had an appreciation for it because I understood to some degree that we needed a little help to get by as a family of refugees. The adults in the family were heavily traumatized by the Khmer Rouge. Some worked and worked to forget the pain. Others drank and drank. And some, like Mr. Dith, took it out on their own family.

For some, the pain and injustice of their situation is helped by religion—belief in a supreme deity who is omnipresent, omniscient, and omnipotent, and has a purpose behind every action or inaction. Religion was, at times, the light in my mother's life when things were very bad. My mother, who at times attended my godparents' Cambodian Christian church when living in California—my godfather being a Cambodian pastor and all—found a new church that sent around maroon buses and eighteen-passenger vans to all the neighboring towns.

This Baptist church, located somewhere in the Freeport area, was a part of my life off and on while I lived in the area. We kids never wanted to go. The vans and buses would show up and, at times, they would literally chase us down and cram us in and ship us off to Sunday school. Depending on what the statute of limitations is, I may have a case against them for false imprisonment and kidnapping (joking!).

One elderly couple from the church took an interest in my mother and me. I don't know why. The few times I made it to Sunday school, they would swing by and say hello. They became attached to my mother and me in a certain way, so much so that the first time I remember receiving a Christmas gift was when they stopped by to pick me up and take me to Toys"R"Us in South Portland. It was the very first time I'd ever set foot in a store filled to the brim with new, shining toys. I don't know how long I browsed with these new friends of my mom, but I emerged from that store with a brand-new red fire truck.

The couple continued to be involved in my mom's life, even after we moved to Riverton.

Riverton Park, Portland, Maine, 1998

●◗◖○○

Eventually, our part of the family had grown too large, and my mother, Brandon, Seyya, Mr. Dith, Tanya, and I moved into a small four-bedroom home in Riverton Park, a low-income housing development.

If you were to arrive in Portland along I-295 after crossing the Fore River, you'd see Thompson's Point on the left, old brick warehouses where now there is a concert venue during the summer and an ice rink during the winter, and the modern brick and beige arches of the Northern Light Mercy Hospital campus. Looming behind this facility is the towering campus of its rival hospital, Maine Medical Center, standing proudly—or menacingly, depending on your perspective—on the steep and rocky ledges of the Western Promenade.

You'd pass these as well as the tennis and volleyball courts of Deering Oaks park on the right and the University of Southern Maine's Wishcamper Center and the seven floors of the retro-looking Glickman Library on the left. This is where you would take the exit to go north along Forest Avenue, the parking lots and strip malls a vague remnant of what used to be known as Portland's "car (dealership) corridor."

For about ten to fifteen minutes, depending on the traffic, you'd ride along the corridor and pass through Woodfords Corner with its iconic clock tower atop the old brick Odd Fellows building. Further down you'll pass Baxter Woods, a bird sanctuary and popular dog-walking destination, one of two Cambodian grocers, and yet another classic five- or six-way intersection common in old New England towns and cities, called Morrill's Corner. At this point, you begin to transition into the lower-density parts of Portland, with multifamily homes along the Forest Avenue corridor and single-family homes on the streets that shoot off to either side of it, like branches on a giant oak tree.

It's not until you pass through the bulk of the single-family homes on lanes and cul-de-sacs, and then under the I-95 highway bridge, that you make it into the part of town zoned for industrial uses and the city dump, namely on Industrial Parkway and Riverside Street. It is here, also, where Riverton Park and other low-income housing projects are located.

This is different from an earlier period in time when Riverton was more forested, less populated, and seen more as a retreat by those who lived in what is now considered Downtown Portland. There was a trolley that ran from Portland proper along roughly what is Forest Avenue, all the way to the Riverton Trolley Park on the Portland–Westbrook border, carved by the Presumpscot River. Once there, retreaters had access to a grand building that housed a casino, a gazebo, and a boat launch.

But the Riverton "Park" that exists today is situated slightly more inland and built atop what was previously wetlands. The move to this low-income housing project was the beginning of the end of our lives with my birth mother, in a way. We had left the watchful and protective eyes of my grandmother (and her broomstick).

How we ended up moving into Riverton Park is unknown to me, but I believe it was something to do with refugee resettlement in Maine. I wonder to this day whether it was Mr. Dith who convinced my mother to move out. It is a pattern of many domestic abusers to remove their victims from safe spaces and isolate them from family and friends.

Domestic abusers are sociopaths. They are not always the dumb, beer-slugging, La-Z-Boy-lounging thugs that reek of body odor, depicted in TV shows and movies. They come in all shapes and sizes, and they are smart, manipulative, and very good at putting on a show when they need to. They know the power of isolation, what it does to a person's brain and psyche, and employ all kinds of tricks to lock a person up in their own minds and in their own homes. In a weird, effed-up way, they understand people and what makes them tick, while at the same time not knowing how royally screwed up they themselves are.

It got so bad that at one point, the elderly couple from the Baptist church talked to my mom about having me come live with them for a bit. I don't know how the conversation went exactly, but I do remember that they came over to our house in Riverton and sat me down to talk to me about living with them. I said yes, not because I knew what I was agreeing to, but because all that was going through my head was the awesome red fire truck this couple had bought for me the Christmas before, and how nice they seemed.

And just like that, with a "yes" and the presence of our guardian ad litem, I hopped in with a few belongings and we drove to their condo in Freeport, in the Somerset development on the left just before where the Freeport Police Department is today. I had a small room there and was given new clothes and plenty to eat. They also enrolled me in a small, private Christian school somewhere nearby, which I hated, because the teacher I had was mean and abusive. When I didn't get a math problem right, or just plain couldn't get something she was trying to teach me, she'd reach under the table and pinch my arm or my leg. This hurt, of course, but it also made me so mad. It didn't help me learn anything because I was more focused on trying to avoid her pinching than making sense of what she was trying to teach me.

I think this was the point when I realized that I missed home. I missed my mom. I would cry in my small room at night. The older couple began to worry, and eventually I told them that I wanted to go back home. I don't remember staying with them very long, but by the time I got back to my mom at Riverton Park, things there had gotten much worse.

There is one dark memory that I am reminded of as I write this, a memory that, thankfully, has lost the sting that many such traumas carry with them.

One cold and dark evening, my mother had taken us to a friend's house on St. John's Street, where they were drinking and singing karaoke. My sister and I were asleep in one of the bedrooms when we began to hear clamoring and shouting. Mr. Dith had shown up and was shouting and arguing with my mother, about what, I don't know. But my heart began to race and my instincts told me that it wasn't going to turn out well. Grandma wasn't there with her broom or her sandal. It was just my mom and her friend, who didn't seem to be doing anything to stop what was going on.

The room we were in was dimly lit, probably by a night-light. I pulled the covers over my head and tried to shut the noise out and go back to sleep.

That's when I heard it. A *smack*. No, a *crunch*. Or both. Then a thud as I heard my mom fall to the floor, shocked. Then I heard her sob—and I began to sob, too, because I knew exactly what had happened. Mr. Dith had hit my mother again.

I came out of the bedroom and my mother was on the floor, sobbing hysterically with her hand over her mouth. Blood was running down. He had struck her so hard that he had knocked out some of her teeth. This was the worst thing I had ever seen Mr. Dith do, and I sobbed even more uncontrollably. My sister Tanya had joined the sad chorus as well. My mom's friend called the cops, and I still remember the blue and red lights from the cop cars and the ambulance flashing through the windows of that second-floor apartment. I sat there in shock, zoned out, my mind spinning to the rhythm of the lights that spun in and out, in and out of the kitchen, blood and tears on the cheap linoleum floor, the pieces of broken teeth on the floor like the broken pieces of our family.

For some reason, Mr. Dith didn't flee, or maybe he tried to but was detained outside by the police. It was either after that point, or sometime thereafter, that he disappeared from our lives. Perhaps a restraining order was issued against him; I don't know. Good riddance.

I wasn't aware of it at the time, but the practice of revisiting traumas and thinking about how you felt then and how you feel now removes that trauma from the primitive parts of the brain to the rational, thinking parts. The trauma gets processed, enabling you to make somewhat rational decisions about what power that trauma will hold over you in the future. It seems counterintuitive, but I would say that processing trauma is quite different from dwelling on it. Recognizing this brings freedom, because no matter how much you want to run from a trauma or ignore it or seal it away, it is a truth that is a part of you. It is something that happened to you, and nothing in the world can rewind and change that. If you run from something you fear, it gives that fear power, which means that it will continue to chase and haunt you. But if you turn around and face it, only then can you begin to see it for what it is; only then can you see it in the light, rather than having it lurk in your own shadow.

This isn't easy, especially when the flight response becomes such an ingrained habit. That's why one of the good things that the US Department of Health and Human Services and the Maine foster care system provided later on was child therapy sessions. Looking back at those sessions now, they were really helpful. The child therapists would do this particular kind of therapy that I remember, using play. I'd show up in their colorful offices and would immediately make a beeline for the sandbox, which I remember was very clean and clear of all toys and encumbrances at the beginning of every session. I'd go in there like clockwork and immediately find the miniature green army soldiers and create an epic scene of army soldiers versus toy dinosaurs. Sometimes, toy cars would come into play, but I soon realized that their wheels would get clogged with sand and become useless.

I realize that I would typically arrange my army soldiers in lines or in organized clusters. It's interesting, and probably something the child therapist picked up on: Despite the chaos swirling around me, I gravitated toward creating some order and sense of control through play. According to proponents of play therapy, there are many benefits, but one psychologist and academic suggests that therapists can utilize play therapy to help children express their thoughts and feelings in ways that they cannot through verbal language.

Life got worse for my mom and me and my siblings after Mr. Dith left. She would disappear, oftentimes for days at a time. There was one time when she disappeared—I remember it clearly, because I was in pain with some sort of infection. I was running around to all of the other Asian families in Riverton Park, trying to find her. Our neighborhood of low-income homes was arranged in six circles to mimic, in a cheap way, the cul-de-sacs of wealthier suburbs. When I reached one of our cousins' houses in 4th Circle (we lived in 6th Circle), I was told that my mother had gone to Boston.

I once walked in on her and another man who I knew was married to a family friend. I remember being livid and my mother asking me why I was so mad at her. I'd like to say I was mad because I knew it was wrong. But I think by that time, despite the other men in her life, I had grown accustomed to doing what I could to take care of my mother and my siblings. I felt I had assumed the mantle of the "man of the house," which may have been in part due to our culture, but was also forced by the circumstances, especially when my grandmother and uncles weren't around.

I became protective of my mother and remember holding a lot of resentment toward the other men she brought in, one just as verbally and physically abusive to her as the last. There was this one white man she dated, Scott, who spoke Cambodian fluently. I hated him. Scott and my mom had a fight once in the kitchen. My mother had a butcher knife in her hand and they were arguing about something. He was closing in, trying to make some point, and she slammed the butcher knife down. I think it was pretty close to his hand or something, because then they started arguing about how she almost cut his hand off. I remember thinking at the time, *Good—now maybe he'll finally leave us alone!* But alas, that didn't lead to his departure. No, he was around for a while. Annoyingly so.

I was angry at all the men she chased. To this day, she's still chasing after them. I get the sense whenever I talk to or visit family, even they don't know exactly where she is, or they will mention casually (in a dismissive way) that she's staying with a boyfriend. So, no, it was not some noble morality that drove my anger. It was a feeling that I had been replaced. It was a feeling that things were out of my control and I was powerless to protect her from her own demons, one of which was alcohol.

I remember one night when she was drinking and we were all sleeping downstairs in the living room. I woke up to her puking on the floor. I remember it was the cheap whiskey in plastic containers with yellow and red labels; to a kid of seven or eight, it looked like brownish-gold pee. I remember that I made the call, picking up the old beige plastic telephone to dial 911 and talk to the operator, who in her sympathetic voice asked, "What's wrong?"

I told her, "My mom is sick. She drank too much, and she puked on the floor."

Next thing I know, the red lights of the ambulance were swirling in and out of our living room, empty save for a small TV and a small, dirty couch that tried in vain to fill the cheap linoleum floor with some semblance of habitation. Only now, that floor was covered with the pungent refuse of alcohol poisoning. The smell of it was enough to make my stomach turn. I wanted to vomit myself, like the repeated scenes in *Family Guy* of Peter, Brian, and Stewie retching at the sight of one another retching.

My mother was still haunted by her experiences in Cambodia and would watch Cambodian movies about the Khmer Rouge, which I knew was dangerous. One movie she watched was of a Cambodian woman being subdued and raped by soldiers. It wasn't the movie that I remember clearly; it was how fixated she was on it. I tried to change the channel on the TV, but she snapped at me.

I have always wondered how some Cambodians seem to remember the Khmer Rouge like it was all in the past, and they keep it there, while others continue to live it.

The Khmer Rouge broke the spirit of the Cambodian people

in unimaginable ways. They tore the fabric of Cambodian society apart. They targeted intellectuals, monks, people with glasses, business owners. Then they forced Cambodians, particular young people, into re-education camps and subjected them to brainwashing. They were taught to turn on each other, their families, friends, and neighbors, and to tear each other apart. They demanded absolute allegiance to the Khmer Rouge and their ideology, and they rooted out all signs of disloyalty.

And when they couldn't abuse the Cambodian mind and spirit, the Khmer Rouge abused the Cambodian body through forced labor and starvation. Cambodians faced endless torture throughout the years that the Khmer Rouge was in control, the effects of which impact them to this day, including the refugee population. It also affects their children and newer generations through intergenerational trauma and through workaholism, alcoholism, and domestic abuse.

These struggles were felt by my grandmother and mother. My grandmother copes better, I think, perhaps because she experienced the traumas of the Khmer Rouge as an adult, while my mother was born into the mayhem and experienced it during her childhood. The Khmer Rouge broke my mother's body, mind, and soul, in many ways leaving her with the brain of a traumatized child. This means that as an adult, she is dependent on abusive relationships and unable to hold down a job, unable to provide a stable home for her children and put food on the table.

While I didn't experience the trauma that my mother experienced, I did experience the trauma of an empty stomach. The number of days that I went to school hungry swirl together in an indiscernible haze. The feeling of my empty stomach, growling and aching and twisting in knots, certainly did not help my feelings of stress and anxiety. I'd often get free breakfast and lunch at school, but not all the time, if I remember correctly. There was a mixture of shame and fear involved—shame in knowing that I was different from the other kids because I was getting free lunch or breakfast; and fear in wondering what others would think if they saw me trying to get breakfast and lunch and was somehow refused, in front of the entire line of kids.

When my grandmother wasn't around, full meals were few and far between. I learned how to cook eggs and boil rice, often topping it with too much sriracha sauce. Other times, I'd eat raw Maruchan instant ramen that came in different flavors, and was color-coded: beef (red), chicken (orange), and shrimp (pink). Everyone knows about boiling water or putting them in the microwave, but little Asian kids like me would open the thin, plastic packaging, take out the bricks of sodium-packed ramen, break them into pieces, and then sprinkle the seasoning mix over the chunks. My group of friends and I would crunch on this snack regularly. When I needed a treat, I'd either pour a glass of milk and mix it with sugar, or I'd take a piece of toasted bread and pour a healthy (or unhealthy) amount of sweetened condensed milk onto the warm surface and take a bite of the crunchy, sticky goodness. Sometimes, if we had avocados, I'd slice them in half, just like my mom taught me, take the pit out, and pour sweetened condensed milk into the little hollowed-out green bowls.

While these memories of food, or the lack thereof, have bright moments, they also highlight the food insecurity that my family and other low-income and working-class families experience. As many psychologists and social workers have pointed out, food insecurity has a tremendous impact on childhood brain development and outcomes.

The connection between food and the brain dates further back than just me and my family. As suggested by Harvard anthropologist and biologist Dr. Richard Wrangham in his book, *Catching Fire: How Cooking Made Us Human*, the combination of fire and cooking helped spur the evolution of the human brain to become bigger and to support more complex cognitive processes. According to Dr. Wrangham, cooking food made calorie intake more efficient, freeing up more energy to devote to brain functions. Dr. Wrangham also argues that this seemingly simple change heavily influenced social relations among humans.

Author Michael Pollan takes this to the next level in his book, titled *Cooked: A Natural History of Transformation*, which has its own Netflix-adapted documentary series. "Cooking", Pollan writes, "is all about connection, I've learned, between us and other species, other times, other cultures (human and microbial both), but, most important, other people. Cooking is one of the more beautiful forms that human generosity takes; that much I sort of knew. But the very best cooking, I discovered, is also a form of intimacy."

So what happens when this form of intimacy, of togetherness, is lost or not consistent? Studies have shown that poverty, hunger, and trauma—especially for children who are in the midst of brain development—are linked to mental health issues. Which leads me to wonder: How many societal problems could we overcome, or mitigate, if we ensured that everyone, especially children, had access to healthful food?

Anyway, it was during this time at Riverton Park that I began to see other people enter our lives—caseworkers, a guardian ad litem, interpreters, and social workers. These visitors would ask me if I was all right, how much food I had to eat, if I felt like I was being taken care of, and if I felt my mom was doing okay. I'm sure they meant well, but it felt like they were snooping around for any wrongdoing on my mom's part, and I knew she was struggling. Again, my protective side came out during these times. Yet, I also grew accustomed to and perhaps even fond of these people, who seemed to have my best interests at heart, especially the guardian ad litem, a lawyer named Kevin.

Things finally reached a point where the State decided my mother was incapable of taking care of all four of us. She was increasingly absent. The house was crawling with cockroaches and generally unclean. There was one section of the house filled with black garbage bags containing clothes and belongings, just heaped up in a big pile. My academic performance was slipping, and caseworkers questioned us about how often we were hungry.

Things really escalated when the caseworkers noticed that my sister Tanya had cuts on her neck from when she'd been playing with curtain drawstrings and had slipped while they were around her neck. The caseworkers eviscerated my mom with questions, almost insinuating that it was her fault. Part of me wonders if cultural bias came into the equation, because surely children from white families must have gotten cuts or broken bones without their parents being threatened with having their children taken away. I guess the difference here was that my mom was already in hot water with Child Protective Services.

My two youngest siblings, Seyya and Brandon, were the first to be put into foster care. This was around 1998 or 1999, a time when the State was pulling kids out of homes left and right. (Thankfully, in the past decade, the policy has shifted toward trying to keep kids in their homes, which I believe is better in the long run, with the exception of the major cases of neglect and abuse that make headlines.)

We didn't completely lose contact with Seyya and Brandon when they were removed, especially when they moved in with Bob and Tracy Berry. Tanya and I and my mom would get rides with the Regional Transportation Program (RTP) to see our younger siblings when they lived with a foster family in Lewiston. It's sort of odd that I associate those trips mostly with the radio commercial, "Whenever you need us, call 1-800-East-West." As if I needed to know how to call a mortgage company! Perhaps it was some type of premonition; our home life was collapsing, and Tanya and I would ultimately be moved from foster home to foster home. Perhaps I really needed someone to understand how effed-up our situation was, even if it was just some random person answering the phone at a mortgage company.

At Riverton, I made friends pretty fast, most of them of Asian background and some of African backgrounds. Riverton Park was made up of mostly immigrant families from African and Asian regions. There were many Cambodians, Vietnamese, Thai, Somalis, and Kenyans. I can only remember one white family; they operated the neighborhood candy store in their unit.

My friends from that time were extremely important to me. We did everything together. Being with them was my escape from the absence of any home life. We would walk the mile to Riverton School or hop on the bus and sing at the top of our lungs. I remember very clearly those golden days of simply walking down the street with my friends, joking and laughing all the way to school or back home. I remember feeling the adrenaline as neighborhood dogs gave us a run for our money, or when we would try to take on some older, bigger kids and found out all too soon that we were going to get whooped. Or the times we felt like we owned the world, going where we wanted, playing where we wanted, being friends with whomever we wanted to hang out with.

One of the clearer memories I have was when I was eight. It was during this time when I first experimented sexually with one of my good friends, whose family was from Kenya. But before I delve into this story, I want to warn those who would try to "explain the gay away" through the hardships of my childhood, or to somehow say that being gay is the result of bad nurturing and not something that is a part of someone's essential nature. In fact, I tell this story of my earliest gay experience to make the opposite point. You see, I experimented with girls as well—the usual "I'll show you mine if you show me yours" dares and the like—but I remember more clearly my time with my best friend, a boy. It was as strong of an emotional connection as a person could make at that point in time—one that, at my age, I couldn't explain or put into words. It was something I just knew. Something I just felt. Something I just ran with.

When I kissed him or hugged him, I wasn't confused. My eight-year-old feelings and thoughts were unadulterated by societal judgments or moral abhorrence, free from the self-hatred I would later feel as a teenager. I did what I wanted. I did what I felt. I loved who I loved without fear. I was experiencing love with childlike wonder, a love untainted by the coming years—at least when we were alone. There was this one time I remember distinctly. We had been wrestling on the bed in the bedroom with a window facing the circle of houses. The light was on and the shades were down. After a while we collapsed in a heap and started to kiss.

The next morning we both walked to the basketball courts where we met up with my predominantly Asian group of friends. As we walked up, one of my friends, who happened to live directly across from me on the other side of the circle, jeered at us and said he saw our silhouettes wrestling in the window. Both my Kenyan friend and I panicked and came up with some story to rebut their presumption—but it was for naught. I suppose we were a little ashamed. But any kids caught messing around, at least before that age where boys began to boast about their exploits, would react in that bashful feigning-of-innocence way, regardless of gender.

Somehow, I don't remember how, we got them to get off our case and walked the mile or so to Riverton Elementary. Sometimes we took the main way, by walking to the Riverton Park entrance across from the 7-Eleven on Forest Avenue, and following that major road (also known as Route 302) until we got to the intersection with the fire and gas stations, which also was the entrance to the school. Most of the time, we'd go through the woods behind 2nd and 3rd Circles and weave through the cul-de-sacs and working- and middle-class neighborhoods that lay between our low-income housing development and Riverton Elementary. Oftentimes, we'd also walk back that way, making sure to avoid the white kid on that block who had chased us once, with his dog. We also took the bus until we figured out we could pretty much walk and have adventures along the way.

But one time after school, we were all riding the bus back home and Britney Spears' "Baby One More Time" came on. We boys loved that song and belted it out, most likely to either the amusement or disdain of the bus driver.

Man, did I love to sing! But it was something I kept to myself. Music would become a big part of my life later on, especially as a way to cope and process emotions. Although I have never had trouble making friends, I have always had that introverted trait of wanting just enough attention, but not too much. When I sang, people stopped to listen. I rarely sang for attention; I sang because it made me feel good. Which is why it took some guts to join the Riverton Elementary chorus group. My guy friends all made fun of me when I told them we should join (I didn't want to go alone). But one of my friends went along with me. I think he was Chinese, although I am drawing a blank on his name. He didn't live in Riverton Park with us but joined our group of friends when we figured out he had Pokémon cards.

Before that, he had endured our consistent bullying when, on the first day of school, we found out he ate cereal with orange juice. Like, who does that? Maybe our behavior was some sort of initiation hazing so common among boys (and men). There was a thrill to it—being part of a group of friends banding together to pick on someone. It wasn't that I necessarily knew what I was doing but more that I felt I was a part of something, even though it was bad. I got approval from my friends when I joined them in ridiculing and bullying others. It was the feeling I had when I was alone that ate me up. An innate sense of guilt and shame that I had done something wrong. I hope today, if that boy is reading this, he knows I am deeply sorry for making fun of him, and that I am glad we became friends, albeit briefly.

I took part in my share of childhood mischief; I should say *we*, the Riverton boys, took part. Learning to slip Pokémon cards up our sleeves after asking to sift through another kid's deck. Sneaking into the 7-Eleven and stealing Pokémon card packs. Like many kids during that time, we were really, really into Pokémon, a trading card game that featured cute little animal-inspired creatures that evolved into more powerful Pokémon the more you trained them. It became even more popular when the Game Boy games came out. For those of us with Asian backgrounds, it was especially a point of pride because it was one of the few things that we knew came from Asia, because some of the cards came in Japanese. It was all the rage, learning to do Pokémon battles and trading cards.

One kid from the middle school, one of the few white boys in the neighborhood, enticed my group of friends, a bunch of Asians and Africans, to hit up the junkyard for bike parts. He described the junkyard as if it was the Promised Land of free stuff for the taking. But what sealed the deal was the promise of bike parts.

Bikes and bike parts were another popular craze at the time for us kids. It was a rite of passage if you could bike all the way up the big hill near the basketball courts in Riverton Park. It was freedom in many ways because of the feeling you would get soaring down the hill or riding with your friend while standing on their bike pegs. So when someone said there was a treasure trove of free bike parts, how could we refuse?

When we got there, the white boy found a bulldozer with the keys in it. I was with my uncle Salut—I was eight, and he was probably seven—sifting through a pile of odd parts, when the white boy came around the corner with the bulldozer, crashing left and right into piles and piles of junk. We ran as fast as we could, diving underneath the tall fence we had dug under. We turned one last time, afraid to be caught in front of the monster machine, and in a split second, we saw him crash into the very fence under which we had escaped. Our adrenaline was at its peak as we booked it back to Riverton Park.

Later we heard that the kid had done considerable damage to the junkyard, and for the next few weeks, we all scattered every time a Portland police department cruiser would roll through the community. We knew full well that the police were searching for the junkyard culprits.

My friends and I already feared the Portland police. In fact, every time we would see a cruiser approach, we would go out of our way to avoid it, running into the woods, jumping into a little marsh and hiding among the cattails, or climbing into a culvert underneath the road. In part, it was a child's game, but the anxiety was also there. To us and the community we grew up in, they were the kind of authority we feared. Pile on top of that the fact that we had been at the junkyard and the officers were looking for the group of kids who had been a part of the incident, and my anxiety was through the roof.

Riverton had an Asian community liaison who also translated for my mother sometimes (I don't remember which nationality in particular). Somehow she had gotten wind of our mischief and made it a point to reach out to us and let us know that everything would be okay as long as we cooperated. She even arranged for me and some of the other boys to get out of town, getting us tickets to ride on the *Songo River Queen* in Naples, Maine, which I think was a way of trying to convince us to fess up. I remember the entire ride up 302 to Naples and on board the *Songo River Queen* that I felt this immense feeling of fear, that I was on the run—that the big men in blue with shiny badges would take me away from my family and all I held dear.

It was 2000. It's odd, thinking back now, that at the age of eight I visited the very town where I would spend my adolescent years living with my adoptive family. A few weeks after the chaos at the junkyard and that ride on the *Songo River Queen*, my mind was temporarily relieved of anxiety, but only because a new worry had come onto the scene: The Maine Department of Health and Human Services (DHHS) had finally had enough with my mother and swooped in to take me and my sister Tanya away.

When I arrived home from school that afternoon, I walked into the house to find my mom sitting on the couch with my sister, crying. The DHHS caseworker was there, so I instinctively put two and two together. Mom crying. Caseworker sitting there, as if waiting just for me. My four-year-old sister not really knowing what was going on.

"I need you to put your things in this bag," I remember the caseworker saying as she handed me an empty, black garbage bag. She had a look on her face that told me she was not enjoying this at all. Who would?

What does she mean? What do I take? My thoughts raced as my heart beat faster and faster inside my chest.

"What's happening?" I asked, half-knowing what the answer would be.

"We're taking you somewhere for a little while. You'll be well taken care of."

As I put random items into my black trash bag, all I can remember feeling was absolute shock. My sister Tanya was crying at this point as she, too, was given a trash bag to fill with items, as if she was supposed to know what she needed to take with her to this new place. Everything happened pretty fast, although it felt like a slow-motion scene.

We piled into the caseworker's small sedan and weaved through the Riverton Park neighborhood. The feeling of shock was still coursing through my veins, my heart pumping with stress and anxiety as we made it onto the highway and headed away from the city I had come to know and love. I stared through the car window during most of the drive to what would be our first foster home.

PART TWO

Acton, Maine, 2000

● ◗ ◑ ○ ○

I fidgeted in my seat. It felt like the seat belt was slowly transforming into a shackle, a feeling of impending doom. There was a churning, a sea of turbulence in my stomach. A tensing as the cords in my shoulders and neck began to draw tight, as if my body was trying to cut itself off from my mind. In actuality, I was losing breath; with every passing minute, the glimmer of life began to fade as I was overcome with feelings of unwanted change.

I didn't look out the window. I didn't look anywhere but at my hands. Fidgeting. As if I were trying to clasp and cling to what was becoming a distant memory. As if the air between my hands could somehow whisk me back to what I knew. My mother. My home. My family. My friends. My neighborhood. As if the way in which my hands turned and turned upon each other would turn back the clock of time, turn the car—and my life—back around, returning tears already shed.

It was dark. It was night. The silhouette of trees haunting as they guarded the road that stretched ahead. Black against the dark blue of the night sky. Their hands stretched upward and waving as if wailing to the murmur of the wind. So dark that not even the stars or the moon could overcome the solemn procession.

I began to feel the cold creep into my heart, that icy fear of the unknown. Of uncontrollable circumstance. That cold, unfettered fear of helplessness and abandonment. Of utter loneliness in the chasm of unwelcome change.

I usually pride myself on having a sixth sense about things, but I really fell for this one—at least for a while. The caseworker had said something along the lines of "We're taking you to stay somewhere else for a while."

In my little head, that didn't register as forever. I was used to this whole bouncing around from one home to the next. For most of the trip to this "better place," it didn't really dawn on me what was in fact happening. But there was a point along the way when I began to get a sense of what was going on. I may have been eight (going on nine) at the time, but I was pretty darn smart. Many of my teachers saw this in me, despite their constant chiding to do better and to apply myself.

I began to connect the dots. We were being taken "to a better place" for a while. That place, if measured by the immense amount of time we were spending in the car to get there, must be pretty far from Riverton Park. The environment couldn't have been more fitting. It was getting darker and darker. The sun had set and the trees, once green and friendly, had now turned into dark shadows with waving arms. They were like a funeral procession mourning the end of the life I had lived up until then.

Eventually, we slowed down and turned into a driveway. A light appeared at the end of the open-air tunnel of night. Was it the spark of something new, or was it a burning reminder of what we had lost?

Out on the porch stepped a white couple, Mark and Debi. Mark was in his forties at the time, balding, with blue eyes, probably somewhere between five-foot-nine and five-foot-eleven. Debi, also in her forties, had blue eyes and blonde hair that was cropped short, and she stood a few inches shorter than Mark.

The caseworker walked my sister and me up the stairs, doing her solemn duty to deliver these two children into the loving care of a foster home. But despite all the reassuring words and love showered on both of us that night, heartbreak set in with the clang of confusion as we met our foster sisters, Heidi,

Tanya, our foster sister Alexis Rix, and me, all dressed up for a church service in Acton. I'm around eight here.

Erika, and Alexis, the two dogs, and the cats. The floodgates opened even more as we shuffled into our new bedroom.

I lay there sobbing, staring at the night-light. I was crying "Mommy, Mommy," until my voice grew hoarse and disappeared altogether, at which point it seemed like my very soul and body sobbed the words with every heave of my heavy heart. While it would seem that my life thus far should have prepared me for this inevitable separation, given the many times I was separated or distant from my mother, it was as if my whole being knew that this was, in fact, the separation to end all separations, that there would be no more back-and-forth. And while the custody battle would continue far from our view, and there would be many more transitions ahead, the truth was, we would never live with our mother again.

The resentment and anger that I woke up with the next day slowly softened over the coming weeks and months as my new family gave us love in abundance. Mark was kind and nurturing. Seldom was he stern. Even if I committed some childish act of disobedience or disrespect and was met with firmness, it soon faded.

In a recent visit with my first foster family, Debi retold the story about how the authorities investigating the junkyard incident eventually found me. We laughed quite a bit as she told me how I used to want to answer the phone every time someone called. But this time, Debi answered first and a voice came on the line.

"Hello, this is the assistant district attorney. Is there a Marpheen there?"

As their conversation continued, Debi said my face grew pale and I began to shake my head vigorously. I had been found! And from the looks of it, Debi was in cahoots with them, as she went on to explain that she agreed with the authorities; I needed to face the consequences of my actions.

The day arrived when I was scheduled to appear before the judge and the owner of the junkyard. Debi said it was painful for her to watch how anxious and nervous I was, but she stuck to her guns, realizing that this was a good learning and disciplinary opportunity.

What I remembered from this meeting or hearing (or whatever you want to call it) was me sitting in a room with a bunch of grown-ups. I remember repeating, "I didn't do it; I didn't mean to." Somewhere in the conversation someone mentioned that it didn't matter if I *meant* to do anything: I was an accomplice; I had trespassed; and I had been on the scene when the incident happened. At this point, I just bawled. I sobbed uncontrollably, most likely sniffling out sad arguments of it being unfair and all that jazz.

The crying must have done the trick, since I was not sent to juvenile hall or assigned community service, as was done for the other kids. My guess is that, in light of the circumstances, with me being in the type of home environment I was in at the time, and being transitioned into a foster home, the judge must have decided that to pile on more would not be in my best interest. I don't even remember if there were any serious repercussions from this event. I chuckle now, because I say that this was my first victory in a court of law (although I don't remember being in an actual courtroom; I think it was the judge's private chambers).

Afterward, Debi took me out for an ice cream. And you know

what? I totally agree that she did the right thing, and that the ice cream must have worked, because it took her retelling the story for me to remember how awful it felt.

One of my fondest memories from this time was with my foster dad, Mark, one that makes me chuckle

My foster dad, Mark Rix, and me at Wells Beach in 2000.

to this day. It was an afternoon on a lake or pond, and Mark and I had taken to the water on a kayak. I remember it was a pleasant summer day, the sort of pleasant where every breath feels easy, as if you were inhaling the very gulps of life for the first time. The sun, golden and warm, set the ripples and waves ablaze with dancing light. The trees were serene and waving, as if begging us to come back to shore so we could wave with them. They, too, seemed to glow with summer. It was the kind of day where you couldn't help but hum with happiness. Like a bumblebee, buzzing drunkenly after hitting a jackpot of pollen.

I was at the front of the kayak. It was so pleasant that I had stopped paddling and closed my eyes, listening to the sounds of the water, the seagulls far from the sea. All I could see was the warm glow of sunlight through my eyelids. And there it was. A sigh. *Un Sospiro* ("A Sigh" in Italian, the title of one of my favorite classical pieces, composed by Franz Liszt). It felt like I was slipping into a trance. As if I was falling.

SPLASH. Indeed, I was falling … sideways into the water. After who knows how long—it felt like hours—I had fallen asleep and had tipped the kayak over. Everything went overboard. Including Mark.

But what I heard was the oddest thing. He was laughing! Of all the responses you might have expected from such an incident, it wasn't laughter. Despite him losing his wallet, and everything being soaked, he was laughing. Next thing I know, I was laughing too. We both laughed all the way home in the truck, and the whole family laughed as we tried to relay the story (through more fits of laughter) of how we'd ended up getting soaked.

Another time Mark was following the GPS with me and Tanya in the car. We were driving along when all of a sudden Mark veered toward the right and off the road into a field. The tiny Honda was bumping along until we rolled to a stop, at which point we all burst out laughing. Who knows why? It was just that darn funny! When Mark reminded me of that incident recently, it brought back all of those cozy and warm feelings I felt at the time.

Life was different for us there. My sister and I were truly allowed to be kids, without having to worry about being cold or hungry or neglected. Their home was always filled with warmth and the comfort of the wood stove (thanks in small part to my newly acquired skill of wood stacking). We were introduced to a whole new array of American food, which I admit was a little bland compared to my grandmother's cooking (many Asian dishes are spicy). But as long as I had the black pepper shaker within reach, the blandness was somewhat tolerable. (Boy, did I learn to love pepper!) All joking aside, Debi's cooking was phenomenal. Homemade mac-and-cheese (none of that fake, boxed stuff). Meatloaf. Pies. You name it, she made it—and I ate it. My favorite, though, was Mark's barbecue chicken. I don't quite remember what made it so re-*mark*-able. Perhaps because it reminded me of some of the scaled-down barbecues I had with my uncles and grandmother.

There is one funny food-related story. Well, I suppose it depends on whom you talk to. But we were having a grill night and relatives were coming over to feast on Mark's famous barbecue chicken. Debi was preparing the table and seating for the guests and arranging the placement of potato salad, green beans, and all the other fixings for a proper grilled meal.

I sauntered into the dining room, which, if you were to walk into the house from the front porch, was at the back of the house, past the living room and to the left of the kitchen. But instead of taking in the sight of the side dishes and the smell of barbecue chicken sizzling on the grill, my eyes fixated on a can of Pringles on the counter. With my mouth watering for those salty, crunchy, thin wavy chips, I reached for them, only to be stopped by Debi's voice.

"Uh, uh, uh," I remember her saying. "You're not having chips. It's almost time for dinner. We're going to have your favorite barbecue chicken."

I stomped my foot down hard and looked at Debi with my scrunched-up face and a determined look in my eye. "I want chips," I said as I grabbed the can of Pringles and opened them.

Debi pried the Pringles from my fingers, saying sternly, "No, we're about to have dinner. Go outside and help Mark with the chicken."

I stomped, stomped, stomped through the sunroom and down the steps that led to the lawn below to sulk and *not* help Mark, who caught on pretty fast to what was going on. When I wouldn't help, he walked me through the front door and we stood there, the living room on our left, the kitchen toward the back, and the hallway to the bathroom and bedrooms on our right.

"You can help me cook outside or help Debi in the kitchen— or you can go to your bedroom," Mark said.

Unbeknownst to either of us, Debi was around the corner. When she heard me walking down to my room and slamming the door, she started to cry because she had hoped that I'd make the right choice and join them for dinner.

Instead, Mark and Debi, my sister Tanya, and the rest of the family sat through dinner hearing me wailing and crying "I want chips! I want chips! I want chips!"

After dinner wrapped up, Mark collected me from my room

My school photo from 2000, when I was at Acton Elementary.

and sat me down at the kitchen to have a talk.

"Debi, Marpheen is hungry," he said as Debi watched us from the kitchen.

She reached up into the cupboard, grabbed a box of cereal and a bowl, and made a pit stop at the refrigerator to get some milk before heading over to the dining table.

As soon as she'd set the items on the table, I grabbed the box of cereal and chucked it across the room, yelling "I want chips!"

I don't remember what happened after that point, but I do know this was one of the few times all of us remember where I acted out in such a manner. Apart from that, they recalled me being a pretty easygoing and lovable kid. Apparently my sister Tanya was the stubborn one!

In addition to a new family, I also had to adjust to a new school, Acton Elementary. And what an adjustment it was!

Just months before arriving at my first foster home, I was a second-grader in the Portland Public School system, which served the most populous and most diverse district in the entire state of Maine. At Reiche and Riverton Elementary, there were Somalis, Kenyans, Vietnamese, Thai, Cambodian, and Lebanese. It was a melting pot, and I didn't feel out of place at all.

But at Acton Elementary, my sister and I were like grains of sand in a sea of white. I mean, it was a school that served one of Maine's quintessential small towns. I felt out of place. I felt shy, it seemed, for the first time in my life. There were no other kids who looked like me, other than my sister. It was hard enough being the new kids in a new school in a new town. On top of that, we were "the Other." We weren't like everyone else. We had different skin. Different eyes. Different hair. Even if we were met with kindness, stereotypes and biases still exist for many who grow up in predominantly homogenous communities, and they tend to appear when someone who doesn't look like them shows up.

I remember quite clearly during my third-grade year at Acton Elementary, in the middle of a snowy, wintry recess, when those feelings of being different from everyone else—having different skin, different eyes—reached a climax. A kid with dark brown hair in a sort of cropped bowl cut, pale skin, and light brown freckles came up to me and poked fun at me about my eyes. It was as if the feelings that were all bottled up just came pouring out. The next thing I knew, my hand, which must have been curled into a fist already, swung back and knocked him in the face, giving him a bloody nose. I had crossed a red line in the snow; I knew that much. But so did the other kid, I felt. I, of course, was suspended for the day.

My assimilation into whiteness didn't come without bumps in the road. While I may have begun to talk white and act white and dress white, in my mind, I was still brown. I was the kid who'd shown up at the tail end of a school year and was just plopped in the middle of a bunch of elementary school kids who'd had an entire year to get to know each other.

Not only was I new, but I looked different, talked different. I still spoke a little Khmer. I had yet to adjust to my surroundings and still had all the fury of a fish out of water. I was a disruption, and felt it in the way that I got "extra attention." I was the kid who needed a little extra help with his English lessons and math problems. I was the brown kid who had white foster parents, the one other kids asked their parents about.

But just as Acton and the people were new to me, so was I new to them. And as time went on, Acton, at least the school community, surprised me. In later conversations with Mark and Debi, they reminded me of how an entire elementary school in rural Maine had organized a Cambodian New Year celebration to help my sister Tanya and I feel welcome. Debi recalled fondly over some lunch at the Honey Paw—an Asian fusion restaurant in Portland—that during that time, I came home and told her, "I'm proud to be Cambodian," and started to own that part of myself.

Still, we were no longer surrounded by our Cambodian family and friends. The language and culture I was born into and grew up with leading up to that point in time began to slip my mind. Something I deeply regret to this day is that I no longer know a single word in Cambodian. This makes it extremely difficult to converse with my birth family members, especially my grandmother and birth mother and father.

But I am jumping ahead slightly. The beginning of a new life in a small town in Maine was initiated by my foster parents, who encouraged me to try baseball and basketball. I was okay at baseball (I was much better in fifth and sixth grade, playing for Gorham Savings Bank in the Babe Ruth League). I didn't like basketball much; I got too many finger jams. One thing I did like was music class. Although I was shy, I had always loved singing. I remember quite clearly the Christmas concert we put on for our parents and how I discovered one of my favorite songs, "My Favorite Things." I still hum it sometimes to this day.

Church was important to Debi and Mark's family. We went to a small church every now and then, but we mainly attended Curtis Lake Christian Church in Sanford, one of Maine's larger towns. We went to Sunday school and family nights and summer Bible camp, and I joined the children's choir. They presented a fully produced Christmas pageant in which baby Jesus is born, grows into a man, and is ultimately nailed to a cross.

Tanya and I celebrated our first American Christmas with our new foster family. It was our introduction to new Yuletide traditions and was indeed a magical time for us. From venturing out and finding our Christmas tree, making strings of popcorn, decorating our own ornaments, and arranging all the lights, Tanya and I were truly enamored by everything. We had an upright piano in the living room and learned Christmas carols, sat by the fireplace, and had Christmas Eve dinner. I remember not being able to sleep that night, having heard the stories of Santa Claus and the gifts he would bring.

The next morning, I remember shaking with excitement and wanting everyone to wake up. At long last, they did, and we all rushed to the Christmas tree. And there they were: more presents than we could have imagined, and stockings stuffed to overflowing! What a sight it was! We had never seen anything like it before. It was truly a time of joy and giving. Everyone was in good spirits.

But even with this new world and all of its comforts, there was a shadow. I had a lot of anger and resentment. In a conversation with Mark and Debi when I was an adult, we talked about the winter of my first Christmas as a time of breakthrough, when my bottled-up emotions reached a breaking point.

I stood out, even in the back of the Acton Elementary basketball team's photo.

It was sometime in March when my foster sister, Alexis, and I were having an ordinary snowball fight. But when a snowball landed on my ear and slid down my neck, I got very angry. So much so that she ran into the house and locked me out, which made me even angrier. As bad as it sounds, this was the point where I expressed all the feelings that I had bottled up since being separated from my birth mother and moving to my first foster family. This was also a turning point in many ways. In letting my anger out, I also began to let go. I yelled and yelled repeatedly and eventually started crying in that angry-kid, gulping sort of way.

I remember that, in that moment, I came up with one of the plans that many kids my age come up with when we get that angry: *I am going to run away and make them miss me, and we'll see how they feel then.*

I ran into the woods nearby and down toward a brook that I often visited. It flowed through a culvert under the road and snaked its way through the woods down past the house. I especially loved this one spot during the summer. There were big, huge boulders on either side of the brook that gave an onlooker a good view of the tiny brook. Sitting atop one of the bigger boulders and taking in the greenish-gold that filtered from the fusion of sun and leaf, accompanied by the soft hint of moss and forest floor, was a favorite pastime of mine. During my outburst in the winter, it became my "runaway spot" where I thought I would hide in order to make my foster family miss me.

It didn't take long for me to calm down and realize that my plan had backfired. I missed *them*. Not only because I wanted to get back into the warm house, but to feel the warm embrace they were more than ready and able to give. To feel the warmth of a home-cooked meal made with love. To put up with having to constantly nag me to clean my room and take out the laundry so I could sleep in a bed with clean sheets and pillows. To sleep without being

I'm around age nine here, in the kitchen with Mark Rix, Brandon, Bob and Tracy Berry, Seyya, Tanya, and Debi Rix.

woken up by shouting and fighting or people drinking, smoking, and gambling. To feel safe—to feel stability and consistency. But most of all, to come back to people who I knew wouldn't disappear, just like that. Who were just around the corner when I'd wake up from a nightmare. I would miss all of it. Something I hadn't had for a very long time, not since I'd lived with my godparents for a while. Things that many of us take for granted, as routine and expected. Things that, although seemingly mundane or small, all translate as part of the language of love.

Reflecting on it now, Mark and Debi offered me a life I had never known in so many ways. Not only because they could, as a middle-class family, but because they wanted to. I think that's a key distinction. They didn't have to upend their lives, change their routine, devote less time to their own biological children (teenage girls going through puberty, dating, soccer and field hockey games, etc.), to take in two kids from a severely broken and traumatized background. But they did, and they were committed to sticking it through. They made it a point, and still do to this day, that we really became a part of their family. That it was not a sacrifice. That despite all the trouble they went through to adapt and change, that we brought love and light into their home just as much as they brought love and light into our hearts.

So I went back. The door was unlocked and Debi was home. When she saw me trudging in, staring at the floor and a little embarrassed, she simply said, "Do you feel better now, bud?" Then she made me a cup of hot cocoa to warm me up.

Debi explained to me later that my child therapist had said this was a breakthrough moment for me. Up until that point, I had bottled away my anger and feelings about the entire life situation I was in. Getting into a rage about a snowball to the ear was in fact breaking the dam that I had built to keep back and hide the immense turmoil of emotions swirling inside me. She explained that things began to change after that, as if a burden had lifted and I had begun to breathe again.

When spring came into bloom, our situation was beginning to change. As I found out later, we were only supposed to stay at Mark and Debi's for a few days, but it turned into a whole year. It was then that the DHHS decided to transfer my sister and me to a group home in Windham, Maine.

At the time, the DHHS was being accused of racism—taking a disproportionate amount of kids of color away from their parents and placing them with foster families, most of them white. This was not only a problem of the 1990s and early 2000s. The problem still exists today because of the way the US child welfare system is designed. Northwestern University School of Law professor Dorothy Roberts wrote in an essay for *Frontline*, "If you came with no preconceptions about the purpose of the child welfare system, you would have to conclude that it is an institution designed to monitor, regulate, and punish poor families of color. ... The child welfare system is designed not as a way to assist parents in taking care of their children but as a way to punish parents for their failures by threatening to take their children away. ... It should be noted that child welfare practice became increasingly punitive. … As the child welfare system began to serve fewer white children and more children of color, state and federal governments spent more money on out-of-home care and less on in-home services." In a national study that Roberts references in her essay, the report found that "minority children, and in particular African American children, are more likely to be in foster care placement than receive in-home services, even when they have the same problems and characteristics as white children."

When faced with allegations of racism during my time in foster care, however, the Maine DHHS didn't look internally at how their policies and procedures led to this, but instead had a knee-jerk reaction. Instead of adopting a new policy that would revamp the review process for determining when to rip kids out of their homes, and especially the policy that kids of color should be placed with other families of color, they committed a colossal fumble. Their first mistake was thinking that they could achieve this in one of the whitest states in the country. The second mistake was rounding up kids that they had initially placed with white families and throwing them once again into the administrative hellhole of the foster-care system.

In my case, the DHHS had actually succeeded in placing my sister and me with a perfectly good and loving family. At a point when I was just starting to heal from the initial trauma of being separated from my birth mother, when I was learning to love again, the Department ripped us from our new family and placed us in a group home. Not with an Asian family—in a group home.

The idea then was to either look for an Asian family or to try and get my birth mother to a point where she could take us back. But meanwhile, my sister and I sat in group-home, foster-care limbo, nursing our broken hearts. If I sound angry, I am. I can forgive and reconcile with people, but when it comes to a system or process or government, I am wholly within my rights to be angry. Mark and Debi both had tears in their eyes when they were recalling what happened to me.

Sometimes I wonder what goes through their heads when the DHHS decides to tear families apart, and then foster families, and then second foster families. Not only that, but when the agency—by chance—happens to place kids in a good home, I wonder how some administrative concern or policy can blind them, leading them to pluck kids from a good situation and place them under the enormous strain of transitioning into yet another new home. You could not design a better system to create a fractured sense of self, with all of the resultant anxiety, trust, and attachment issues, if you tried.

We all packed into Mark's truck and rode to the group home together. The drive from Acton, through Alfred, Sanford, and Buxton, to Windham, felt like it took ages. I expected at any moment during the trip that Mark and Debi would turn around and take us back home, so when we drove into the driveway, the feelings hit us all like a Mack truck.

Saying good-bye to a family I loved, one that loved me, was so much harder than being separated from my birth mother.

Park Place, Windham, Maine, 2001

● ◗ ◐ ○ ○

My anger toward the DHHS did not mean I was angry with the people who lived and worked at the group home. In fact, I grew to love each of them, and the other kids provided much-needed company and playtime. Among my favorite staff were Ellen, Ken, and Dana.

Ken was in his early to mid-twenties, and we recently reconnected on Facebook. I was the oldest of my four siblings, so Ken became something of a big brother figure to me. For someone his age, he had a deep and caring heart and took his job seriously, treating us as if we were family. He was also the only male worker at that group home, so he was the only male role model I had—and I couldn't have asked for a better one.

Dana and her husband were looking to adopt and had the difficult task of choosing between my sister and me and two other siblings. They had us stay overnight at their huge house in Gray, to sort of test the waters. Life would have been good there, I am sure, but they ended up going with the two sisters. Surprisingly, I wasn't upset. I knew those two girls very well and I was happy for them; for me, the saddest part was that I was no longer able to see two of my friends regularly.

One memory from the group home days always finds its way back to me in moments of solitude. The room I stayed in had white laminate flooring speckled with blue and gray. The room itself was sort of weirdly designed, with an open closet full of hangers off to the right, at a right angle to the window. I remember standing in the middle of my room staring at the dust floating in the panel of sunlight that sliced in from the window. I often did this, by the way—stared at specks of dust floating in the sunlight, that is. In my hand was a baseball card, and I remember looking at the man on the card. I was surprised by the feelings that surfaced.

I brought the card closer so I could see his face. *He's handsome,* I thought to myself. Then I lowered my head and planted a kiss right on his face. I passed no judgment on myself for thinking he was handsome, or for kissing that baseball card. I merely stood in that shaft of sunlight, pleasantly warm on the outside and on the inside as I admired the man.

I had just turned ten. It's probably a good time to remind folks that most of these transitions happened around my birthday, in June. The progress I had made while living with Mark and Debi had all but vanished. I'd begun to hurt emotionally again, which had an

Tanya and me, posing with Mark and Debi during one of their visits to the group home.

effect on me physically. One photo of me and Tanya, taken when Mark and Debi were allowed to visit us at the group home, shows that I had become pudgy compared to when I lived with them in Acton. But one thing shines through in that photo: If what I've said about Mark and Debi up to this point hasn't convinced you of how happy I was when living with them, then the big smile on my face in this photo would probably do the job.

That smile also reminds me of something I didn't realize until I'd heard it said multiple times by all the people I've met along the way, throughout my story. Although I was in pain and hurting, my smile seemed to shine through and lighten their lives. I say I didn't really realize this because when I remember those transitions and difficult periods, I focus on the pain and the hurt—not that I don't remember the good times and moments of joy and happiness, but all of it swirls together in the fog of memory. It's been a revelation to learn that I had an impact on people as an eight-, nine-, and ten-year-old.

Mark and Debi and those who worked at the group home all

recall me being a sad boy, but very sweet, kind, and considerate. I had a big smile to prove it. It's heartening to me to know that even then—as I do now—I was able to find the positive in things, and to be optimistic. That I did not forget to hope.

A dark memory from this time was at Jack Elementary School. It was September 11, 2001, and suddenly the school was bustling. We were told school would be closing early that day. Being kids, we rejoiced, knowing nothing about what was unfolding that fateful morning.

One of the group home employees picked me and my sister up and drove us home. The ride home was odd. The day couldn't have been more perfect in terms of the temperature and the way a golden tinge seemed to light the air with an invisible glow. The breeze wafting in through the window also carried with it the faint smell of summer coming to an end.

But the noises from the front of the car were distracting. The group home employee's hand was covering her mouth, as if she had witnessed an unsightly scene on the road ahead. I knew she was responding to what was being said on the radio, which honestly sounded monotonous, the same story being repeated over and over again, the employee trying in vain to cover her gasps.

When we made it to the group home, the TV was on. I finally connected the images on the screen to what was being said on the radio. America had been attacked. Two planes had rammed into the World Trade Center. Thousands of people had died.

Our peace was shattered—violated, in a sense. My reaction was a little absurd: I remember "praying" to George Washington that we would make them pay. (Then again, I was a ten-year-old with an imaginative mind.)

Probably the memory that most makes me cringe out of embarrassment is when I woke up one morning sometime after September 11 and placed my little stereo in the open window of the TV room. I put in a CD of patriotic songs that I had somehow acquired and cranked up the volume for all to hear. The group home was smack dab in the middle of a quiet, suburban, residential neighborhood in Maine. This was also in the early morning hours. Perhaps the neighbors were not all that upset to hear "God Bless America" blaring through the neighborhood. I was a kid caught up in the wave of patriotic fervor that swept the nation, and it only served to further fuel my fascination with history and current events.

Aside from this huge event, life at the group home seemed to settle down for the next ten months or so. The building was an odd piece of architecture. It had a flat roof with outer walls covered with masonry and an entrance with floor-to-ceiling glass windows that led into the kitchen. If you turned to the left, you could walk down carpeted stairs into a huge living room that looked more like a small lecture space. If you passed through the kitchen, you eventually entered an open area surrounded by the kids' rooms, two bathrooms, and the TV room. My room was the first on the right, the TV room on the right after that, then, going counterclockwise, there was a bathroom, four other bedrooms, and then another bathroom. The group home also had a huge lawn, a garage, and an in-ground pool surrounded by a tall, wooden fence.

This was where I first saw the movie *The Princess Bride*. I laughed until my stomach hurt when I heard the priest say the word "marriage." This was also where I got one of the kids to trade me his Charizard for my Articuno, which he later found out was a bad trade. A year or so later, when we'd both moved on to different foster homes, I ran into him at a Walmart. He began to tug on his foster mom, saying, "Hey! He stole my Charizard!" It was disputes like this that caused many schools to ban Pokémon cards from the playground.

Tanya and I languished at the group home for fifteen months until one of the workers there, Sheila, took us home with her.

Gorham, Maine, 2002

It has taken a while for me to process and write about moments from this period of my life. Part of me was holding back to protect Sheila, since it is not my intention to imply, nor is it my view, that she is a terrible person. The way I see it, reflecting on it now as I approach the age of thirty, she was a single foster mother who most probably had bitten off more than she could chew by agreeing to foster me and Tanya. She was a high school special education teacher, so imagine doing that all day and then coming home to kids who were dealing with emotional trauma.

Sheila brought us to her home, adjacent to the University of Southern Maine, as a sort of testing period. Tanya and I were enamored with how big the house was—a New England home built in the 1800s with two barns and a large, and I mean *large*, field that sloped up toward the university. The backyard had this neat patch of land with a screened hammock house nestled in between the trees. Sometimes I would imagine it as my own private jungle. The yard gave us more than enough space to play. But there was also a lot of responsibility involved, and this was where Sheila and I often butted heads. The huge yard required a lot of raking and maintenance during the spring, summer, and fall, and, like many other kids, I hated chores.

Despite how large the house was, the barns and about one-third of the house were uninhabitable due to lack of insulation and heating. Upon entering the mudroom, you saw a flight of steep stairs that went up toward my room. To the right was a doorway that led into the kitchen, the floor of which was covered with linoleum like many other old, New England homes. The next room was a dining room with a large table and chandelier, with windows that looked out onto College Avenue. A bathroom was on the right. Farther down you would take a right, and on the left you would have the front door—which we didn't use—and more narrow stairs on the right that led upstairs to the bedrooms. Straight ahead was the living room. We each had our own bedrooms, which all had doors that led to a bathroom located in the center. I mostly used the stairs by the entrance to get to and from my room but would often travel through the centrally located bathroom to get to my sister's room to pick on her or tease her.

We spent time with Sheila's parents throughout our stay with her, which was always memorable. We would visit for Thanksgiving and Christmas, and other occasions. Her parents lived in Damariscotta, about an hour's drive that takes you along I-295, branching off at the Brunswick exit, and continuing over the giant bridges of picturesque Bath and Wiscasset. It was a treat to go there to visit. The salt air was thicker in those parts, less polluted by the mixture of cigarette smoke and car exhaust out of Portland, or the bustling university town of Gorham.

Sheila's father was a man of few words, but we found something to bond over: World War II documentaries. If I recall correctly, he himself had served in the armed forces, although I'm not sure which war. We'd sit there together and watch hours of the black-and-white footage of the battles that were waged across Europe and the Pacific. The struggle against the Axis of Evil. D-Day. The Battle of the Bulge. The triumphant liberation of concentration camps and the fall of Adolf Hitler.

I have always loved older people—grandparents. There's a tenderness that comes with age, born of wisdom from a life lived and lessons learned. Sheila's parents embodied these qualities.

I was a fourth-grader by this time and was enrolled at Village Elementary School in Gorham. I walked a mile back and forth to school each day. I remember we were studying the Civil War in history class and I found a poem in a book on the Civil War. For reasons I still do not know, probably an impulsive need to be recognized and appreciated, I told my teacher and classmates that I wrote the poem. Well, of course that didn't pan out well, as they caught on pretty quickly that I had not written it. Both my teacher and Sheila were flabbergasted. Sheila sat me down and asked me something like, "Why did you lie about the poem?" To which I responded with a guilty look at my lap.

My lack of response did not sit well with her, and she asked again. And again. And again. Instances like this occurred more and more often, and each time she would become more flustered with my inability to explain why, exactly, I had taken a certain course of action. Her face would get visibly red and puffed up as she got angrier and angrier. Somewhere along the way, her words became like poison. Not that the words themselves were that atrocious, but rather, the way she said them. Her face with that angry, red flush. Her eyes getting bloodshot and fierce. It scared the hell out of me and made me even more speechless.

Her words dripped with venom, hot coals that burned and melted through my self-esteem like butter. It felt like an unfair game of Jenga, where with every word and scathing look she was tearing me down, piece by piece. I knew I was crumbling.

When I received some failing grades on my math homework, she sat me down at the dinner table to go over each problem, to try to show me how to solve them. I wasn't quite getting it, and I could see her frustration on her face. Her jaw was clenched, and her lips were trembling with annoyance and festering anger. The ends of her curly brown hair looked like they were violently shaking.

"Why can't you get this?" she said. "Why can't you focus? What's wrong with you?"

Again, not terrible words *per se*, but it was the way they seethed out of her eyes and ears, not just her mouth, like steam from a hot engine ready to explode. I knew she was angry. I knew she was impatient. I knew she felt that there were better things she could be doing with her time. It was precisely this knowledge that made every word a wound that whittled me down. I felt small. Really small. Like a speck of sawdust floating through the vast and empty halls of a home whose walls and rooms were stripped of life. I felt humiliated. Stupid. Dumb. I felt like I had a mental block, where I couldn't put two and two together.

I absorbed it all, and over time I learned to shut down in the face of it, and, under my skin and out of sight, how to curl up into a ball and escape the emotional hell. I learned how to deafen myself in a way, to lessen the pain. The art of staring blankly at her, or at something else in the room, just focusing on that one feature on her face or the chandelier hanging from the ceiling in the dining room. I became numb. Unable to feel anything—especially any pride in myself. I learned to just emotionally check out, which made her even angrier. I felt my insides become like walls stripped down to Sheetrock, gray and lifeless, like a silent motion picture.

As things escalated with Sheila, I felt stuck, with no control over the situation or myself, my thoughts, my feelings. I didn't know how to feel about Sheila or myself. I felt depressed, reclusive. I retreated into the deepest, darkest corners of myself, into an emotionless cell that would protect me from feeling the sting of Sheila's words, and her frustration.

In other words, I tried to feel nothing.

It also felt tremendously confusing, because at the same time, Sheila was also challenging me to be active and to get involved with things. Thus, during the summer of my eleventh birthday, I tried out for the Babe Ruth baseball league. I was incredibly anxious, because a baseball is small and extremely hard. When I showed up for tryouts, the coaches had us cycle through various tests to see which positions we might be good at. I remember waiting in line to catch a fly ball and being petrified. So many thoughts ran through my head. *What if I don't catch it? What if it hits me? What would the other boys think of me?* I caught it all right. But not in my newly broken-in, leather baseball glove that held my hand prisoner. No, I caught it right in the face. *THWAT.* Right against my chubby cheek.

I could hear the other boys in line behind me snickering. But what made it worse was that across the gym, the other boys had their dads looking on and watching, nodding as they saw their sons face the trials. I had no father to cheer me on. Sheila was single, and I don't even remember if she herself was there at the time.

I felt an emptiness after getting that fly ball in the face. Even if the other boys messed up, I could hear their dads saying, "It's okay, son, you can do it. You're all right." All I heard was that *THWAT* as the hard baseball smacked my face and sent ripples across my brown, *brown* cheeks. No familiar voice rang through the pain or the shame, which hurt more than the physical sensation sizzling through every part of my body, burning up my cheeks and my ears like a teapot coming to boil.

After the tryouts, I felt like none of the teams would want me. But to my surprise, the coaches of the Gorham Savings Bank team, dressed in their blue GSB caps and windbreakers, called me over. I was stunned. I'm sure they saw my wide-eyed surprise as they asked me which position I wanted to play. To this day I don't know why, but for some reason, I picked right field—a position where fly balls were a common occurrence.

To be honest, the first two-thirds of the season, I sucked. I barely caught a fly ball. I barely hit a ball. I was no good. But the coaches kept encouraging me, and my teammates did the same. I remember one game, near the end of my first season on the GSB team, when I smacked one deep into center field. I barely even remembered to run for first base, but I can recall the surprised shouts from my coaches and teammates as they yelled for me to run.

This was a game-changer. All of a sudden, I was catching fly balls and making plays, and as the season came to an end, my team and the other teams expected me to smack it deep into the outfield, or even to hit a home run.

The next baseball season, I got even better. How things had changed from that day in the Gorham middle school gym, when I'd faced the music of a fly ball in the face and the snickers of the other boys. By this point, I was standing underneath the lights, everything else around me, the sounds and murmurs of the crowd and the players, blurred and drowned out by my focus on the pitcher, whose eyes peered above the rim of his glove. Time seemed to slow in that moment. The only two people in the world were pitcher and batter.

Breathe. Feet firmly planted, shoulder width apart. Find your balance. Knuckles aligned. The words became like instinct in that moment, the product of many, many practices.

Then came the pitcher's dance, a double-edged sword meant to both distract and deliver. I answered in kind, shifting my weight between my left and right foot, swaying my bat slightly in a pendulum arc to keep time.

One pitcher in particular, tall, blond, and blue-eyed, had a dance different from the others, which climaxed in a lightning-fast throw. His pitches would fly low and were easily missed if your eyes wandered. I got to know this pitcher and his style. He didn't pitch with his arm swinging up and over in an arc, but rather with a fast sidearm swing. While I'd once feared him and his fastballs, with my newfound confidence that was no longer the case. He may have been lightning-fast, but lightning has its weaknesses. It longs to connect to something, to anything. The metal bat is the perfect rod to catch that lightning and cast it out beyond.

Around this same time I discovered a love for fantasy novels, especially Brian Jacques' Redwall series. My imagination flourished as I painted pictures of talking animals living in abbeys and castles and towns. My boyish sense of adventure was emboldened as I imagined scenes of mice and moles fighting off rats with swords and sabers.

And, boy, did I love the badgers, a warring clan of mighty heroes who often wielded battleaxes.

Books were my escape. They carried me into far-off lands where I knew there were happy endings, despite the mishaps and tragedies along the way. Books inspired me with heroes who rose from obscurity and adversity to face daunting challenges and obstacles. I delved into fantasy and, whether it was Redwall, Harry Potter, or The Lord of the Rings, I lived in these worlds. I also loved history and read voraciously about the greatest leaders in the Western world. I would sit for hours and hours, burning through books. Sometimes that was all I would do all day long.

There is something to be said about the power of reading. Through reading, I found heroes and role models. I found people from small beginnings who struggled through trials and tribulation to overcome the seemingly impossible. The heroes I found inspired me and helped me feel something other than misery and shattered self-esteem.

Reading also expanded my horizons. It encouraged me to learn a new language while being exposed to different points of view and different ways of thinking. You learn how to think by piecing it all together. Even if they are fantasy novels, they present an author's view of how things happen and the story or lesson they wish to convey.

A child who has grappled with learning a new language and how to speak it begins to encounter another world of ideas, often at their own pace, at a stage where they can begin to comprehend more complex issues. The journey into this world is a struggle at first, because one is already predisposed to thinking a certain way, in terms of where one lives, who one is surrounded by, and even *what* one is surrounded by. Wading into the world of an author's ideas creates a sort of cognitive dissonance at first, because one is inundated suddenly with new perspectives—like an ancient explorer who begins his journey in a fishing boat, only to discover that, the farther out he goes, the more treacherous it can be. And so, he returns to shore and endeavors to build a bigger ship that will carry him farther.

Books weren't my only escape. I had friends, too—well, a few. I also had my first girlfriend in fifth grade. Her name was Dani-Le, and we got to know each other in our after-school recreation program at Village Elementary. I honestly can't remember why we started "dating," but I do know I just wasn't into it. Looking back today, as a blossoming and successful gay man, I have a clearer picture of why it didn't work. Dani-Le and I happened to have a class together in college, and we keep in touch to this day. She once threatened to share an embarrassing photo of me on Instagram. (Fortunately, she hasn't—yet.)

I bonded quickly with another kid named Noah, probably because we were both having a hard time. His parents had just divorced and I was in foster care. Both of us were big into the video game *Yu-Gi-Oh*, as were all the other kids at the time, and we would often play the PlayStation version together. I'd go to his house sometimes and we'd play the video-game adaptation of The Lord of the Rings on his machine.

As kids often do, we acted out our imaginations and video games in real life. I remember one time we ran off into the woods behind his house and made an adventure out of knocking over dead trees, mostly birch trees rotting from too much moisture. It was such an adrenaline rush at the time to run up to one, hit it as hard as we could, and see how the tree splintered and fell over, to hear the crash—the snap, crackle, pop, the creaks and groans, and the final thud on the forest floor—that would send vibrations through the ground. A feeling that crept into our toes and feet and up our legs. As if we were giants who could make the Earth shake. Exhilarating.

One time Noah came over to Sheila's to play PlayStation. We were laughing and talking and celebrating either our loss or win against each other—I can't remember which—and an overwhelming urge came over me. I wanted to kiss him. It was a powerful feeling, as if my heart itself was trying to claw its way out of my chest. But it was fleeting, and nothing ever came of it, unless you count the brotherly bond that grew between us.

I think it was important for me to experience that feeling, if ever so briefly. I only wish I could have explored it more in depth throughout my adolescence, like many heterosexual kids get to. Stumbling home after school with rosy cheeks after saying hi to a crush in the hallway at school. Hearing yes when you ask them to sit with you at the lunchroom table. Going to the movies and bumping arms, or maybe even the clichéd putting your arm around their shoulder in that classic awkward, motion-picture way. Or even just being rejected and figuring out that you're better off as friends.

Times have changed since then in terms of the acceptance of LGBTQ+ people, but many kids like me who identified as such in the 2000s, before gay marriage and new LGBTQ+ rights and broad social acceptance, had to delay this part of their adolescence—the social and dating rituals middle schoolers and high schoolers go through, the ups and downs of all the hormones and awkwardness. Getting "the talk" about how all the parts fit together when it comes to opposite-sex relationships, and not the one about how all the parts fit together when it comes to same-sex relationships. Talking openly to your parents about your dating and sex life. A lot of this, for those of us who experienced being in the closet during middle and high school, was put off until we "came out."

Like the song says, "You don't know what you've got till it's gone." I think that was definitely true for my friend Noah and me. It was a powerful friendship that gave each of us the sort of brotherly affection we needed to get through the hard times we were both going through, he, with his parents' divorce, and me, living with an emotionally abusive foster mother.

It is a wonder how we sometimes meet people in our lives as if by fate. Some say it's a higher power, but I think there are good friends to be made in every circumstance and at every turn. I think that giving God all the glory for these relationships belittles how much goodness there is in humanity. Have we lost faith in humankind, our hearts and dreams broken too many times? When we look to the heavens for answers, perhaps we have lost hope of finding the answers here on Earth, around us, and in us. Saying so does not diminish the importance such friendships have. The role of coincidence does not make a chance meeting any less important. There are those who argue that "reducing" everything to random chance and probability strips life of purpose and meaning.

But what is purpose and meaning? For me, it is something that emerges from the dialectic between society and self. Society imposes upon us what one must do to feel as though one has purpose and meaning. In America, for example, a good-paying job is tantamount to what American society perceives as adding purpose and meaning to one's life. When we ask, "What do you do for work?" we're really asking, "What are you doing with your life?" It is a loaded question, underpinned by the assumption that what one deems as purposeful and meaningful is deemed by another as the same. As we grow up, there is a clash between the external world and the internal world— the thesis of self and the antithesis of society—and what emerges varies for each of us.

Coincidences and chance meetings—I don't attribute them to God, or to some higher power, or to karma. I see them through the lens of probability and proximity. When you step in one direction, the probability of meeting a certain person or a certain event occurring is increased by your proximity with that person or event. For me, moving from California to Maine, from home to home, brought me within proximity—and increased the probability—of meeting people who would have an impact on my life. Many of these are shining lights who helped me, befriended me, loved me through it all. They form the constellations that helped guide me, a moon among the stars.

Eventually, social workers and child therapists began to notice that Tanya and I were emotionally deteriorating. We were becoming shells of our former selves, as expressed in our child therapy sessions, which used play to bring out what we wouldn't have expressed otherwise. I was changing physically, putting on weight, and my performance in school was also suffering. So moves were made to get us out of our placement with Sheila. The foster parents of my two youngest siblings took the lead on this, having heard stories from me and Tanya during our visits and sleepovers with our siblings.

Since 1999, the same year that Tanya and I were living with Mark and Debi Rix, Bob and Tracy Berry had been fostering our two younger siblings, Seyya and Brandon. The Berrys lived in Naples, in the Sebago Lakes region, about an hour north of Portland along Route 302. They had worked hard to keep me and my siblings in contact with each other, and it was at this time that they started to take the first few steps toward reuniting us as a family.

The process was arduous and involved an exhaustive and thorough vetting process. I suppose the State had to assess whether our adoptive parents could bear the burden of supporting four foster children with all of our traumas and insecurities—and whether it was, from a legal standpoint, "in the best interests of the children."

I can only imagine what Sheila was going through at the time. I do remember that she tried her best to make it up to us, including taking us on trips to Gettysburg and Washington, DC, and to a botanical garden with many types of butterflies. But at some point, she had to realize that fostering us was more than she could handle.

Sheila had taken a risk, and it came from a good place. She had recognized that my sister and I had spent too much time in that group home, so she opened her home to us. She fed us, provided a roof over our heads, beds to sleep in, and clothes to wear. She took an interest in our well-being and our education. But sometimes that kind of responsibility is too much for one person to handle, especially when it's two foster kids with emotional trauma.

As she later recounted to me when I visited her during my college years, Sheila felt immense guilt at how she had treated us. I keep a letter from Sheila to this day that she wrote to me while we were still living with her, in which she apologized for how she had acted and admitted that the situation wasn't ideal for any of us.

Being a foster parent is no easy task. And not all foster parents are in it for the right reasons. Some do it simply because they can. Some do it for the state benefits that come with foster kids. (And boy, did I run into some of those, like a couple that lived in a trailer park in Gorham. Their house was an absolute pigsty, and their two foster kids were pale and sad-looking, emotionally and physically. I can't count how many times they took us to McDonald's in that one weekend.)

And then there are some, like Mark and Debi, who do it because they're willing to throw their hearts and souls into being foster parents, with its ups and downs, its successes and challenges.

No one should become a foster parent without being prepared to be pushed to the brink while caring for a child who comes with a lifetime of experiences and heartbreaks that they cannot fully articulate. A foster parent with a foster child of a different ethnicity or race also takes on the challenge of raising someone who will be treated differently, and will look in the mirror and wonder *why* they are different. No foster parent should ignore the biases or stereotypes that they themselves might hold, whether consciously or subconsciously, or that their friends, family, neighbors, and community may hold. Being "color blind" and not considering the emotional needs of a child of color is no better or worse than looking specifically for a white child "to fit in with the family."

PART THREE

Naples, Maine, 2003

● ◐ ◑ ○ ○

Taking Route 302 past Sebago Lake in Raymond, average-looking rural gas stations and strip malls suddenly give way to views of a startlingly blue lake. At the crest of a hill looking down slightly over the town of Naples, Long Lake (which stretches eleven miles to the towns of Bridgton and Harrison) is on the right, as are a small grocery store, bank, and pharmacy. Brandy Pond, and Bray's Brew Pub in an old white farmhouse, are on the left.

As you drive over the bridge separating Long Lake from Brandy Pond, there's an enormous American flag. Back when this was my hometown as a teenager, there was a drawbridge that twisted sideways to allow boats to pass between Long Lake and Brandy Pond. The *Songo River Queen*, a replica of the old-fashioned Mississippi River paddle wheelers, would squeeze through what was then considered "the smallest river in the world"—a point made in opposition to the installation of the new bridge that was being proposed and was, in fact, built while I was in high school.

I rode the *Songo River Queen* shortly after the Riverton junkyard incident in 1998, and, five years later in 2003, I was back in Naples. Tanya and I were moving out of Sheila's and in with Bob and Tracy Berry, who had been fostering Seyya and Brandon for four or five years. The Berry family had a double-wide ranch house with beige siding and a green-shingled roof. The unpaved driveway was marked by a rough-hewn cross marked with a white-painted "108" on it. The house itself sat atop a hill of sorts that, in the back, overlooked the rest of the five-acre, largely wooded parcel of land.

To get there, we often took Lakehouse Road, which wound through some hills and valleys and streams and would often incite an "Oh, they must be on Lakehouse Road" comment whenever a cell-phone call was dropped. There was an S-shaped bend dubbed Dead Man's Curve because more than a dozen people had died there. Little crosses marked where fatalities had taken place. Once we passed Dead Man's Curve, we would descend into a small valley and pass Trickey Pond and Sebago Cove. From there, we would climb up and up, then down a little, and then up a large hill until we reached the top and turned right onto King Hill Road, which is surrounded by a small tract of open land.

We rarely ventured into the woods behind our house, largely due to the thick brush and thorn bushes that lined the slope. We were also discouraged by the stories of the angry man who lived with his family on the piece of property behind us. We would hear him yelling at his kids to behave or to come back inside or things like that when we were out feeding our two female pigs in their pen that we'd made out of old wooden pallets.

At the time we moved in, my adoptive dad, Bob, was in his mid-forties, and my adoptive mom, Tracy, was in her early forties. It's easier for me to write the word "dad" than to say it. And while I always refer to him as "Dad" otherwise, I find it's not a go-to word I use when having conversations with him. For instance, on the phone I'll just say "Hey" instead of "Hey, Dad." Or just "Love you" instead of "Love you, Dad." To this day, it's an uncomfortable word for me, for reasons I can't explain, other than the fact I went my first eight or nine years without knowing my own birth father and having no reason to utter the word as a young child. That, and when I think of "my father" or "my dad," I think of more than one person. Not only Bob, but also Mark. On the other hand, I'd grown up saying "Mom" from a very young age, and was conditioned into knowing who was considered a mom.

Bob is on the shorter side, probably somewhere around five-foot-eight at the time (and slightly shorter now). He had red hair and a red neck beard most of the time, with some signs of gray coming through. He had a stout build, which lent itself well to our family and church's characterization of him as "Bob the Builder" (because he was a handyman), and jokes about him being a leprechaun (which he would attribute to his Irish family background). His ancestors, as detailed by my grandfather, Peter Berry, came to America in the early 1900s seeking economic opportunity, arriving in New York before making the trip north to Maine.

Bob worked as the maintenance person at both our church, Windham Assembly of God, and its affiliated Christian school, Windham Christian Academy. He also worked on the side for The Gutter People in Raymond, and even picked up a third job to help pay for an eventual addition to the house and our yearly winter trips to Florida. I generally got along with my dad, but, unlike my mom, he tended to be a bit of a talker—a gossiper—which made me angry.

There was one time during high school when we had to come up with projects for a science fair. I looked and looked for a project that would blow everyone else's out of the water. In other words, I aimed high. After some Googling, I found my project: a homemade hovercraft that involved cutting a circular piece of plywood, drilling a hole in it big enough to mount a leaf blower, then taking some plastic sheeting and stapling it in a donut shape on the bottom side. When the leaf blower was turned on, the air would blow into the donut hole beneath the wood and force itself beneath the plastic inflated portion. The result was a makeshift hovercraft.

While I was building this, I heard from a classmate that my dad doubted whether it would actually work. I remember this hurt me a lot, causing a burning feeling in my chest. A feeling of betrayal, in some ways. I decided then and there that I would show him. My hovercraft would work.

When the science fair rolled around, it was time to show the world what I had created, and boy, did I ever! The leaf blower roared to life, and as I was standing on the plywood platform, it filled the plastic donut, lifted the hovercraft ever so slightly off the ground, and I went zooming across the gym floor! I felt triumphant. I had succeeded in bringing something to life. I felt like it was the best damn science project in the entire room, and better yet, I had proved my dad wrong! And then I got to watch him boast about it to the other parents.

Tracy hails from The County (Aroostook) and is of French Canadian background on her father's side. I know little else about her father; she and her mom, Grammy Anita, endured a lot of abuse from him and are estranged. My mom is taller than my dad and has long dark brown hair that grayed a bit more each year she spent with me and my three younger siblings. She was thin and fit, always going to the gym or riding her bicycle around the hilly and mountainous parts of the Sebago Lakes Region.

My mom was an RN before all of us moved in, but we became her full-time job once all four of us were reunited (with adoption subsidy assistance from the State, thankfully). She took some periodic cleaning gigs and worked at our private Christian school's kindergarten house to supplement our income, but most of her time was spent driving us around—me to piano lessons in Windham, beginning in eighth grade; my sisters to horseback riding lessons; weekly volunteering at the Fryeburg animal shelter; and later, during high school, to our jobs. If you look at a map, that's a lot of territory to cover within a week. The red 2003 Toyota

Sienna was pretty much driven into the ground before they got a new one after I started college.

My mom and I had a difficult relationship. We clashed and argued a lot because, in many ways, we are alike. My sister Seyya and I resemble my mom the most. Stubborn and opinionated. I remember one time my mom and I argued about when to brush your teeth, before or after eating breakfast. She said before, I said after. My reasoning was, why brush your teeth if they're about to get dirty eating breakfast. We had a pretty heated argument about that, going back and forth in front of the entire family. While it's not definitive, I later found out that it's generally better to brush before eating breakfast, so she was right. (But don't tell her I said that!)

Every now and then we would get into some really explosive arguments. I was a young teenager dealing with a lot of anger issues that I'd bottled up. Underneath it all was the anxiety and stress I was feeling about being gay. Sometimes, when she would nag me like mothers do about laundry or doing the dishes, I would just explode and start yelling and arguing with her. It was definitely scary for her, having a teenager that was almost her height and weighed more than her, yelling at her. I think it was traumatizing for her, as well, as someone who had an abusive father. When I would get into arguments with her, she always had this look that I was about to take a swing at her or start throwing things around.

The truth is, while I would get very loud at times, never once did I think about hitting anyone or being violent. She would make statements like "You're a big boy; it's scary sometimes," which made me feel bad, because I didn't want to be that. Those words crept into my brain and made me feel like I was a monster. And there were ways she'd reinforce it, by telling me that she "knew me," and what I used to be like in the other foster homes and the group home. She reminded me of things like the junkyard incident, painting it like I was a little thug. Or when I'd be playing

Me and Seyya, picking apples in 2003.

with my little brother after seeing a *Star Wars* movie, using sticks to re-enact a fight scene, and he'd run in crying, saying that I'd hit him. The horrified look she'd give me, as if I was a violent monster.

Instead of seeing an angry boy who just needed some help, and love, all the words she said and the looks she gave me warped my thinking, gaslighting me into believing that I was a violent person, and coloring the way I thought of my childhood before I'd moved in with the Berrys. I think that's why, later on, I was surprised to hear that people in the Riverton school and my first foster family had only seen me act out every now and then—that overall, I was a sweet, kind, and polite boy.

This isn't to say that I didn't have a lot of anger inside of me, because I did. I sought to change this, starting in middle school. This is where religion helped me. Not the beliefs *per se*, but the practice of prayer and meditation, and reflection. I knew I was hurting and angry inside because of my life circumstances, and so praying, meditating, reflecting, and playing music were ways I found to nurture myself on the inside, to calm myself, and ultimately to bring back that sweet kid everyone kept talking about.

Today, I can look back with grace, empathy, and understanding for both my adoptive mom and myself. We both were hurting and neither of us realized it. She, with the pain of having grown up with an abusive father and not being able to have children, and me, growing up knowing abuse and being taken away from my birth mom. We each had our own truths and experiences and reasons, but not excuses, for how we both behaved. And that's healing.

I had two older adoptive sisters as well, Laci and Laura, who were out of the house by the time Tanya and I moved in. They were from my dad's previous marriage. At the time, Laci had had my niece Reilly, who grew up loving to cling to my legs while I walked through the house. At the time of this writing, she's a freshman in college. How time flies! Laci now has four kids and Laura has two; add in my sister Seyya's two sons and my brother Brandon's two daughters, and that makes me an uncle of ten!

But back to the story at hand. Shortly after Tanya and I moved in, my dad decided to build an addition to house all of us. It would take many years before we were able to spread out. Tanya and Seyya had to share a room for most of my teenage years. The new addition doubled the size of the house by adding a breezeway and a two-car garage, with the master bedroom and living room on the second floor above the garage. Construction began in the years leading up to the recession of 2008, with the laying down of the concrete foundation.

I helped with installing the radiant heating, opening the rolls and rolls of orange tubing and crisscrossing them over the first portion of the concrete foundation after it was poured. We had reconnected with Mark and Debi, and Mark came over to help us install the radiant heating tubes.

Over the years we watched as the rest of the foundation was poured, and slowly but surely, my dad brought in the two-by-fours and frames and plywood. The walls started to go up, and eventually we had a contractor with a crane come and raise the walls for the second floor and the rafters for the roof. My dad did most of the work, with my brother and I helping out in small ways. As the years progressed, I became less interested in hammers and nails and screwdrivers; I was mentally unable to grasp the details that went into constructing and building things. I gravitated more toward books, drawing, and music.

We were also heavily involved in our Pentecostal church,

Windham Assembly of God, which was under the larger, umbrella organization known as the Assemblies of God. Our denomination believed in the "power of the Holy Spirit" and speaking in tongues, which, when talking with other Christians, I felt was the defining element that separated our denomination from others. Our family went to church every Sunday, I started going to youth group on Sunday nights, and we went to family night on Wednesdays.

Religion played a big role in the Berrys' decision to foster and adopt. They would always tell me that they had prayed and prayed before deciding to foster my two youngest siblings, and later, to adopt all four of us. They sincerely believed that God had led them to do what they did. Throughout the years I spent growing up in that church, I felt that adoption held a special place in their belief system, second to "saving" sinners through conversion, because if you raised adoptees right, they would become God-fearing Christians, too! The message to adopt was especially compelling when viewed in light of the statistics pastors and evangelists would highlight in terms of declining church attendance in New England, and the United States overall, along with the declining US birth rate (at least among white Americans).

And so while I believe that my adoptive parents were sincere in their belief and their love, I think the broader message in the evangelical world—to have lots of kids, or to adopt kids (especially from Africa and China)—is part of a larger strategy supported by the message that good Christians are warriors of God, here to expand His kingdom on Earth. There are several good articles that cover this topic more in-depth, including a *Mother Jones* article titled "Orphan Fever: The Evangelical Movement's Adoption Obsession," and a *New Republic* article titled "The Trouble with the Christian Adoption Movement."

I remember our family sat in the second row nearly every Sunday. Barely anyone sat in the front. Sitting in the front is awkward; you're exposed, and there's nothing to put your hands on. But we were sitting in the front row (for one of those few times), shortly after we'd moved in. The pastor spoke of how the world was suffering because of this thing called Sin, which came about as a result of Adam and Eve partaking of the fruit of the Tree of the Knowledge of Good and Evil. Ever since then, Sin has been passed down from generation to generation. In short, Sin was what created a "God-sized hole" in your heart that only God can fill. All the troubles of the world are the result of human nature and the corruption of Sin and our rebellion against God. All of Nature was created in a certain order, and humanity, with all of its faults and failures, acts against what God intended.

Just imagine what a twelve-year-old kid might think while sitting there, having just moved in with a new family and having experienced what I had lived through. All the complications and complexities of life, all the pain and suffering and awful things that happen to people, neatly packaged into one grand narrative of why everything is so messed up. For a beaten-up, broken-hearted kid, God was an answer to all of life's uneasy questions. The problem, in a nutshell, is that we are all sinners. Each and every one of us. With all my pain and suffering neatly bundled, I didn't question how I was to blame for something that supposedly occurred some ten thousand years ago (according to Creationists). I didn't have to face the hard questions or process the pain and trauma. I didn't have to dive into all the complexities of human nature and psychology.

Not only did this framing of the human problem explain everything, it also offered a solution. All we had to do was realize that God took pity on mankind and sent his one and only son, Jesus Christ, who was also God in the flesh, to Earth to sacrifice himself for the atonement of our sins. From this realization, we then must confess our sins and accept Christ into our hearts. During the first few sermons I heard in our church, the opportunity to do so was offered toward the end of the service, during what was referred to as the "Altar Call." The pastor would sum up his sermon and refer to the doctrine that I laid out above, and then ask if anyone wanted to give their life to Jesus, thereby turning it around. If they did, they were asked to raise their hands and to repeat the prayer, which went along the lines of: "Dear God, I am sorry for all that I've done and all the sins I have committed. I realize now and believe with all my heart that you sent your one and only son, Jesus Christ, to die on the Cross for my sins, and that if I accept him into my heart, you will forgive me."

For many people, this invokes an emotional reaction. The first time I raised my hand, I remember peeking around to see if anyone else was doing it, and noticed a hand or two. I uttered the little prayer and heard a few sobs. I was waiting for my moment, but it never came. No emotion, no nothing. This frustrated me. I felt like something was wrong. Maybe I wasn't sorry enough, or maybe I had to list every sin in my head that I could think of. I couldn't figure it out, so the next Sunday, I raised my hand again. Still nothing.

Eventually I asked the pastor why I didn't have the same reaction, and he said that it was different for different people. As long as you believe that Jesus came and died for your sins and you accept him into your heart and turn your life around, you're good.

While this somewhat tamped down my worries, I had also stumbled upon the theories about the Rapture and the End Times, and how Jesus would come back one day to take his followers home. Middle school me—no longer allowed to read Harry Potter books or collect Pokémon cards—read the Left Behind series and began to panic inside. *What if I am not truly saved? What if I didn't say it right? Will I miss the Rapture and be left behind when all the bad things happen in the End Times? What if I died right now—would I go to Hell?*

I began to have night terrors. I'd wake up in the middle of the night and feel like I was being choked or that I couldn't breathe. I'd feel a presence off in the corner or see a shape. I'd feel like something was leaning on my blanket. I'd "wake up" in my dream (cue the music from the film, *Inception*) and get a strong sense of fear and that something was in the room, so I would jump up and try to turn the light on. The only problem was, in my dream, the light wouldn't turn on. I would flip the switch up and down and up and down, but no light would come on. I'd then run into the laundry/bathroom area just outside of my room and try to do the same thing. Still nothing. Things like this happened so often during that time.

I wasn't able to explain it to myself until years later in college, when I picked up Michael Shermer's book *The Believing Brain: From Ghosts and Gods to Politics and Conspiracies*, which is about how we construct beliefs and reinforce them as truths. It was from this book that I learned of the evolution of the human brain and how and why we think the way we do. One particular chapter spoke of how people under high levels of stress are more likely to report or tell of instances of hearing God's voice or seeing things that aren't really there.

Research like this helped to lift a huge burden off my shoulders. Without this knowledge, I had no explanation as to why I experienced these terrors. Years ago, when I would tell people about my night terrors, they would say I was under attack by Satan, or I was being tested like Job, or perhaps there was something in my life that was creating a tension between me and God. Whenever I heard these things, I panicked a little, because it was around this time I was also wrestling with my sexuality in a way that I had never done before. In some ways, it was typical of all boys going through puberty, with sexual hormones coming to life—but with a twist.

Although homosexuality was never a frequent topic while I was growing up—it was almost a hush-hush issue—it did make its way into sermons and church events, and discussions at the family dinner table. Whether it was a family friend who "went through a phase" and had recently come back to Jesus, or whether it was whispers of an older church member whom young boys like me were warned to stay away from, the stigmas were there.

Our church would have traveling evangelists and ministry leaders visit and give guest sermons. One such minister and his wife and children happened to be sitting in front of us, and had introduced themselves. I noticed the minister had an effeminate voice, which wasn't really that odd until he started to give his sermon about how he had been saved from homosexuality. For him, it all started when he was collecting baseball cards and, in his words, he was "tempted." I immediately started squirming on the inside and my stomach sank. As I mentioned earlier, a couple of years before, when I was living in the group home, I'd had the same experience when I'd glanced at a baseball card and kissed the player's picture.

The pastor continued with his sermon, raising the same arguments I'd heard before when our Christian high school teachers would uncomfortably skim over the topic, which was often lumped with in-class sermons on Planned Parenthood and abortion conspiracies. The Roman Empire, with all of its glory and accomplishments, collapsed because of a moral and societal decay spurred on by its embrace of homosexuality. The argument, therefore, was that if America embraced homosexuality, then America as we know it would crumble and God would punish us with hurricanes and floods and famine and fire and brimstone.

Homosexuality was also seen as a symptom of men losing their traditional roles in society. We were taught that feminists, in addition to convincing women to abandon their domestic duties and abort their babies, would downplay the husband's role in the household, ultimately feminizing men. Without strong male heads of families, single mothers—you know, the ones who didn't abort—would rely on food stamps and welfare, and their children, without proper male role models, would turn out to be gay. Like me. We were told that accepting homosexuality would lead to the acceptance of pedophilia and polygamy and other "sins." We heard about gays getting HIV/

AIDS, or even prostate cancer, and having higher rates of suicide as proof that same-sex relationships were against "Nature" and "Nature's God," and, therefore, expanded the God-sized holes in our hearts.

And if sermons during church services weren't enough to drive home the point, I also got the same message in the private Christian school that we were enrolled in. Whenever gay rights came up in the news, the teachers would all get up in arms, and next thing you know there was a week of classes and chapel services focused on praying for the salvation of the gays, and how God forbids being gay, and that if we were gay, we were confused and should seek help. One teacher had read something in the morning paper about gay marriage and proceeded to tell the class that he didn't hate gay people, that he in fact knew some gay people. That those gay people seemed fine, but he knew, deep down, they were unhappy with their lives and that was because God didn't approve of gays.

Recounting this story tells you the impact this one statement had on me at the time. This was one of the reasons why I turned against myself and was afraid to come out.

Middle-school me didn't know how to counter these arguments.

Middle-school me was not taught the version of Roman history where Rome had overextended itself. Rome's system of administration and governance, as innovative as it was, was unable to bear the crushing weight of a vast empire that was also dealing with income inequality, in the form of massive land grabs by the patrician class, food shortages and famines, maintenance of the world's largest military force, and frequent and devastating incursions by ravaging, foreign forces.

Middle-school me didn't know how to counter the other arguments based on traditional values and mores. Insulated against anything but preapproved textbooks, books, movies, and television, I had no ability or courage to access resources that would inform me otherwise. Everything that was true was everything in the Bible, or everything that was based on a Christian worldview. Everything else stemmed from flawed human reasoning and the corrupt influences of the "world's philosophy" and the utter lack of "Godly wisdom."

For instance, Harry Potter books were banned from the household because they interested children in darker things and taught them spells. Of course, as I found out later, the "spells" were merely Latin words. An expansive education would have enlightened us to this fact, but ignorance made us all fools, subject to our flawed way of thinking. Religious rhetoric overtook reason and clarity, clouding the judgment of our collective hive mind and poisoning our longing for a higher purpose—in many cases, driven by our collective misgivings of the temporal world and the imperfect condition of humanity.

Do I think there is something wrong with Christianity? Not entirely. Religion, broadly speaking, has its purposes for those who need it and seek it. It is at its best when it echoes the deepest instincts of humankind, that deep sense of the reality of the human condition and the compassion and collective action needed to mitigate its more crude and cruel features. But its value ends when it departs from the near-universal principles of loving your neighbor as yourself and treating others with dignity and respect. Once religion transcends private practice and enters into the public domain and becomes institutionalized, that is where its evils can be realized as an instrument of power and control. When it becomes less about an individual and their God (or gods or higher power) and becomes a mission or crusade to wield influence over public institutions and to then enter the private realms of others, it transforms into something less sincere and soulful and becomes more sanctimonious and sinister.

I think that Christian churches, including conservative evangelical ones, that have organized their congregations into mini political parties cross this line, going beyond free speech and instead dangerously toward trying to establish a theocracy of sorts, where their form of speech, ideals, and values are the law of the land (as we have seen recently with the anti-abortion laws in Texas).

So when someone would mention that my night terrors and anxiety could be the result of a "thorn in my side," as alluded to by the Apostle Paul with regard to some unknown affliction, or some sin that I was struggling with, I immediately thought of my attraction to boys my age. No one told me then that those night terrors and anxiety were actually the result of my being gay in a world that shunned and looked down upon homosexuality, no matter how many times they would say: "We don't hate! We love the sinner, but hate the sin!"

I didn't know at the time that the inner turmoil was this clash between my identity—who I was inside, which I was trying to suppress and hide—and the identity that my family, community, and church wanted to see in me. That the subtle (and not-so-subtle) demands of those around me to be just like them was suffocating what my mind, body, and soul were all screaming at me on the inside: *I am attracted to other guys. I am gay.* Instead of listening to my inner voice, I believed what was preached and taught and told to me: Those were the voices of temptation trying to make me stray from the one true path—their path.

What made it worse was that I had no one to talk to who would understand the situation I was in. In many ways it was similar to those who find themselves caught in a cult and cut off from "bad influences" (those they consider heretics—people with different views). It was ingrained in me that being gay is unnatural; that it's a choice; that gay people are just confused. There were times when I almost felt I should talk to the pastor or youth pastor. It was fear of being exposed and fear of the unknown that held me back.

I truly believe it was my inner voice telling me to hold back, in order to save myself. Because had I told my family and church, there's no telling what would've happened. Maybe I would have ended up in the conversion therapy camp that the pastor with the effeminate voice ran.

Ultimately, what kept me trapped and a part of the church was not only that I felt like I had no other option, but also because there were positive features, too. What drew me to church was the sense of togetherness and belonging, so long as you accepted Jesus into your heart and believed what was accepted as doctrine by that specific denomination. Within those four walls, the sense of common purpose was real. We all yearned for the God that we created with our doctrine, rituals, sayings, and services.

One question that nagged at me throughout my time in the church was why Christians were referred to as the "Body of Christ," despite their numerous denominations. For instance, I got the general feeling, going to a Pentecostal church, that being Catholic wasn't enough. Or that being Methodist or Unitarian or Mormon wasn't enough. That being Baptist, and not hearing the voice of the Holy Spirit, was just boring.

When our family discussed the differences between us and Catholics at the dinner table, for instance, it often boiled down to Catholics not necessarily believing in being "born again." Instead, Catholics sought the forgiveness of their sins, not by uttering a prayer to Christ, but by confessing to a priest and uttering a "Hail Mary"— which, according to our version of Christianity, was taboo. We were taught that Catholics had strayed from the path, worshipped saints as idols, and were too ritualistic. We believed that the only way to be "born again" was to sincerely pray to God and accept Jesus into your heart.

What set our denomination apart from Baptists or Catholics and other denominations was that we, as Pentecostals, believed that in addition to being born again and baptized by water, Christians should also be baptized by the Holy Spirit (by fire) and speak in tongues. In addition, the denomination also believed in divine healing.

Which church you attended and which denomination you belonged to had so much weight and so much power that when you revealed yours, you could see someone's eyes either glisten with recognition or fall with a subtle dismissiveness. Sure, they talked a big game about belonging to the Body of Christ, but it seemed to me that the variety of practices and doctrinal beliefs served as clear rifts that cut that body into tiny fragments. While God was said to bring us together, religious dogma and sectarian details split us apart.

By the time eighth grade rolled around, I had all but thrown myself into being the best-darned Christian I could become. My attraction to men became "my cross to bear," and my battle against those feelings and belief that I could pray it all away was partially what spurred me on to pursue God so passionately. That, and some sense of gratitude to my adoptive parents, an instinct to survive, and to just do the easy thing and fit in. My zeal was noticed and commended, and I began to express my faith publicly through music, which led to my being more and more involved in our youth group.

I was in pursuit of understanding who I was in this world, trying to discover and navigate feelings and emotions that seemed to pile on with puberty and age. I threw myself wholeheartedly into religion, not realizing that I had given up, for quite some time, an essential part of my personal identity: who I can love.

If there's one thing that holds true with almost every American, it's that shared experience of adolescent angst. Rich or poor, gay or straight, Black, brown, or white, nature indiscriminately strikes us all with puberty, pimples, and puppy love. There is some comfort in the fact that life delivers this stage of life to all of us. However, nature's twisted sense of equality lasts but briefly, as popularity becomes ever more prominent when the hormones are pumped up to full power.

As an early teen, I was, in my view, painfully average. Shy. Overly polite. In other words, a threat to no one. In a way, you could say that I was a survivor. I knew what it took to survive, adapt, and deal with what life handed to me.

At this point, I knew that my life was more or less a good thing. Tanya and I were reunited with our two younger siblings.

Me, Tanya, Brandon, and Seyya celebrating Christmas at Grammy Anita's in Mapleton, Maine. I was twelve years old.

Our parents weren't rich or middle-class; they just barely made it into the working class with the aid of state subsidies. As I have previously mentioned, Bob worked three different jobs to finance the addition to the house and provide us with a solid, blue-collar life in rural Maine. Tracy gave up her work as an RN to take care of us full-time. The only time she had to herself was at the gym, biking for miles, and running. We had a dog named Jake and a fat orange cat named Zack. Later on in high school, we adopted a pug we named Sadie and two Maine Coon kittens. In short, we had a lot of mouths to feed—a reality that became more stark when our baby nephews and nieces from our two older adoptive sisters would sometimes spend the weekend with us.

Some might read this and think, "Oh, well, that doesn't sound too bad," or "That's much better than what he experienced before." To some degree, that is true. But the stability and serenity on the surface came at a great cost to me, and involved in many ways the deception of both myself and my family. I could have fought for myself and come out as gay in middle school or high school, but that would have disrupted the picture-perfect family I've portrayed above. Some would say that I had everything I could have wanted, but the price I had to pay was living a lie to keep the peace. The price was suffering those night terrors and the anxiety, the ever-present fear that I would be caught glancing too long at my cute classmate or blushing when the handsome store clerk smiled at me. The price was losing out on experiencing what other kids my age got to experience openly and freely, flaunting their heterosexuality in my face on a consistent basis.

As I have hinted previously, our family's life revolved around our church, Windham Assembly of God, which was also home to the private Christian school we attended, Windham Christian Academy. That meant church on Sunday morning, youth group on Sunday night (which I used to hate attending until I started high school), family night on Wednesdays (which was pretty much a daycare for the kids while the adults went to Bible study), and private Christian school from 8:00 a.m. to 2:30 p.m., Monday through Friday. Add in soccer practice for me, and you get the picture. We were the typical evangelical family, and very Republican. The least conservative thing about us was that Dad didn't like guns.

The summer when Tanya and I moved in, before school started, I spent most of my days following Dad around as he went to work at the church. He would fix this or that, repair some of the school's lockers, buff and shine the floors, and mow the soccer field, which was also the outfield for the baseball diamond on one end and the softball field on the other. It was on the first day of one of these "shadow Dad" days that my dad introduced me to another boy who was also twelve: Peyton. Peyton mowed the lawn and stacked the church chairs in the hall that doubled as a basketball court for our school. Peyton was also adopted, and Black. So, almost like me. He was taller than me. Lean. He had big, dark brown eyes and his hair was short, black, and curly. He would grow it out sometimes and have a 'fro. And when he found something funny, he would do this half-chuckle, half-chortle kind of laugh. He also had a reputation for pulling pranks and getting into trouble.

We hit it off pretty fast—especially after a certain accident with a golf cart, which he would never stop reminding me about. I had offered to help, and one of the jobs I had to do was load the back of the golf cart with cut grass and dump it in the woods. All I had to do was back up to the edge of the parking lot, where the ground went downhill for about three feet into the woods. After unloading the grass, I enthusiastically jumped back into the golf cart and slammed on the gas. But instead of going forward, the golf cart shot backward and into the woods. Long story short, Dad had to pull the golf cart out using our blue, slightly beat-up, mid-1990s Plymouth van. Peyton was laughing hysterically, and the incident became a recurring joke for the rest of the summer. It was also one of the real bonding moments Peyton and I shared.

Peyton was also friends with Carlton, another boy from the church and school. Carlton's mother was white and his father was from Jamaica. Peyton, Carlton, and I made a trio of boys of color entering seventh grade in our small, rural, conservative church and school. Whether it was church or family night or school or soccer, people rarely saw the three of us apart. Sometimes all three of us would ask the teacher to go to the bathroom or to take a water break at the same time, and then we'd conveniently forget to come back to class. Or we'd spend the church service with the two of them flirting with the three girls we hung out with all the time. In my defense, I was usually the one who tagged along and hung back, observing. I was the only voice of conscience they would have at times, which often meant I served as lookout, watching for any adults who might appear.

Carlton and Peyton both loved sports. Baseball, basketball, soccer, you name it. I used to play baseball, but I found I liked it less since starting at the new school. Soccer was more fun. Peyton played forward, and Carlton and I played defense as fullbacks, most likely due to our larger builds. Both of them were great at these sports, while I was average.

Peyton and I had another thing in common: He had been adopted by white parents. The difference was that he had been adopted at birth and never really knew his birth family. His father was an ordained minister and sometimes preached at our church. He was also a teacher at the Christian school. Thinking of it now, it really did have an isolating effect, going to the same church and school where our teachers and friends all came from the same place. Indeed, that was most likely the intent. We were specifically sent to the Christian school to insulate us from the world's corrupting influences.

It was drummed into us that we had the answers, being born-again Christians, and that we were "not of this world, but in the world." "The World" was seen as if through a telescope or a magnifying glass that zoomed in on the bad and the "evil." Everything, it seemed, was a sin that could jeopardize your born-again-ness. Smoking, drinking, swearing, asking too many questions were common but easily overlooked taboos.

But sex outside of marriage? Oh boy. That was like Hell on Earth. Later in high school, I remember a one-day sex education presentation where the women impressed upon us the images of gonorrhea, chlamydia, syphilis, and herpes. These pictures were all blown up and zoomed in to show the nasty warts and pus-filled lesions. They even took the time to show photos of aborted fetuses and drive home the message of how evil and heartless women who sought abortions were. The most uncomfortable part of that presentation was when they somewhat glossed over homosexuality. It seemed like they jumped immediately to the HIV/AIDS part, as if your first contact with another boy or man would instantaneously transmit the viral disease to you, which was ludicrous, of course.

I was downright frightened. All of this, and the angst and

anxiety I had about having feelings for other boys, was probably what caused me hesitation during one particular encounter.

It was a sunny afternoon, the summer after seventh grade, and Peyton wanted to hang out at my house after my dad was done working. So when 2:30 p.m. came around, I hopped into the van with my dad, our brown Lab Jake (who always went to work with Dad), and Peyton, and we drove home.

When we got to my house, Peyton and I ran around outside for a bit, after which we went down into the basement where my bedroom was located, next to the laundry room. It was the first time he'd been in my room, so it was awkward, which may be common for many other boys. The first time you have a friend over and they get to see your room and how you've decorated it, what kind of stuff you have and so forth—it's like you're opening up your entire inner world to them. Adolescent angst.

Peyton did the usual things. Poked around. Picked up a book. Looked at my collection of (contraband) Pokémon cards. The room was pleasantly cool, and it was late afternoon when the light outside was starting to tint with shades of orange and gold, and rays of sunshine gleamed golden-green through the trees. We were joking about something and laughing when all of a sudden it got quiet and awkward. The kind of quiet and awkwardness boys display as they shuffle their feet around and kick at random things.

That's when he popped the question: "I'll show you mine if you show me yours?"

You could cut through the angst in the air. Not like butter. No … this could only be described as a thick, juicy, rare steak like they showed in those Applebee's commercials, as a feminine hand slices slowly and seductively into the perfectly seared piece of meat, revealing its tender, pink inside, the droplets of bloody gold seeping downward and mixing with the marinated juices.

I was a flustered hot mess. Every instinct in my body wanted to say *yes*. But everything in my head, from the sermons, classes, and Scripture, screamed *no*.

Peyton must have seen the hesitation on my face as I gave him a quizzical look, but then he just whipped it out and told me, "Your turn."

Not only was he quite big for our age, he was also circumcised. I wasn't, and I blushed with the shame of being different and weird. But the pressure was on, so I sheepishly lowered my shorts.

"Now hold mine," he said.

Again, I was shocked to be asked such a thing, even as every ounce of hormones and adrenaline in my body was screaming "YES!" The church taught us that this was the voice of the Devil, tempting us to commit an abomination in the eyes of God.

I hesitated. I was so deathly afraid in that moment. And yet compelled. Slowly I reached out and touched him and felt a storm of emotions. My face burned with both guilt and a blossoming realization that this was pretty damn gay.

We heard footsteps upstairs and floorboards creaking.

"Boys!" Dad said sternly. "Get up here—it's time to go."

Hearts pounding, we yanked up our shorts and went upstairs, where my dad ushered us outside. We hopped into the Plymouth with the peeling blue paint. The drive to Peyton's house was about fifteen minutes, and it was one of the longest fifteen minutes of my life. So much angst was in the air you probably could have lit it on fire. Dad, who was usually a chatterbox or singing along to Christian radio, was quiet.

When we dropped Peyton off, Dad went inside and chatted briefly with Peyton's father before coming back out and turning the Plymouth back toward home. Again, more awkward silence as we hit Route 302 toward Naples.

"Hey, bud," Dad said. "I don't think I want you to hang around Peyton anymore. He's a bad influence on you."

I hung my head. He must have heard us. That's the only explanation I have, to this day. This marked the slow decline of my friendship with Peyton and Carlton. I'm not sure if my dad ever told anyone else. It's really unclear what happened after that. I would run into Peyton every now and then at school or church, and it was almost like nothing had ever happened. Life just went on. We continued to hang out at school, but we never bothered to invite each other over anymore.

It also marked the moment when I wanted to make up for what I'd done, and to make my dad proud. Telling myself that I wouldn't make the same mistake again, I began years of hiding who I was and how I felt about other boys. Years of catching myself gazing too long at boys in gym shorts and jolting back to reality once I realized that someone might notice. Years of prayer and thinking that I would end up in Hell, or that my family and church community would all be chosen during the Rapture except for me, because of my secret.

I wasn't completely friendless. Despite no longer hanging around as much with Peyton or Carlton, because our church and Christian community was so small, we still ran into each other just about every day. Peyton and Carlton were in the same grade as me, and there were only four other students in the seventh grade. Even as I tried to make my dad proud, it was unavoidable that the only three kids of color would band together.

While those two were the instigators of a lot of funny mischief, I remember one instance in seventh grade that I initiated. I have a fondness for history and had found an online game called *Conqueror*, where you run a province in medieval Europe and try to conquer the other European provinces. During the computer class taught by Mr. Earle, who was also a church elder, I showed the game to my entire class of seven. We used the old boxy computers with boxy monitors arranged with their screens pointing away from Mr. Earle's desk. We were supposed to be practicing typing, but Mr. Earle didn't walk around the class much. All seven of us, five boys and two girls, got hooked on this game. It's sad to think back on this time and realize that three of my classmates from that small class are now resting in peace. At least two died in connection with substance use. But I will remember their middle-school selves and how they made bearable a time that was so often full of melancholy and angst.

It was also in middle school that I met two lifelong friends. I think it was the summer after my seventh-grade year when I received two phone calls. The first was from my classmate Chris. We hadn't hit it off immediately in class, but we played co-ed soccer together with the others in our class. His phone call came randomly in the time before the proliferation of personal cell phones, and the conversation was awkward and short, something along the lines of "Hey, umm … Want to come over and swim in the pool and play video games?"

That call was the start of a friendship that has lasted to this day. Granted, we have become busier, and he now lives in DC, working for Maine Sen. Susan Collins, but deep down, I know he understands who I am and what drives me. Going to a small school and living in a rural community can be challenging when it comes to making friends. Chris lived in Standish, which is nearly a thirty-minute drive from our home in Naples. Coordinating our schedules—and our parents' schedules and their to-do lists—was a bit like moving a mountain. But we managed. It helped that my family went to church on Sundays in Windham, which is close to Standish, so I'd sleep over at Chris' house on Saturday nights and my parents would pick me up Sunday morning.

The other phone call that summer that made me a new friend was from Jennifer, a church member who had three sons: Travis, Braden, and Kyle. The Cushman brothers. I was mildly surprised that she would want to talk to me. Essentially, she wanted me and Travis to be friends, and for me to come hang out with him and the family. I thought this was odd, for a mother to try to make friends for her son, when obviously Travis already had friends. She would probably say it was divine inspiration. Perhaps it was a mother's instinct.

Travis was an all-American kid who went to our church but attended public school in Gorham, where there was a much larger pool of potential friends. He played soccer and baseball and ran track. In my eyes, he was one of the popular kids. Me, on the other hand, I was awkward. Painfully so.

That first time we hung out at his house, I was in full awkward mode. I didn't think we had anything in common. I thought he'd see me as just some weird kid from church that his mom wanted him to hang out with. But the awkwardness faded over the years. In fact, I soon felt so at home at their house that I practically spent every other weekend there. They lived about a forty-minute drive from Naples, but the fact that our families went to the same church made getting together easy. Dad would drop me off Saturday before dinner. Travis' mom would bake brownies and make us spaghetti before heading off to see friends, and Travis, some of his other friends, and I would settle in for a night of video games and movies. This was around the time that *Guitar Hero* was becoming popular, so a handful of thirteen- and fourteen-year-olds would gather in their finished basement (where Travis' bedroom was) and pretend-rock to "Sweet Child o' Mine" by Guns 'n Roses, Queen's "Killer Queen," or Joan Jett & the Blackhearts' "I Love Rock 'n Roll."

These nights would often last until four a.m., when not even our youthful energy could keep us up any longer, or when Travis' father would come down to tell us we were either too loud or it was time to go to bed. We would begrudgingly settle in. All of us teens would whisper and snicker as if we'd be overheard or get into trouble, until one or all of us passed out and didn't return some snide or funny reply. Those were the kinds of nights as a kid when I'd look up in the dark toward the ceiling and sigh, heart warm and vibrating with that sense of knowing I was not alone in the world. It was a feeling evoked by authentic connections and friendships. Those sorts of feelings can grow and build and become something more, if you're not careful. And I wasn't.

The Sunday mornings I'd wake up at Travis', his mom more likely than not had the griddle out and was churning out pancakes for a bunch of sleep-deprived teens. Pancakes with chocolate chips, bananas, and strawberries, with whipped cream if you wanted it. His mom would always be chipper and happy as can be, singing some Christian worship song or saying a prayer or whatnot. She was also ushering all of us to get ready to leave in time for church.

Travis, like kids often do, gave off a slight air of rebelliousness while in the presence of his friends. He always used to have some snide or snarky remark, which his mom took in stride. I, on the other hand, felt so embarrassed for Travis, almost apologizing for him. I most likely gave off a sheepish and overly polite vibe to make up for the gruff and grumpy protesting from her own son.

Once we'd showered and finished breakfast, we would try to cram in another round of video games before church. Mind you, this was before we were driving, so we'd have to go in early on most occasions, especially when church included Sunday school classes for every age group (from toddlers to seniors), held an hour *before* the Sunday service that began at ten a.m. or so with music, followed by preaching at around eleven a.m., for another hour. But it didn't stop there. *After* church there was a potluck lunch in the cafeteria that the school and church shared. Once that was over, Travis and I parted ways for a few hours as we both went home with our families, returning later that night for youth group with Pastor Brian, or "Peebs," as we called him.

Starting out, youth group used to be another thing I *had* to go to. I was really shy then, and when you combine that with a bunch of kids who were in high school, and older than you? That made me even more nervous. Adults were okay; being polite to them came easy. But high schoolers? The big kids? Middle-school me didn't know what to do.

So many questions clanged around in my head whenever I would come into the presence of one of these older kids. *How does one act like a high schooler? How does someone talk to a high schooler? How can I impress them so they'll want to talk to me? Oh God, am I cool? Should I shake their hand or give them a fist bump, or do that grasp-and-slide thing they do?* It was a serious matter, then—how, as a middle schooler, to impress a high schooler. I mean, who wants to be uncool? Even in the evangelical world there is an awareness of popularity, a quality that didn't necessarily stem from how "Christian" you were. The same dynamics of whether you were a football player or were hot and pretty still played their part with evangelical youth.

Truth be told, I am not sure if I ever resolved this monumental existential question. Being accepted was something I always struggled with in an evangelical world, where I had a big secret. I would catch myself gazing at an older high school guy, wondering what it would be like to be his girlfriend—because back then I knew, or believed—that a guy couldn't date a guy. So when one of those guys I considered handsome would notice me and give me one of those smooth, upward jerks of the head as a greeting, my mind would just go blank and my motor functions would melt down in a cluster of clumsy, awkward hellos and waves and miscalculated handshakes.

What I did enjoy about youth group was the selection of soft rock songs geared more toward young people. The adult church service always had to maintain a delicate balance of older, more outdated songs. Any change, and you could have church members threatening to go to a different church (and, of course, they would take their tithes with them). But at youth group, they played songs from Hillsong and Hillsong United, an Australian-based church that churned out a tremendous amount of worship music and Christian music artists.

Soft rock was my jam. The right kind of mood or notes or chord progression combined with the right kind of lyrics was enough to send me into melancholy ecstasy. Especially slower love songs, and boy, church and youth group services were amply supplied with those.

One of the church members, Matt, who was in his late twenties, played the keyboard and sang for the adult church service (his mom was the worship leader and choir director). At youth group, though, he was the worship leader and had assembled a band consisting of his wife, Danielle, and a few other younger church members.

The youth worship band became a serious obsession of mine. They were young and on fire for God, and middle-school me, expressing myself through the world of ideas, books, history, and music, wanted to be like them. So while hiding my burgeoning sexuality in part drove my deep dive into evangelicalism, so did my being surrounded by it and the role models I found there.

Deep down, I also wanted to do something with my life, and in the evangelical world, the answer was easy. God had something planned for each and every one of us, and I wanted to know what it was. I wanted to know what my purpose was in life. What was the purpose of all the pain that I had gone through? I wanted to know what the hell was going on.

The message of lost souls in search of salvation, that pain and suffering existed because humanity rebelled against God, resonated with me. The sermons and the Scripture all said there was a reason for everything—that things didn't happen unless they were ordained or allowed by God. An example would be the story of Job, when God allowed Satan to "test" him with all manner of trials and tribulations, to see if Job would curse God in the end. Long story short, God conveniently interrupted before the trials could go on any further, showing Job that He was all powerful. Despite everything, God was still in control.

This appealed to a young person like me who had already seen a lifetime's worth of painful events and circumstances. For so long, I had been rudderless, riding the rough seas of poverty and the foster-care system. There was comfort in the idea that all of this upheaval and loss had happened to me for a reason. That nothing was left to chance.

I wanted to find out for sure. Peebs, our youth group pastor, took notice of this and began investing time and effort in helping me find my way. Music became a thing we discussed a lot, especially as I gained enough confidence to ask to sing on the worship team.

The first time I practiced and sang with the worship team, when I was in eighth grade, is something I'll never forget, and will always be proud of. My desire to express myself through music was bigger than my awkwardness. I have a good voice, mind you, but my confidence was low. When I was presented with a mic stand, I probably stood ten feet back while barely whispering out a tune. Matt and Danielle, especially, encouraged me and affirmed that I had a good voice. Over time, the investment of patience and effort that Peebs and the others put in started to pay off as I gained more confidence.

I also took up piano lessons around this time. My piano teacher, Ruth Stokes, came on the recommendation of the pastor's wife, who herself was quite the pianist. Classical music was already something I quite enjoyed, especially the slower, more dramatic, and exhilarating pieces from the Romantic Period, such as Pachelbel's "Canon in D" or Schumann's "Träumerei." My piano teacher took great interest in me and pushed me beyond my comfort zone. Piano recitals were terrifying. I would emerge a little shaky, but with near-perfect marks.

To this date, I still remember my very first piano recital in which the panel of judges in the recital hall at the University of Southern Maine told me that I had "a special sensitivity." That was one of the proudest days of my life. Not because I had made it through a recital or received a little certificate and beams of pride from my family, but because someone had acknowledged me— who I *was* inside. Throughout life, despite the ups and downs, I could never bring myself to harden my heart. Music was one of the ways I processed emotions and how I expressed my true self, along with doodling, gazing at sunsets, and writing.

These moving pieces shaped and molded me at this critical juncture in my young life: The Berrys adopting me and my three siblings and giving us a stable home; the friends I made, and the community I found at that time through the church; and the angst and secrecy I felt about my sexuality. This tension continually pressed me to figure out my life. Meanwhile, I was on the precipice of entering high school and beginning a lifelong struggle with the concept of time, and feeling like there was never enough of it. To paraphrase Scripture, "There is a time and a season for everything" (*Ecclesiastes* 3:1).

While I no longer cling to my parents' faith and the religion I grew up with throughout my teens, the trust in God and a higher power that I experienced at that time helped to center my attention and allowed me to expand my existence beyond pure survival, beyond just existing, to truly embrace *living*. I stopped worrying about when I'd have to move to the next home, and I didn't have to expend quite as much energy building up walls to defend myself emotionally.

This security meant I could finally look inward to discover my true self and to begin building the foundations of who I am today, as an adult.

Windham Christian Academy, 2005

The summer of my fourteenth birthday, before my freshman year in high school, cell phones were becoming popular among my classmates and friends. Not one to be left out, I decided to ask my dad for one.

"No, you don't need one," he said, without missing a beat. "And I am not paying for it."

I didn't give up. I employed a timeless strategy that has been tested in nearly every home by kids with parents who say no: Keep asking until they say yes. And so I embarked on a relentless campaign to change my dad's mind, to convince him that I did indeed need a cell phone, and could afford one.

By that time I had picked up a gig at the church stacking chairs after service, on Sunday afternoons. If I recall correctly, I was paid about $20 a week for a few hours' work, so about $80 a month. This argument eventually seemed to sway my dad, although it could have also been resigned exasperation. Either way, I didn't get an actual cell phone; I got my very first Nokia TracFone, which I filled up by purchasing cards at Rite Aid, across from Bray's Brew Pub. This allowed me to text and talk with friends without being limited to the one hour a week on the computer on AOL Instant Messenger. But this wasn't enough. I wanted a real cell phone with a real plan, like my friends.

My dad said if this is what I wanted, I needed to get a job to pay for it. My two older adoptive sisters, who were out of the house by the time I moved in, had both worked at Point Sebago, a family-friendly lake resort. My dad knew Bruce, the general manager of the restaurant there, so we drove the ten minutes or so to Casco, down a long, windy road and past the checkpoint, toward the restaurant. We walked through the back door, and my dad introduced me. Dad and Bruce made some small talk, and then we got down to the business of getting me a job. I had just turned fourteen on June 8, so the season had already somewhat started for them, but I ended up getting a summer job working with the restaurant janitor.

I applied myself doggedly to that job. I was most likely the slowest vacuumer, mopper, and bathroom cleaner they had ever encountered, but I obsessed over doing a damn good job. This alone wasn't what made me enjoy work. Bruce was a good manager, and he and I bonded, talking about my dad's not-so-picture-perfect past. Bruce was a jovial guy—stern when you screwed up, but good-humored nonetheless. The head chef, Matt, was also much the same, along with their top cook, Andrew—who was eighteen or nineteen. I'd catch myself sneaking longing glances at him every chance I could get. Those three guys were my work family. They joked and cussed and played pranks on each other, and the more I settled into the job, the more they bore the brunt of my pranks and puns.

There was also Mary, the dishwasher, who was in her late sixties. She was scary. Whenever I would go into the dishwasher room to fill a bucket or whatnot, she wouldn't say a word to me. By the time summer was ending and I opted to work on the weekends until the end of vacation season, I had been "promoted" to dishwasher. I was clumsy and nervous around her, but that drove me to work even harder to prove I was a valuable employee. By the end of that first summer, she and I had bonded in a way. The dishwasher room was our mini comedy club, and we had fun at work. When the season ended, she announced that she was retiring, which set me up to be the only dishwasher the following summer.

I was fifteen by then, and with Mary gone, I was *the* dishwasher. Juggling that with being the busboy and helping Matt and Andrew with special events like barbecues, weddings, and so forth was daunting. I was a nervous wreck most of the time, but I still tried to do the best damn job I could do. Even when I messed up—and boy, did I have some snafus—I made sure to learn from those failures and improve.

I looked up to Andrew, the younger of the chefs, who had worked there throughout high school. He knew my dad and adoptive sisters, so we were already off to a good start. I loved being around him. He had slightly curly brown hair with tinges of blond. He was white, but bronzed and tan, somewhere around six feet or so, and man, was he muscular. He'd wear our green work polo shirts with the short sleeves slightly rolled up, which made his biceps stand out even more.

When we worked together, I followed him around like a puppy. I ate up every word he said as he showed me how to lay out charcoal on a long, brick grilling station on the beach nearby. I learned how to do food prep, and would set up tables and supplies for big events. Yeah, I was attracted to him. I didn't know it quite clearly at the time, but thinking of it now, I was! I'm not sure if he knew it. I feel like he was one of those confident guys who just ate up attention and took everything in stride.

I remember another female chef who had short hair, was lean, and joked around with the guys as if she was one of them. Before I even knew of such a thing as *gaydar*, all the bells and whistles went off in my head, telling me that Miranda was a lesbian. She was strong, demanding, and skilled; the people she worked with accepted her for who she was; and, deep down, I wished I could be like her. Instead, I tried to shower her with the love of Jesus—which, to me and my family, mostly meant being nice and smiling even if we didn't really agree with someone's lifestyle (passive-aggressive evangelism?).

Miranda knew I was a Christian and liked to push my buttons. Not because she loathed Christians, I don't think. Like many out LGBTQ+ people at the time, she liked to challenge the status quo. They could also smell a closet case from a mile away. And that was me: a big gay closet case who was in love with another man—and his name was Jesus! I was so full of His love and wanted everyone else to have the love of Jesus inside of them. It's funny how ironic it is that evangelicals belittle homosexuality and homoeroticism, but the way evangelical men talk about Jesus—it's like we're all gay for Jesus.

Miranda pushed as many buttons as she could. At times, I felt like she was working me to death, to test me. Sometimes the restaurant would get so busy she'd call me in to grab dishes for people and send them out. Miranda and I ended up becoming quite good friends. And boy, was she funny—snarky and sarcastic. Bruce, Matt, and Miranda would always play pranks on me, and I was only too happy to return the favor. Although in my head, and through what I was taught at church, these people were considered "unsaved," "lost," and "different," deep down I didn't really see much of a difference between them and the churchgoers, other than they probably prayed less and had fewer rules to follow.

I had been taught that no matter how much fun the unsaved had or how much they loved, laughed, and lived, they still had a God-sized hole in their hearts that they were trying to fill with all the corrupt ways of the world. What really set us apart from them was that we "had Jesus," as if that were a tangible thing we could pull out and show the rest of the world. The idea is, we are so full of the love of Jesus that it overflows into other parts of our lives, most visibly in the form of joy and love. People see this and wonder why we are so joyful and happy, which gives us a window of opportunity to tell people about Jesus.

I am chuckling as I write this, thinking about how much effort I put into being the best I could be so I could find an opportunity to save those around me. The ultimate gesture of love that a Christian could make was to try to save every person around them, telling them the good news of Jesus Christ and how he died for our sins so we can go to Heaven. Weirdly, however, there was so little that differentiated us from those in the world that we'd resort to things like no swearing, no drinking, no smoking, no wearing revealing clothing, no sex outside of marriage—all of this to show that we were different. So I would ask someone who was using cuss words not to do so around me. Or there was the time I asked the manager to play Christian music instead of the classic rock station.

It is interesting how we were taught to frame things in a way that quickly led to proselytizing. Questions like "Don't you think there's more to life?" would lead to "Don't you feel like, aside from everything, you have a hole that can't be filled?" or "Why do you think there is so much evil in the world?" These are clever devices, really, because they tap into the uncertain nature of our reality and the human condition. I think there is a reason why people tend to believe more in God when deeply traumatic, emotional, or stressful events trigger our biological, psychological, and physiological responses.

Michael Shermer's *The Believing Brain* opened my eyes to the evolutionary origins of such things as fight or flight, a tendancy toward what he called "patternicity," and our susceptibility to, as he put it, "magical thinking." Patternicity, for instance, is the human tendency to extract meaningful patterns from otherwise meaningless noise. This can lead us to make two types of errors. A "type I" error, or false positive, is believing a pattern is real when it is not; and a "type II" error, a false negative, is not believing a pattern is real when it is. Shermer gives the example of a rustle in the grass, and how it triggers a type I error in believing that the noise came from a predator, rather than the wind, and how that is less costly than a type II error, whereby we believe it is the wind when it is actually a predator.

But what really jumped out at me was Shermer's explanation of "agenticity;" the belief that there are invisible, intentional agents behind the patterns that we extract from the noise around us. Hence, our human tendency to believe in ghosts, myths, monsters, and gods—or God.

Studies suggest that the human tendency to believe in the supernatural, a higher power, or deities is an advantageous evolutionary adaptation akin to walking upright. Religion, some researchers suggest, was important for early and primitive societies to develop, and some even suggest that religion and social evolution together produced what we now know as modern life.

British Anthropologist Robin Dunbar has conducted research on the size of animals' social networks in relation to brain size. Dunbar has found that humans can maintain significantly larger social networks, as compared to other primates, than brain size alone can explain. To support this, he has found evidence that this reflects the social network sizes of our hunter-gatherer ancestors.

Cooperation and the forming of societies, villages, city-states, and civilizations are explained by evolution, according to Dunbar, as a survival adaptation. And of course, when, say, 150 people come together to form a commune and have to cooperate to survive, that has an impact on behavior, customs, mores, technology (remember fire?), and, most probably, diet—which, according to some studies, has a strong correlation with brain size. Some scientists even point to the invention of cooked food; with less energy devoted to digestion, it was advantageous in terms of freeing up energy that helped to make our brains bigger than those of other primates.

But, according to Dunbar, brain size alone doesn't explain our biological ability to maintain up to 150 friends—that is, to cooperate and form societies. Dunbar and his colleagues have identified three things that have aided in releasing endorphins, which are powerful hormones that help with bonding: laughter, singing, and religion. Dunbar's research has found that religion often incorporates both singing and laughing—perhaps why preachers often start with a joke—and, therefore, is an especially potent tool that activates and triggers endorphin production, and, as a result, increases bonding with other humans. He has even found that laughing, singing, or engaging in repetitive motions in synchronization with others can induce a trance-like state.

This is all to say that religion echoes the deep longing in all humans for bonding, connection, and authenticity. Science suggests that humans are social beings who have relied on cooperation to gain evolutionary advantage in order to survive in a wild and chaotic world. With humanity as the dominant species, wielding great power and responsibility over the future of the planet, I believe that our collective efforts should be channeled toward the betterment of every living creature on Earth.

To this day, I still catch myself saying a little prayer or beseeching God at certain times. I lean toward the idea that religion is a natural tendency, that it still serves a purpose for me, and possibly others, who find support in prayer when needing direction or a will to do something. But beyond that, I am less forgiving of dogmatic, fundamentalist religion that twists social cooperation and becomes, instead, a spiritual and mental prison in which the masses are enslaved to archaic ideas wielded by charlatans and false prophets who profit from and even drive people to commit history's most heinous acts—inquisitions, witch hunts, purges, and, yes, terrorism.

Just like when my birth mother and I were caught in a prison of domestic abuse and isolation, humans can find themselves trapped in the prison of a belief system. Our longing to belong and be a part of something bigger than ourselves can make things seem irresistible and right. But whether it's cults or conspiracy theories or groups that harbor them, one of the ways we are held captive is when these groups make us feel alone, or isolated. That the whole world is on fire and is set against us. That we're the only ones with the answers, and that those who don't listen to us are corrupted, which then forces us to only commune and interact with others who agree with us.

Sound familiar? We can see strains of this in our political climate today, when everything is presented as so black and white.

That was very much how I operated back then. With clear lines in the sand. I was saved; my co-workers, who had tattoos, swore, drank beer, had sex, and smoked, were not. All I had to do was save them, too. As easy as that. If I saved enough souls, then maybe God would see that as compensating for me being gay.

After the summer season died down, rather than wait for next summer to roll around, I applied for a job at Aubuchon Hardware in Raymond. The manager, Mr. Zarecki, was a Catholic priest who had majored in history. I remember that because we would often discuss history and politics when it was slow.

Though I knew next to nothing about hardware, carpentry, plumbing, or mechanics, I set my mind to being the best vaccumer, organizer, and loader there was. Soon, I knew where most things were, and I eased into assembling wheelbarrows and furniture, helping a co-worker named Gerald in the equipment shop, cutting glass and keys.

One proud moment I remember was when a couple came in with a children's book made of thick compressed cardboard. One ring held the pages together, sort of like a keychain in the corner—or it had, until it broke. We didn't have anything that would perfectly match, but I took them to the hardware aisle and, after thinking and rummaging for a few minutes, produced a metal ring that could serve the same function.

I was still in the hardware aisle organizing and cleaning up when I heard Mr. Zarecki over the intercom saying sternly, "Marpheen, please come to the register."

I panicked; why did he sound so serious, and why was he using the intercom to call me to the front?

I walked as quickly as I could to the front of the store where I saw Mr. Zarecki standing between the two registers, his arms crossed and wearing a frown. But I could see that old-man twinkle in his eyes as I sheepishly approached him.

He broke into a smile. "Marpheen, that couple you just helped were very, very pleased with your customer service," he said. "They went on and on about how creative you were."

"Oh … umm … thanks," I said.

"Good job. Keep it up, Marpheen."

I walked around with pride swelling my chest for who knows how long after that. Working for Mr. Zarecki was fulfilling, and I worked as many hours as possible—almost every night and on weekends, when I didn't have a game or music practice—until my parents noticed that my grades began to slip and threatened to make me cut back on hours. When I did my taxes the following spring, even my dad's accountant looked at my pay stubs with surprise. I had earned about $7,500 that year, some of which went into those oh-so-teenage activities of hanging with school friends at the mall, going to the Tim Horton's donut shop during study hall and breaks, and paying for gas to go to the beach and whatnot.

You might be wondering by this point if I ever thought of my birth mom and my family. I did, at times. But I found that living my new "normal life" rarely allowed me the time or energy to think about my birth family, let alone to focus on who I really was, deep inside. It took a lot to maintain the facade of being "the same" as everyone around me. That's the price of assimilation. Because I could not be fully me, all of my energy was devoted to being someone I was expected to be. I found that working hard and making money was a way to fit in. Having a good work ethic was part of being a good Mainer—a good American. Even if your job sucked, you just muddled through and faked it till you made it.

Not that work wasn't fun for me at times. I actually enjoyed it once I got to know my co-workers. Gerald, especially, was cool. He was in his mid-forties, a little rough around the edges, but we'd hang in the equipment shop in the back, fixing and assembling things. Many times he'd bring his German shepherd along. Ashley and Ryan joked about my being Christian, but we warmed up to each other, and pranks ensued. Ryan especially started to engage with me on religion, and we would have some deep discussions about why he didn't believe in any religion but did believe in a higher power.

Apart from the cussing, drinking, and smoking, I didn't really see these co-workers as inherently bad. One thing that did annoy me, however, was the misogyny. A few of the guys would make some of the most lewd and chauvinistic comments about attractive customers. Those were the few times when I'd get flustered or angry with them. Seeing how badly my birth mom had been treated by abusive men in her life created these strong gut reactions whenever I witnessed misogyny and chauvinism. I couldn't help but protest that kind of behavior.

Now, you may be wondering why I am talking so much about work. It's important to me, because it was a part of my working-class upbringing from middle school on. My adoptive parents weren't swimming in money. My dad worked two or three jobs for many years to help finance and afford the addition onto the house. My mom had a tight hold on our finances, carefully crafting the grocery list and clipping coupons to make sure dinners, lunches, and snacks followed a calendar. Meatloaf, beef Stroganoff, and spaghetti appeared frequently, with tuna casserole, split pea soup, and chicken making appearances every other week. Saturday nights were special: movie night and ice cream!

Our family loved both *Star Wars* and *Star Trek*, and watched the movies over and over again. We also watched the *Star Trek* television show on a weekly basis, along with *Home Improvement* and plenty of Hallmark TV shows and movies. During the summer, we went to the Bridgton Drive-In to get two-for-one movie deals. We would pile into the Toyota Sienna and either watch with the back open, or from lawn chairs staked out in front—or, later, when we had a van, we'd stay inside and avoid the swarms of mosquitoes.

We stuck to the financial plan that Mom and Dad worked out so that, starting when I was in eighth grade, we could go to Florida every year. We would drive down the East Coast, stopping somewhere in the Carolinas or Georgia to crash at a hotel overnight. Then we would finish the last leg of the trip and arrive at one of the timeshare developments in Kissimmee. Another family that went to church with us was also usually in Florida at the same time, so we would meet up for dinner (usually at a buffet) or go to Disney World together.

One year, we brought Grammy Anita, who lives in Aroostook County. She had just had knee surgery and would often use a wheelchair, which had its advantages. Not just handicapped parking at stores, but the much shorter lines for rides at Disney. I felt a little bad as we zoomed past long lines and people glared at us. I wonder now if I felt bad because we were getting off easy while they all had to stand in the sweltering Florida sun with their kids in tow. Maybe not *bad*, but slightly embarrassed. Mom or Dad could have gone with Grammy Anita, rather than having all seven of us in the handicapped lane.

That's the power privilege has—the power to help you get ahead. But it also drew the ire of the rest of the people who had to stand in long lines. This reminds me of something I often hear when talking to folks about food stamps, housing, or welfare. I often hear back: "Native Mainers shouldn't have to wait at the back of the line while asylum seekers and refugees get to skip ahead." While I think that's how it appears to the "native Mainers," I think something that gets ignored is the harrowing and dangerous journey asylum seekers and refugees have had to take to even *get* to Maine, let alone through the doors at the benefits or housing office.

My Cambodian family saw two million of their own countrymen and -women slaughtered between 1975 and 1979. Even at the end of the Khmer Rouge's reign, they weren't immediately flown to California and settled. They languished in a refugee camp for nearly a decade while the world sat around deciding their fate, determining which country would get what number of refugees.

The same goes for refugees today. Their homes and lives were upended by war, famine, and disaster. Many had to secure passage to a refugee camp or a refugee processing center, oftentimes having to bribe guards and enemy soldiers, or paying a human trafficker to hopefully take them to the right place. This in itself can take years. Only when the UN designates and processes them as refugees can they finally step foot in America. Once here, they're faced with language barriers as well as bureaucratic ones.

While I understand the pain and frustration folks may feel when they see someone going ahead of them in line, in this case, there is a lot more to the story than what occurs in a crowded social services office. And there is definitely a lot more to the broader story of how social services and support safety nets are chronically or inadequately funded, which exacerbates situations where people in need are pitted against each other to beg and scrape for scraps.

Looking back now, I am cognizant of some of the privilege and advantage that rubbed off on us. It wasn't our own inherently, but rather what was granted to us because we were an acceptable exception to the unspoken rule. Although we were brown kids, people always knew we were the brown kids of white parents. Their privilege was akin to an umbrella policy—as long as those who saw us were aware of this fact, or as long as our parents were actually there with us. While we carried our brown skin with us, our white parents' privilege was sort of an invisible marker that said to the world, "Oh, they're different, but they're the kids of people who look like us."

In rural Maine, this was easier-to-digest diversity. It meant that we weren't seen as much of a threat to their way of life, their concepts of what makes a good community and a good neighborhood. We weren't as much of a threat to their ideal of what makes up their small corner of America.

Even so, there were still ways in which racism and stereotypes filtered through. When I was sixteen, I started going to driver's ed with Derek, a friend from school, and the "Asians are bad drivers" jokes started popping up. Being a survivor, I employed that ever-so-useful comedic tool of self-deprecation to elicit laughter from my white audience.

All of this probably made me even more nervous when I got into the student-driver car for the first time with Derek and the instructor. All that nervous energy seemed to travel down my right leg and into my foot as I slammed a little too hard on the gas, and the car screeched and jolted forward until I took my foot completely off. Derek laughed nervously in the background while the instructor chided me. After that, it was all pretty much smooth sailing through driver's ed. I always took corners very slowly, something the instructor took note of and commended.

I enjoyed driver's ed mostly because I got to see other kids from other schools—and by that, I mean other boys from other schools. A handful of the guys were from the Fryeburg and Lake Region hockey teams, and the rivalry made its way into the classroom. Each group of hockey players from each of the schools had their leader, both of whom were recipients of my awkward small talk and pretend nonchalance.

But here, too, a multiplicity of things kept me from revealing who I really was. The second I realized I was indulging in this kind of connection with other guys, the butterflies in my stomach would start and my natural defenses would go up. Take the normal teenage angst when it comes to crushes and throw in rural evangelical American values, circa 2007.

My family and my church stood firmly against homosexuality, seeing it as a perversion of what they considered "natural" and in line with "God's purpose." I had internalized the evangelical views that homosexuality was an abomination and something that was twisted and wrong inside of me. To give you a glimpse of what they believed about homosexuality, here's an excerpt from an Assembly of God position paper:

> Scripture consistently identifies homosexual behavior as sin ... Homosexual activities of every kind are contrary to the moral commandments God has given us. ... When people choose to engage in homosexual behavior, they depart from the God-given nature of sexuality. Their unnatural sexual behavior is a sin against God, who established the order of sexuality (*Romans* 1:27). And the social unit they seek to establish is contrary to the divine instruction for the man to leave father and mother and be "united to his wife." (*Genesis* 2:24).

In light of the beliefs expressed in that statement, and the values taught to me through the church and Christian school, I prayed and prayed, hoping it would go away. I threw myself relentlessly into searching for the spiritual answer to the thorn in my side.

The answer never came. But hormones did, and I found myself wanting to kiss a cute boy and to walk along the lakeside, hand in hand. Instead of coming to the conclusion that perhaps I was gay, I threw myself more and more into getting involved as a Christian youth leader. By this time, at sixteen, I was officially the worship leader for our youth group band on Sunday nights. While others had their prayers and other expressions of spirituality, I felt that if anything would help me "get in touch" with God, it was music. So I poured everything I had into worship at youth group.

By now, people in the church were expecting great things from me. I was young and on fire for Jesus. I wanted a return to the revivals of old, for thousands of people in the region to realize the saving power and grace of God. Music was the key to unlock the spiritual hunger that could help spark this type of revival. It all makes sense to me now, given the research on evolution and religion and the endorphin-releasing power of synchronized singing and music.

It was around this time that Brandon (or B-Denny) came into my life. He was first introduced to me and Travis as a friend of some kids who went to our school and church. One of those students was a backup singer in our youth worship band, so Brandon would come early with them to practice. Next thing we knew, he was trained to do setup and to work the soundboard.

The three of us came together through youth group: me as the lead singer and on the keyboard, Travis on the drums, and B-Denny making sure we sounded half-decent on the soundboard. Brandon was seventeen and had a car by then—a silver Saturn—and he joined Travis and me for our weekend soirees playing video games and watching movies in the basement. It became our tradition to head to Travis' house around dinnertime on Saturday evening, B-Denny picking me up on the way. We'd stay up until four or five in the morning, being goofballs, and then go to church the next morning. After that, we'd hop in Brandon's car and drive somewhere in the Sebago Lakes region, do some burnouts in the Walmart parking lot, or go to the mall and hang out before coming back for youth group worship practice.

Travis and B-Denny added a level of risk-taking and troublemaking to my life that had been sorely lacking. I mostly tagged along quietly while they would come up with the most obnoxious noises, like "Ringo! *RINGO!* RRRRRRINGO!" or "Rooster! ROOSTERY!! ROOSTEEEE!" Most of these were directed toward unsuspecting pedestrians on the side of the road, or, something that made me blush with embarrassment for my friends, they would direct them at Travis' mom or Pastor Brian when they were being scolded for being too loud or driving erratically in the church parking lot.

B-Denny had that effect wherever he went. He enrolled in

our school and soon became the prankster and class clown who gave the teachers and the principal quite the headache. He was this way at work, too, which I found out when Mr. Zarecki retired and I applied to work at Hannaford. The benefits of my new job were not having to deal with the new boss at the hardware store, getting a pay raise, and working with B-Denny.

Once we clocked in, we immediately started bagging, cashing out customers, and retrieving carts. We all became parts of a machine, and I despised it. It seemed monotonous and such a bore, lacking anything fulfilling, except for the times when a customer would wait in my line to get some good old-fashioned customer service. As a cashier, I could engage in one-on-one conversations. I took an interest in people and their lives, and they noticed it.

The company had goals to meet and imposed on the cashiers a standard rate at which we were to ring items (something fast, I remember), and even made it into a competition. My ring rate was the slowest because, again, I loved customer service and I was too polite to tell a person that I couldn't chitchat. I was, in fact, taken aside a few times by the shift leader and told that I needed to increase my ring rate—which I would do for the next week while practically throwing customers' groceries down the register's belt. But eventually I couldn't avoid focusing more on the customer rather than speed, and my ring time would drop again.

It's rather dehumanizing for all parties involved, cashier and customer alike. Smile. Ask if they found everything okay. Ring the items through. Accept their payment. And wish them well on their way. The cashier is expected to provide satisfactory customer service within the confines of clear guidelines and goals established by those higher up in the chain. Companies like this also deliberately engineer the store layout to funnel customers in and maximize sales. For instance, the grocery chain where I worked was a subsidiary of a larger corporation that owned other grocery chains up and down the East Coast. A major initiative of theirs was to standardize each of the stores in all of their subsidiaries so that a person who shops at one of their stores in Maine will still feel a sense of "home" in another grocery chain belonging to the same corporation in Florida.

Folks barely give this dehumanization a thought because both the laborer and the customer are bombarded by the expectations and stresses of capitalism and consumerism. Laborers are pitted against each other in what companies deem "healthy competition," with such creative ploys as "Employee of the Month" competitions to figure out who is the most productive. Companies distribute rewards, bonuses, and salary increases to those who, according to quantitative standards, surpass their peers. It's degrading. One of the trickle-down effects of unfettered capitalism is that positive attributes like work ethic and personal responsibility are twisted into a form of manipulative subjugation. Those who cry out for living wages are urged to work a little harder. But how can you, if you can't afford wholesome food, basic health care, and everything else you need for good mental, physical, and emotional health?

I see this especially today, as I'm sure you do as well, when it comes to COVID-19. During the pandemic, Congress passed a number of measures to support American workers and families facing mass unemployment and economic hardship. People received stimulus payments, and those who were laid off or lost work were eligible for generous unemployment benefits. As the economy started to climb back and businesses started to reopen, it seemed social media and the news exploded about a shortage of workers. That's when I started seeing memes (graphics that use images with an often-exaggerated summary of an issue) saying that the unemployment benefits were making people stay at home, choosing to remain unemployed.

I can understand to a degree why this may be cause for outrage for some, but one, the pandemic has killed hundreds of thousands of Americans, decreasing the number of people in the workforce, and two, wages have not kept up with productivity and inflation. Instead of looking at why, systemically, the economy is failing American workers, we instead are playing "blame the victim."

Some will say that if you work hard, you will be rewarded with higher wages and then will be able to afford what you need. But with the cost of living rising much faster than wages, workers struggle to afford even the basics of food, clothing, and shelter on poverty wages. While I am fortunate enough to have rented from the same landlord for many years, and have enjoyed below-market rent, I drive by for-sale signs for houses nearing or exceeding half a million dollars, and for-rent signs for one-bedroom studios that go for $1,500 a month or more. I wouldn't be able to afford any of it if I decided to move, even though I have a relatively good-paying job and consider myself middle class. So I can only imagine what front-line and essential workers are experiencing at this time.

It's usually folks who live comfortably who reframe poverty as a moral defect, saying that someone who works hard and uses their money wisely will have what they need. They point their fingers at those who spend their limited funds on cigarettes and alcohol, rather than pointing to the hamster wheel of systemic poverty. Is it a moral defect—or a defect in the economic and social systems—that the working class and working poor need a couple of jobs just to make ends meet? They are tired. They have less and less time to spend with their families, less time for self-care, and even less time to be engaged with what is going on in their communities, their states, and their nation—as if they are merely machines. When people are isolated and segregated, we are more susceptible to economic, political, and spiritual exploitation. Instead, we can choose to come together as part of the human tribe, to uphold the dignity and value of each human being.

I didn't understand this when I was growing up, because the political beliefs that come with evangelicalism are staunchly conservative. I was taught that if you loved God and Jesus Christ, then it was your duty to vote—and to vote Republican. We were soldiers in the Kingdom of God who were on a holy crusade to return America to its Christian roots. We were anti-abortion. We were anti-homosexuality. We were for any candidate who was "born again" and committed to pro-family, pro-Christian values. In all of this, the idea of individual, personal responsibility and morality were integral pieces of the conservative Christian worldview. Yes, we all came together to worship at church and were creating community around a common set of principles, mores, values, and ideas. But each person either lived up to the standards set by the community or they were ostracized and shunned. This was all coated with such things as "Love the sinner, but hate the sin"—a sort of love that is a pretense for passive-aggressive fundamentalism.

Starving for some sense of identity, to know who I was in this world, I became deeply rooted in this worldview. Being separated from my birth mother and my Cambodian family and being placed in foster care stripped me of the opportunity to grow into who I might have become as a brown kid living with a brown family in a community made up of predominantly Black and brown families. And while neither my foster families nor my adoptive family are to blame for my being separated from my birth family, I think it is important for me, for them, and for the world to know the deep trauma that occurs beneath the surface when your identity is splashed against a white canvas, and that one splash of brown is stretched and thinned and begins to fade. Fitting in allowed me to at least be aware, in some way, that it was still me. That I still had a voice in all of this, even though the sounds around me were drowning me out. For me, surviving, assimilating, and fitting in was a temporary surrender. It was me living to fight another day.

My brown identity—my first language, my Cambodian and Buddhist cultural values, and everything else that I grew up with until the age of nine—began to recede and become less vibrant as layers and shades of whiteness were mixed in, impressed upon me, and pronounced. One identity was shed and another was offered: I could be a brown kid in a white family with evangelical and conservative views, living in a rural state. And I could be loved and cared for.

My adoptive family tried their best to keep my siblings and me in contact with our birth mother, but over the years it became increasingly difficult because we didn't speak the same language. It is in many ways like phantom pain. When I hear Khmer, my ears twitch and I intuitively nod as if I understand. But in the end, like a missing arm or leg, that feeling is just a feeling. Slowly I am relearning very basic Khmer, but it is so very difficult.

Eventually, it was too hard for me to go through the routine of speaking through a translator only to get a general sense of how she was doing; that she wanted us to do well in school; and that she hoped to see us again. I wasn't good at small talk, and in a sense, I was deeply ashamed that I couldn't even converse with my own mother—that I had lost my first language.

I remember the day our family piled into the van to go to one of these translated sessions with our birth mother, over the phone (my birth family had moved back to California). I realized I was not okay with having to talk to my own birth mother through a translator. Although there was really no other way for us to communicate, my frustration and shame had reached a peak. I told my parents, and we turned around and headed home. After all the years spent in foster care, a brown kid who had lost his brown identity, I had little to no connection left with my birth mother. At this time, she began to move around a lot, and eventually my siblings and I lost contact with her for many years.

I became consumed with my new identity as a brown kid adopted by a white, working-class, socially conservative family. I was obsessed with trying to get God to purge me of my sin and homosexual feelings. This, in turn, fueled my drive to get in touch with God through music and Scripture.

My church pastor and youth pastor saw this drive and passion, as they referred to it, and were there to guide me on my journey. I ate up their mentorship, and even though they didn't know of my secret struggle, I wanted to prove to my parents and church community that I wasn't a homo.

I felt in some way that the religious revival I so longed to see happening in my church community was somehow the answer. All we needed to do was to seek God and be consumed by his love and Spirit, and to spread that love to those we deemed unsaved, and "of the World." I cannot express strongly enough how important music was to me in helping to achieve this goal. Dunbar's research on the evolutionary psychology of religion, and how synchronized singing and chanting can induce a trance-like state among participants, explains everything that went on when I led worship sessions at church services, youth conventions, and youth camp.

I remember clearly all the youth group and church members who came up to me with tears in their eyes after a worship session or song to tell me how they could "feel the presence of God in the room," or how they "got in touch with God" while I was leading worship. This often happened after moments during worship where I would play a chord progression over and over again and sing a prayer, ad lib. These moments would come to a crescendo as we moved into what can only be described as desperate cries for the attention of a God whose proof of existence we hungered for and whose validation we sought through prayer. It was the simple act of singing and praying together—with the added power of music—that made us feel God was actually in the room.

This also explained all of those moments toward the end of a youth convention sermon, when they asked if anyone wanted to be saved or to recommit to Christ, or when an evangelist would hold special services at our church, where people would be "baptized by the Holy Ghost," speak in tongues, or be "healed." It is frightening thinking of it now, actually. A faith healer or evangelist would show up and give a sermon about how the End Times were near, as evidenced by all the floods, fires, famines, wars, and immorality in the world, and that "the Church" better saddle up and get ready.

From what I recall, these special sermons were intentionally designed to rile people up and fill them with anxiety and fear about what the world was becoming—how they weren't doing enough to save their families and friends and neighbors. Once they were in this state of fear and anxiety, the evangelist would deliver the message that true believers in Christ need not worry. As long as you were saved by the blood of Christ and were baptized in his Holy Spirit, as the apostles of old were in the book of Acts, nothing could stop you from going to Heaven and bringing your family, friends, and neighbors with you.

That second part is important. Like any good pyramid or multilevel marketing scheme, you had to bring people with you. It was ingrained that if you were truly saved and passionate about God, you would do everything you could to convert the unsaved and ungodly. It was almost as if we wouldn't get into Heaven if we didn't save at least one wretched soul. All of this was part of a cycle that fed on human emotions—on how we are hard-wired to see patterns in otherwise meaningless noise. Our brains have that power to trick us into seeing something that we want to see. Get someone desperate enough, stressed enough, and questioning reality enough, and next thing you know, they've seen God in that cloud in the sky, or Jesus on a burnt piece of toast.

Or you've felt the heebie-jeebies when Satan was sitting on your shoulder, trying to tempt you into disobeying God by looking too longingly at that cute boy at the mall.

It always bothered me that I never experienced whatever it was that made people fall over or become filled with the presence of God. That is another defining belief in the Assemblies of God Pentecostal denomination. Other denominations believe that Holy Spirit baptism only existed in the New Testament times, while denominations like the Assemblies of God believe that Holy Spirit baptism exists to this day. The clearest evidence is when a person begins to speak in tongues.

How do you know if you're speaking in tongues? Who knows. Conveniently, it is left up to the individual to decide whether it was tongues or not. To me, the pattern seemed to be that at the end of a sermon when the pastors would invite us to become baptized by the Holy Spirit, they would say that a sign would be speaking in tongues, and that we shouldn't resist whatever came to mind. So, although I never personally felt that special spiritual force that apparently other people felt, I would utter the most nonsensical things that came to mind. *Dras golalalalal montocasto* or *Sololota manditto*. It's completely ridiculous. I am laughing right now, thinking of a moment when a woman walked up to me afterward and said she thought I was speaking Spanish. I suppose you could say that speaking in tongues is in the ear of the listener.

It deeply bothered me that I never fainted or felt the Holy Ghost inside of me. I am chuckling as I remember the prayers that went something along the lines of, "God, I want to feel you inside of me," or "Holy Spirit, I want to feel you burning inside." The evangelical world refers to God using male pronouns. For a sect of Christianity that despises homosexuality, it sure wasn't lacking in homoeroticism.

I thought at the time that I didn't feel any of this because I was hiding my sin, my homosexuality, and that I wasn't seeking God hard enough. So I dug in even deeper.

India, 2007

●◗◖○○

When I was sixteen and in my sophomore year in high school, an opportunity came up that I thought would help me in my pursuit to become one with God. Our church had an Indian family who wanted to help organize a mission trip to India with our youth group. I joined Pastor Brian, Travis, his mom, and a few others to set about fundraising for the cost of the trip, which was about $6,000 per person. I was more than thrilled to go and spread the Gospel in a third-world country and to grow closer to God doing so, not at all realizing how amusing it was that a boy who was raised Buddhist, who became a born-again Christian after being adopted, was now going to preach to Hindus about who had the best religion.

We departed from Boston's Logan Airport and stopped in Milan, Italy, for a short layover. There wasn't enough time to do much, but I bought an "authentic Italian leather" wallet that I carried and used until I was about twenty-four. From there, we flew directly to Mumbai, India, where we emerged out of the plane and walked into an airport bustling with people—brown people! Immediately the culture shock set in.

Armed soldiers carried what seemed to me to be massive AK-47s. The bathrooms were *very* public, with men standing around peeing into tall stalls with the drains in the ground. And, boy, did I feel like a million bucks when I exchanged my American dollars for Indian rupees! (I believe the exchange rate at the time was forty or so Indian rupees for every American dollar.)

Making our way outside into a warm afternoon in Mumbai, we saw a gaunt Indian man with no legs rolling himself around on a small, makeshift trolley. We felt pity for him and stopped to give him some rupees. But when I reached into the fanny pack beneath my shirt to pull out some cash, a gust of wind swept by and the wad of rupees I was holding flew into the air. Money was flying everywhere. The people in the square all stopped and stared at the Americans as we scrambled to gather up the money. (I still felt like a million bucks afterward.)

Whether we knew it or not, part of the strategy of bringing missionaries (or what I would call "tourist missionaries") to impoverished parts of the world was to shake things up a bit, but also, in an underhanded way, to take sort of a Joel Osteen approach to convincing people living in these countries to accept Christ into their hearts. Thus, we Americans rode into these unknown lands like knights in shining armor—or in this case, on a bus—to flaunt how blessed we were as followers of Christ. If they would just join our religion, they, too, could be like us Americans. All joking aside, it was very colonial of us to think that we could save these people from poverty and hell with a bus tour through the crowded streets and remote villages of India.

Mumbai wasn't where we were going to spread the Gospel. We were headed to the rural regions and villages in the Tamil Nadu province, to Coimbatore, where the Indian family from our church also lived when they were in the region. This was in itself a long trip, over seven hundred miles through dusty plateaus, that reminded me of photos from Mars.

When we got to the center of the province, we traveled up steep roads that hugged treacherous cliffs and through jungles and mountains that led us to Coimbatore. At times, the distance between the wall that guarded the edge and the mountainside was so small it made me feel claustrophobic.

Macaque monkeys sat atop these walls, overly confident, entitled little runts that tried to entice us to roll down our windows and hand them some food.

When we got to Coimbatore, we stayed in a multilevel unfinished building intended for the ministry that the Indian family from our church had started. The first level, which sat atop a porch that jutted out of the hill the building sat on, was where we stayed, along with the host family. We were treated to home-cooked meals with plenty of *naan* and *puri* breads, *biryani*, and even rabbit curry. I loved everything, but some of the others—white Mainers—didn't enjoy it as much.

During one of the meals, we were brought rice and curry wrapped in banana leaves. When I opened it up, I immediately spotted the little red pieces of chili pepper, which I devoured, of course. But another person in our group took a bite and immediately spit it out, loudly proclaiming that they didn't like it.

I remember feeling personally offended. I had an idea of the standard of living in India compared to America, and knew about the cultural differences when it comes to hospitality and generosity. The Indian family had had to cook more food than usual, and they had given us the best portions. And then here was a white person—a person on a mission trip—spitting it out and vocalizing their distaste. I may have lost my birth language and many of the customs and values common in Asian cultures, but I knew that you do not spit out food offered to you in hospitality and tell the hosts that you don't like it. My Cambodian grandmother would have had none of that; she watched like a hawk to make sure you ate every grain of the massive pile of rice that she gave you.

The whole trip was eye-opening for me then, and even more so now, as I reflect on the white-savior complex that accompanies evangelical missionaries. The idea is subtle but simple, really, if you break it down. Those who grow up in the American education system internalize the idea that the United States is far greater than any other country and civilization on Earth. In my private, Christian school education, for instance, I was taught that Western civilization was responsible for the greatest advances in human history because of Christianity and capitalism. We internalize that Western civilization has it all figured out and can solve all of the world's problems.

This has given rise to a trend known as "poverty porn," where well-meaning white folks go overseas to third-world countries to spend a week or two doing "good" in poverty-stricken communities while posting photos of themselves surrounded by white and brown children. This has raised questions about whether these efforts are actually helpful or whether they are mainly feel-good sentimental moments to bring home and broadcast.

While I don't want to compare the white-savior complex to what's happening here in Maine, I think it may help you to understand by putting the concept in a different light. Not in terms of religion and spreading Christianity and colonialism, but in terms of tourism. Folks flock here from Boston and New York and all over the country—and the world—to visit the state of Maine, tucked away in the Northeast in what is "basically Canada." Instead of poverty porn, what are tourists after here? Well, obviously lobster porn, all delicious-looking, smothered in melted butter, with the oh-so-sexy sounds of shells and knuckles cracking and juices squirting. Lighthouse porn, too. Those familiar phallic structures jutting into the sky, pouring their light all over the place. Maine people? No, I don't think we're the attraction here. If anything, I feel like we're merely the accessories to the Maine experience. Or in the way. Or both. Tourists with their "We'll save your economy from falling apart" complex.

In movies, we can see the white-savior complex at play in *The Great Wall*, with Matt Damon as the lead who helps to save the Chinese from zombies, and in *The Last Samurai*, with Tom Cruise as a white man who fights to save samurai culture. Growing up in America, we are accustomed to this; we're prone to being blind to the effect this has in shaping views of the world outside. Many of us associate strong leadership and the rule of law, justice, and freedom with whiteness—with white men, especially—who are painted on the canvas of our more than two hundred years of history as stoic, rational, faithful, and devout men who rise above the masses to take their place as father figures for the ensuing generations.

Even one of the most holy figures in history, Christ, a Middle Eastern Jew, was recast as a white savior—whose Gospel of loving God and thy neighbor was misappropriated to aid Western, European powers in the colonization of lands populated by what they deemed as infidels, heathens, and savages. As Kenya's former prime minister Jomo Kenyatta succinctly put it: "When the missionaries arrived, the Africans had the land and the missionaries had the Bible. They taught us how to pray with our eyes closed. When we opened them, they had the land and we had the Bible."

It was also a form of colonialism when these missionaries from America subtly sent the message that these people, struggling with real and abject poverty, malnutrition, and poor health, would have it as good as Americans if they would simply accept Jesus Christ into their hearts.

All of this is shrouded in our consistent messaging that suffering exists because we are all of us sinners; we are empty, and we have God-sized holes in our hearts. All they have to do to be set on the path toward happiness and joy and relief from all suffering is to say a prayer, accept Christ into their hearts, and *presto change-o*— their lives will turn around.

Before our trip, we had had no cultural competency training. We knew nothing of the Indian people before we arrived in their country. We didn't know about the long-lasting divisions and effects of British colonialism. We didn't understand the overarching political, economic, and social forces at work that create and exacerbate the conditions in which India's population has suffered. We also didn't fully understand Hinduism, and the fact that there are a multiplicity of gods and goddesses. We were approaching them with the message that there is only one God who is somehow made up of the Father, the Son, and the Holy Ghost.

We ran into some interesting situations as we continued throughout southern India and ventured toward the northeast, including stopping at a leper camp to proselytize and try to faith-heal.

We were holding a service in a remote village when a man with white powder or paint all over his body showed up. People began to leave. Some of the Indian pastors began to intervene and confronted the man. Our group was visibly worried, but we focused on preaching and engaging with the few people who had stayed behind. Afterward, when we were on the bus, we were told that that man was the village witch doctor. And, boy, he was not happy.

We did a lot of sightseeing as well. We spotted a wild elephant once, and were warned not to spook it or it would flip our bus. The region was tropical and jungle-like, and we were told to keep an eye out for a Bengal tiger (although we didn't end up seeing one).

Each of us was assigned a security guard. I can't quite remember mine, but he was bald and had a mustache, and he stuck with me throughout the two-week mission trip. One day, about a week into the trip, we were on the bus and he put his hand on my lap and just left it there. I was uncomfortable, but I didn't know what to do. I became visibly more annoyed the longer his hand was there. Finally, he asked, "Do you not like that I have my hand there?" I nodded and he moved his hand. "Sorry," he said.

Later, I asked an Indian pastor about it and he said that it was a gesture of love and brotherhood. I felt ashamed that I had essentially spurned his show of brotherly affection. Reflecting on it now, I probably felt embarrassed, and that it was a little gay to have a man rest his hand on my lap like that. But this also raises questions about American society as it relates to hyper- and toxic masculinity. We have ingrained it in our boys and men that physical displays of affection for other men are taboo. We link it to homosexuality, to make the shame that surrounds it even more potent.

This reminds me of one of the Indian attendants who served

as a guard and aide throughout our trip. He was a few years older than me, probably eighteen or nineteen. He had dark skin, was tall and lean, and quite handsome. I found myself sneaking glances at him when we were on the bus, or when we were sitting around the table or spending the night on an open church floor. I think this was the first time I'd ever noticed feeling attracted to another brown person. Back in Maine, I didn't know many brown or Black people, other than Peyton and Carter.

But, like I'd done many other times before, I bottled up these feelings and went on about my day, trying to spread the Gospel and get closer to God. By the time the two-week mission trip came to an end, I was more and more flustered that nothing had happened—that I hadn't had the spiritual experience I expected. I didn't feel some special presence that let me know that God was there.

I was a little angry when I got home. I kept questioning why I wasn't experiencing God like other people around me were. Again, the message that sometimes what keeps us apart from God is "hidden sin" made me look inward at the deep secret that I was hiding from the world around me. I anguished over this, obsessively reading and praying, wrestling with my homosexuality, mind racing, heart aching, and world shaking—or was it me shaking? The anxiety, as I've said before, gave me night terrors and night sweats. I'd wake up in the middle of the night, my suffering so great that I thought something was lying on top of me, and I couldn't breathe.

It was terrifying, too. Layers of fear. As in some of the stories told by well-known evangelists, like Dwight L. Moody, I thought I was wrestling with the Devil or some demon spawn that he had sent. I believed the Devil was coming to get me because I was an abomination in the eyes of the Lord. This kept me up on countless nights. Combine the fear and anxiety of keeping my secret along with the teenage angst I felt about dating and friends, and it's a wonder I got any sleep at all.

Windham Christian Academy, 2008–2009

● ◗ ◐ ○ ○

The start of my junior year in high school marked a sort of unraveling for me. I was as spiritual and conservative as ever, but I was silently dealing with a new side of teenage angst. My best friends B-Denny and Travis were in their senior year and starting to talk about college—where they wanted to go, what they wanted to study. As a junior, I wasn't ready yet. I also wanted to deny that I could lose my closest friends. As in so many coming-of-age stories and movies, I felt like I was coming to terms with the reality that things weren't going to be the same. I came to dread it. I grew somber, perhaps even depressed.

On top of that, my feelings about being gay, coupled with hormones and puberty, were in full swing, with no outlet. I tried dating a girl once to see if that would prove being gay was just a choice, but it only confirmed even more that I liked guys. I didn't even kiss her or touch her affectionately. Not even close.

I spent a lot more time in my room during the last two years of high school. I'd eat dinner, then head down to my room to read and listen to music. As the worship leader at our youth group and, on occasion, adult worship services, I still listened to and played a lot of Christian soft rock worship songs. But especially by my senior year, I had started to branch out to Coldplay, Snow Patrol, and Radiohead. A lot of their songs made the hopeless romantic in me sob a little at times. I truly felt hopeless then, especially about love and romance. I didn't know it for certain in my mind yet, but I felt deep down that I wouldn't be happy unless I was with another guy.

One day after wrapping Bible class, my principal said to me, "Marpheen, you've been a little down lately. Are you good?"

"Yeah, yeah," I replied. "Just stressed out."

And just like that I moved on.

I expressed how I felt to B-Denny and Travis by making us promise each other that we would make the best of the time we had left in high school—that these would be the best times of our lives, and that our friendship would grow so strong that not even college could ruin it. I invested completely in the time we spent together on weeknights and the weekends even as I dreaded the fact that these hours, minutes, and seconds were running out.

One night we all watched *The Walk* with some other friends and were nearly moved to tears. We'd go swimming at the lake near B-Denny's house at night. We'd slide down the basement stairs on mattresses and pillows. And then there were the times when B-Denny, who was a big fellow standing about 6'3" and probably 300 pounds, would strip down to his underwear, give himself a wedgie, and parade around Travis' house, in front of Travis' parents.

The thought of seeing these two guys, my closest friends, leave for an extended period of time gave me feelings that felt familiar— a coming farewell. This weighed so heavily on me that my family, friends, and teachers all noticed.

I was particularly sad about losing Travis. My bond with him had grown over the years, to a point where it felt like my heart was splitting in two. My other friendships at school and work were mere shadows compared to my friendship with him. I felt deep inside that he understood me when I was quiet, when I'd just stare out the car window on our way somewhere. He knew more than most people my story of going through foster care. He and I both struggled with not having experienced the same spiritual moments as everyone else: the fainting, the speaking in tongues, the palpable presence of God. He understood me and didn't judge me for being sheepish or shy or awkward. He didn't see me just as the youth group worship leader or that super-Christian kid; he saw me as a friend.

But he didn't know everything about me. The part of me that I went to great lengths to hide from the world. That light that I kept shrouded inside but which still burned like an ember buried deep beneath the ash. The light that would spark into a raging fire that I felt sure would consume me if I let it burn for too long. He didn't know that it burned a little brighter when he was around, in those quiet moments when we'd open up our inner selves and talk about our lives. Part of me was afraid that I would lose our friendship if I told him, so I continued to keep it buried.

The moments I treasured the most were the quieter times, whether we were camping, driving around, or lying on the floor, staring at the ceiling. We'd talk about life and purpose and the things we were struggling with; we dug in deep and revealed our inner selves, what we felt, what we worried about, and our dreams and visions for ourselves and our futures. It felt so real, so fulfilling and meaningful—I wanted to hold on to these moments forever. Although it didn't feel this way at the time, adolescence was relatively free of burdens—a time before we had bills, student loans, careers, and mortgages to worry about.

As my senior year began, the inevitable happened. Travis and B-Denny went off to college. I felt like my world had changed completely and turned upside down. My two best friends whom I had spent nearly every weekend with were now gone, and I had made no effort to replace them. There was still Chris, and we hung out every now and then, but I had let that friendship wane, especially when Chris got Lyme disease. Hannah, another one of our classmates, stuck by him and they got a lot closer, which I am thankful for. I also stopped hanging out and going over to Chris' house when his mom happened to glance at the search history on their family computer. (I'd recently entered "gay" into Google search.) She had a brief talk with me about this, and I was embarrassed to go there for a long time afterward.

At that time, the Christian Civic League of Maine was in lockstep with the National Organization of Marriage in pushing for a people's veto after Gov. John Baldacci signed a bill legalizing same-sex marriage in Maine. Maine was the first state to legalize same-sex marriage through legislative action, even if the Christian Civic League of Maine overturned it months later through a campaign of misinformation. It's something I always point to when I talk about how far we've come from the days when kids like me were deathly afraid to come out, to today, seeing our youth able to be more expressive, more fully themselves. It was a historic moment, one that I didn't fully appreciate until I became more involved in politics. I later met and thanked Gov. Baldacci personally for his courage on the issue.

At the time, though, I made a show of decrying the decision. It was a smokescreen to cover the struggle I was undergoing, like a caterpillar writhing in its cocoon, unsure of what it would face on the outside. I still had a long way to go. Members of the church and representatives from the campaign were circulating the petition around and tabling at our church. This worked to cement more and more in my head that the secret I was hiding was not welcome in my world.

My angst and anxiety drove me inward, and I began to further distance myself from those around me. I spent more time in my room reading or playing music than I did with my siblings or watching TV with the family. I would come upstairs for dinner and finish before everyone else, then head right back down to my room.

It was all starting to become a little much—the stress I felt around the transition into a year without my closest friends, and a time when I'd have to start thinking about life beyond high school. I lashed out at my parents and wanted to spend even more time alone. I started to look at kids who went to public schools and envy how much fun—and how many friends—they seemed to have. I had a lot of feelings at the time about a lot of things. Thinking back now, in some ways it was completely normal, teenager stuff. But at a deeper level, my very core seemed like it was tearing at the seams. I missed my friends, deeply. My weekends were no longer the same because they were all away at college. I had more time on my hands, and I didn't know what to do with it.

My mood lifted a little when I started applying to colleges. I knew that I wanted to become what they called a "worship pastor," someone who led worship professionally at a church, and, if they became famous enough, would travel around the world and record worship albums. I applied to Christian colleges in Massachusetts, Pennsylvania, Indiana, and elsewhere—I stuck strictly to Christian colleges because, again, I wanted to make my family and my church proud. I got acceptances from most of them, but I really wanted to go to Valley Forge Christian College (now the University of Valley Forge) in Pennsylvania, where B-Denny was studying digital media.

As high school graduation drew closer, I found myself becoming more and more excited about striking out on my own, and being able to join B-Denny at college. Deep down, I knew this was my opportunity to venture out and discover who I was apart from my church and family, so I set about charting my future. When I told my dad that Valley Forge was my top choice, I watched as he beamed with pride while telling other church members about it. Everyone he told was excited for me. They saw such promise in me, and had come to know me as a passionate and talented worship and youth leader who was on fire for God.

When graduation day arrived, nearly my entire world converged at the graduation ceremony. My first foster parents, Mark and Debi, were there. Sheila was there. And my adoptive family and all three of my younger siblings were there. I could look out and see the sum of my journey up until that point, other than my birth family, who were in California. The ceremony itself was a little different, almost like a marriage ceremony, where they had the parents walk their kids down the aisle. It's almost like they were walking me down the aisle to marry Jesus.

In attendance were the parents and family members of my graduating class of six. Also there were many members of the church, including the deacons and elders. My siblings and I were the only people of color in the room, from what I can remember. The community watched someone they had known for the past six years, a kid adopted by one of their own, walk up onto the stage.

Despite the struggles I was facing with my identity, I got to grow up in one of the most beautiful places in the world, with some of the cleanest rivers, lakes, and ponds imaginable. To this day, I judge other states' waters against Maine's; the same with forests and trees. I learned many lessons that I continue to hold dear: the value of community and giving back. Loving your neighbor, albeit with a different interpretation of it today. And lessons of grit and perseverance, which were not only taught to me by my life experiences, but by Mainers who endured countless cold winters. The land and the seasons, too, taught me that there is always hope on the other side of winter. I learned to appreciate a slower way of life, and the value of contemplation. How I would stop while on a walk through the woods just to listen to the leaves rustle in the wind. Or dangle my feet at the end of a dock and listen to the way the water moved below. Mother Earth has a way of creeping into the cracks in your heart and helping you heal, and Maine is one of those places where you can easily find her.

That summer flew by, and when the time came, my adoptive parents delivered me to college. They drove down in our minivan, and I led the way in my old 1995 Saab 9000 CSE, which, thankfully, had ample trunk space. We drove through New England, through New York and New Jersey, and finally, we arrived in Pennsylvania, weaving through the rolling hills and farmland to arrive at the college.

The air was full of freshman energy as students and their parents moved boxes and goods in and out of cars and into the dorm rooms. Roommates were introduced to each other, and families gathered for meals in the dining hall. Then there was the chapel service, where all the freshmen and their families got together. The school staff and faculty welcomed us with a sermon and had us pray together with our families. Mom and Dad cried, and I almost did, too. This had been a long time coming. They were letting go of their first son, a son they'd put through school, argued with, gone on trips with, and watched grow up in their church and community.

Aside from the angst of being in the closet, it had been a fairly typical working-class American upbringing. I got a job the minute I turned fourteen, fussed over grades with my parents, argued about how late I could stay up, played soccer, took piano lessons, learned the guitar, spent the weekends with my friends, got my driver's license, got a car, dated a girl (for barely a week), and went on a few trips. But through it all, I was always searching for who I was underneath the seemingly Norman Rockwell adolescence I was so lucky to enjoy. I thought I'd found the answer in what I was taught to believe by my family, my church, and my community—but it was still locked away within me, in the prison I had built to contain it.

I didn't get to experience the first love (and the heartbreak that often accompanies it) that most teenagers go through. That first kiss, the first date, getting into trouble with my parents for staying out too late—experiencing the passion and experimentation and pushing the boundaries that I could have felt not only emotionally, but also physically. When I hear stories today from those who came out during high school, part of me wishes I'd had the strength and bravery to come out as a teenager—to have experienced what other, predominantly hetero teen couples had a chance to experience. But I've come to accept that my journey was, and is, different. It's what made me who I am today.

Far from being a straight trajectory, life bends and twists and crosses over rivers, through valleys, and over and under mountains.

We do not have full control over which path we take, when we take it, and who we meet or what we encounter along the way. Sometimes the wind picks up and blows you off your path. Sometimes the rain comes down in torrents and washes away the road you were on. And oftentimes you meet people along the way who make such an impact on your life that you stick by them, and they by you, and you tread down a path together. And then, a storm along the way may drive you apart. Life may give the illusion of inevitability in the short run, but in the long run, it is shrouded in uncertainty.

There is no better time to feel what it means to be at a crossroads than that moment when (if you are lucky enough to be able to pay for and go to college) your parents or guardians leave you in your dorm room for the first time. The past is behind you, and the future beckons, but which road to take? Now I see that the path is actually built by the choices we make and how we respond to the forces that we have no control over while we are walking it. Whatever may cross our path, whether joy or despair, we forge ahead into the unknown.

That is how it felt to me the day I said good-bye to my parents. Bittersweet. They were my family, and I had gotten where I was in no small part thanks to them. It's important for all of us to realize that we don't have to travel our life path alone. In fact, I don't think it's possible. We are social creatures who, deep down, know that we need community if we are to survive in the face of adversity and the uncertainty of life and death. Hopelessness and despair more easily set in when we lose that sense of human connection, that longing to belong and be a part of the whole. We become less human when we turn our backs on our fellow human beings, and we are more susceptible to treating others inhumanely when we forget that we are all part of the human race, and that our individual paths eventually converge into one great unknown.

Death is the one thing we all share, and no one escapes it. The challenge therein, then, is how to live. The inhumanity of wars

My senior photo in 2009.

and genocide and all the atrocities and wrongs committed en masse or between neighbors are rooted in the dehumanization of others. It is so easy to fall into that trap when we forget to hope and to see the good in one another.

We can't just see the bad; we must also see the good. I wouldn't have made it to college if it were not for those who surrounded me, mentored me, and helped guide me. My adoptive parents, church, and school community were well intentioned in the way they raised me. But I think the extra things that came along with the evangelical world—their views on homosexuality and the lengths they went to denounce it—meant that I was only allowed to be a *part* of myself, and not my full self. My authentic self.

Religion is a powerful tool, and helps all of us to tap into our spirituality.

But it also has the power to divide, and can be twisted to conform to the inhumane goals and missions of persecution, genocide, terrorism, homophobia, and racism.

We need to seek religion in its truest and most authentic form, where it can fulfill our longing to connect with our true selves, one another, and the world around us.

PART FOUR

Valley Forge, Pennsylvania, 2009

The first week at Bible college wasn't much different than that of other colleges, minus the drunken debauchery often associated with secular schools. I'm not saying that drinking and sex didn't occur at all on the Christian campus—just that college rules drove these activities underground, so to speak, or off campus. It did seem pretty mainstream that within a week of meeting each other, freshmen were already dating—walking around campus holding hands, kissing, and spending inordinate amounts of time together. Our dorms were slightly different from those at secular colleges, in that they were separated by gender and there was a curfew. And the college convenience store didn't sell condoms.

My first roommate was from New York. He was cute and fit, with a button nose, and he drank a huge amount of Diet Coke. The guys on my floor were fun, except for one know-it-all show-off upperclassman. But there was another guy on the floor who was the sweetest guy on the planet, it seemed. And as the semester progressed, I developed a sort of crush on him.

As a church music major, my first semester was filled with music courses such as Applied Piano and Applied Voice, as well as ensembles like Gospel Choir and hours upon hours of practice. I would be in practice rooms until curfew, squabbling with other music majors for the room with the best piano. Other core requirements mainly focused on biblical studies, with courses such as Foundations in Christian Thought, Foundations in Biblical Interpretation, and Christian Philosophy. The biblical interpretation classes dove into hermeneutics and the origins of Scripture in the languages of Hebrew, Arabic, and Greek. We debated the merits of various translations, noting when and how they were translated. This historical context laid some important groundwork for me, as I learned to dig into how the Bible was interpreted and, especially later on, to figure out why the Word of God was used to oppress.

As one month followed another, I became more and more discouraged as I saw other students walking around hand in hand, kissing and spending time together. I was also flustered, realizing that I was attracted to a few guys on campus (especially the captain of the soccer team) but knowing that what I held in my heart was considered an abomination and abnormal among evangelical circles, including the Christian college I attended. In my heart and at the deepest levels imaginable, I longed to be like everyone else—free to be myself, to live unapologetically, and to love whomever I chose to love. Instead, I strove to be like everyone else in a very different way: by hiding my true self, and hating who I was inside, all the while trying to cast myself in the image that man—not God—had created.

My own fear was strangling me, cutting my heart and soul off from the oxygen—the love—that I knew I wanted and needed, but didn't think I deserved enough to turn against the beliefs of my family, my church, and the person I felt I was trying to be. The idea of coming out and going against the family that had reunited me with my siblings and the church family that had rallied around us was crushing me.

The very thought made me feel like the earth beneath me was shaking and being torn asunder. It was a war for my heart, mind, and soul.

No, it was a war *between* my heart, my mind, and my soul. My heart longed for the love I knew I deserved as a human being. But my mind knew the reality in which I lived and broke my heart every time it raised the improbability of my family and church accepting who I am. My soul? My soul just wanted to live free.

For a little while, I resorted to my usual habit of ferociously seeking change. Some of my friends and I held small worship and prayer circles all over campus. We were, as the elders would say, young, dumb, and "on fire for God." There was a palpable excitement on campus, mostly among the incoming freshmen. The exhilaration of being on a new campus, with new people, helped to drive this, but as the semester progressed and winter approached, that energy waned.

When Thanksgiving rolled around, the other kids from Maine and I packed up in my car and headed home for break. Our family Thanksgiving tradition was to head to Fryeburg where the Berrys gathered with extended family at the Legion Hall to feast; the number of people attending approached one hundred, including kids. It was a time for everyone to catch up and laugh at the kids all running around banging into things and whatnot. Like many other Thanksgivings all across the country that night, it was also time to answer questions like "What are you studying?" and "What would you like to do with that degree?" and "Do you have a girlfriend at college?"

I didn't know how to answer that last question. Instead, I would feign deep interest in my studies, or say I was focusing on growing closer to God. This was always an unsettling question, but this time, it packed a little bit more of a punch. What had helped me stay in the closet up to this point was my belief that God had a special someone meant just for me, so I had to save myself for that person. In fact, to suppress my gay feelings, I would pray to God to send this girl my way, and soon. I felt deep down that she would be perfect; surely she would make the gay go away when we fell in love at first sight.

My family didn't seem to suspect anything—of course, I kept it all well-hidden. They were bursting with pride, especially since I was the first kid to go to college.

When I got back to campus, I continued to slip further into my somber mood, and the rest of that semester soured to the point where the professor teaching our choir ensemble noticed that I was actually sighing a lot. In fact, he made a big announcement that no one should sigh, since it gave off the wrong vibe, especially since we were putting on a Christmas concert. We were "ministering" to the audience and our community; we needed to be joyful, and celebrate the season.

Frankly, I was glad when the semester was over. I was all packed up and heading home, intermittently messaging my friend Travis. I told him that it had been a rough semester and that I was glad to be on break. Somewhere along the New Jersey Turnpike (before texting and driving was illegal, mind you), we were texting our good-byes when I saw his last texts, saying "I miss you, man," and later, "I love you."

Immediately, my eyes started to water. I felt like the wind had been knocked out of me, so I pulled off at the next rest area to catch my breath.

I don't remember what was running through my mind—I only remember what I felt. Love, in all of its forms and in the many ways it is expressed, is powerful. It truly is a mystery how love is able to move mountains, it seems, or break down walls. It's easy to forget this and to take it for granted. When we tell someone we love them, whether as a family member, a friend, or a lover, we are telling them that they exist. They are heard. They are seen.

They matter. In a sense, it is a play on Sartre's "I think, therefore I exist." Except that here, it is "I am loved, therefore I exist."

So in that moment, pacing back and forth at a New Jersey rest stop, I felt alive. I felt like my existence had been proven. That I was heard. That I was seen. That I mattered.

It wasn't necessarily "gay thoughts" that were running through my head. It was the power and depth of our friendship of five years' time, expressed verbally (well, via text), which previously had been expressed through time spent hanging out and talking. It's amazing, the power we attribute to those three words. It boggles my mind, how saying them can build one up, just as withholding them can tear one down.

I drove the rest of the way home for Christmas break with my heart pounding in my chest.

But when I visited Travis and his family, I was introduced to a new person: Travis' girlfriend. Whatever initial displeasure or jealousy I felt was lost once I'd settled into the old routines of hanging out, playing video games, watching movies, and getting ready for church.

This wasn't the most significant event that happened over Christmas break. No, that was when I took the first step toward being honest with myself and who I am.

One night during break, when I was browsing Netflix, I noticed they had an LGBTQ+ genre. My mind and my heart were in a tug-of-war as to whether or not I should click the damn link. I felt as if God were watching me the entire time, and I shrank inside myself with the slightest bit of shame. Eventually I clicked the LGBTQ+ genre link—heart racing—and began to browse the small list of LGBTQ+ movies and shows. The one that piqued my interest was a movie by the name of *Shortbus*.

The setting is early 2000s New York City and centers mainly around a gay couple, James and Jamie, and an Asian woman,

Sofia Lin, a couples and sex therapist. James and Jamie are clients of Sofia's, and while they argue during one of their counseling sessions, Sofia snaps and reveals that she is "pre-orgasmic." She describes how she fakes orgasms with her partner, Rob. As the story progresses, James and Jamie open up their relationship to include a third partner, Ceth, a young and attractive man, while Sofia follows their recommendation to attend Shortbus, an artistic, sex salon hosted by a drag artist. At some point later, Rob also joins as they try and find answers for their relationship.

James and Jamie's third partner, Ceth, who plays the guitar, sings a song in the movie that sticks with me to this day, the chorus of which goes:

> "They say your body's a temple, well, boy, were they right.
> This feels so simple, I could kiss you all night.
> And I could spend forever in the palm of your hand,
> But when the clock strikes twelve, oh, you'll go home
> to another man."

The phrase "body's a temple" struck me in a special way because it is a phrase from the Bible that is often used to condemn homosexuality, drinking, smoking, and so on. It comes from *First Corinthians* 6:19–20, which reads: "Do you not know that your bodies are temples of the Holy Spirit, who is in you, whom you have received from God? You are not your own; you were bought at a price. Therefore, honor God with your bodies."

This song from *Shortbus* is brilliant, really. It reminds me of the song "Hallelujah" by Jeff Buckley and "Take Me to Church" by Hozier, both of which take biblical references and deliberately turn them on their heads. To me, this song expresses both an in-your-face, yet subtle rebelliousness. Watching this film showed me the human side of sexual orientation, expression, and freedom. Seeing people, albeit actors, living so openly and freely was vital to shifting my perspective.

By the time I returned to campus after break, my heart was chipping away at the belief system that I had constructed inside myself. My rather free-thinking Christian Thought professor openly challenged our mainstream beliefs about Christianity, which I found interesting. When it came time to write a ten-page paper, I chose to explore the Trinity, and how the Father, the Son, and the Holy Ghost could be three separate entities but still exist as one God. This led me to the writings of St. Augustine and St. Thomas Aquinas, but then somehow I went down the rabbit hole of Greek philosophy, particularly Aristotle, and Zoroastrianism.

Around this time I also discovered *The History of Western Philosophy* by English philosopher Bertrand Russell, who traces Christian symbols, icons, and stories and reveals similarities they have with other ancient religions. For instance, the idea of Christ and the importance and symbol of wine is not unique to Christianity. Russell points to the Greek god Dionysius or, as the Romans knew him, Bacchus. Dionysius is quite literally the son of Zeus and the god of wine in ancient Greek and Roman mythology. Russell highlighted how the Christian faith developed while incorporating beliefs, holidays, customs, and practices of other religions and faiths that were believed by the people of the time.

My mind was opening, and thus, in chaos. This was reflected in my emotional and physical health—and my grades. Serious doubts were now filling my mind, and I needed to clear my head somehow. So when February break came, I chose to stay on campus while most everyone else went home. I spent that winter break alone with my thoughts, and, at night, tossing and turning, praying for some relief. More and more, one big question kept coming up: "If God is love, then how could he not condone love between two men?"

For the first time, I was cognizant of the fact that I wasn't scared to consider this question outside the framework that I had been given—that homosexuality was an abomination, a sexually deviant practice that resulted in getting HIV/AIDS and all sorts of other health problems. I was considering the emotional and spiritual love a man can have for another man, in addition to physical love.

For the first time, I began to see that love between two men could be as pure and wholesome as love between a man and a woman. The very idea felt both exhilarating and terrifying all at once. It became so unbearable at times that I would go for long walks at night, to help clear my mind.

What I had thought was a house built on solid rock was instead a castle built on sand, and it was beginning to shift beneath me. Now that I was away from family, my church, and the community I'd grown up in, I was beginning to see faults in the foundation. Looking back now, I can't help but feel sympathy for my younger self and the obstacles I had to overcome to climb out of the mind-set I was in.

One night, I was walking through the middle of a snowstorm. Snowdrifts, stirred by the wind, swirled beneath the lamps that lined the path in front of me. The brick campus housing buildings stood gray and shrouded in the background, the sky a dark and muddy pink from the distant lights from town.

I flipped out my phone and started to type a few words, delete them, and then type the same ones again, for who knows how long. The message was directed to one of my high school friends, Hannah, who I'd known since middle school, and who also attended the same church back home. I finally ended up sending a message saying, "I need to talk to someone."

Next thing I knew, we were on the phone and I blurted out, "I'm gay."

The silence was thick and heavy.

Finally, she said, "It's okay, Marpheen. It's okay. It's fine. I'm your friend. I am here for you."

Relief broke like the light of day through the darkest of nights, despite the snow and darkness around me. And for the briefest of moments that night, as I was settling into bed, I felt a little bit of the weight I had been feeling lift. The room around me felt less claustrophobic. Instead of plastering arguments to God against the ceiling above me, the words I heard that night ran through my mind on repeat until I drifted off to sleep.

It was one of the best nights of sleep I'd had in a while.

But as I woke up the next day and realized that winter break was coming to a close, I reminded myself that Hannah was just one person in my life. In order to be truly free, I would have to tell everyone.

Nonetheless, I walked around with a little more hope in my heart, knowing that the first person I'd told hadn't totally freaked out.

Over the course of the next few months, I wrestled with my God. Or the idea of God. Or, rather, the construction of God that had been built in my mind through all those Sunday services, my fundamentalist Christian education, and the limited access I'd had to books and movies and even people who didn't fit into my church's "Christian worldview."

Working on my paper for my Christian philosophy class, I exposed myself to the idea that perhaps Christianity—at least the version of it that I'd been sold, and bought into— is not all that unique. Despite its claim to being the one true religion and path to God and everlasting life in Heaven, my research exposed me to the fault lines in that claim, and how they had been there all along. Those fault lines were hidden amid the shroud of half-truths, buried truths, and misinformation in order to advance a pseudo-Conservative Christian movement in the United States.

Up until this point, I had been taught that the Bible contains the inerrant Word of God, meticulously passed down through generations and with the divine guidance and inspiration of Providence somehow written, rewritten, transcribed, and translated without error through the ages.

The problem that arises with this belief is that instead of an overwhelming body of evidence, both scientific and historical, that supports the claims that apologists make, we are directed to a few historians who make vague references to Jesus in their work. We are taught that this is proof that the Bible was inerrant and accurate, that Jesus existed—which could very well be, though I believe he's been mythologized—and thus proof that the Christian faith rests upon a solid and unshakable foundation. And, if all else fails, then we must have faith that the Bible is indeed the Word of God, and it is infallible.

This was circular reasoning, and I was like a hamster stuck on a wheel. But as impossible as it seemed, the more I started to doubt—and subsequently, allow my horizons to expand—the more I started to deconstruct, pick apart, and examine the individual pieces and pillars that held up the belief system I had been raised with. To aid me in that journey, I turned to history, philosophy, and texts outside of what I was being taught, including Russell's *The History of Western Philosophy*.

Another important event happened during this spring semester. An LGBTQ+ rights group had been touring across the country to rally for gay rights and protest abuses of LGBTQ+ students, demonstrating outside of Christian colleges. They stopped at mine that March. The entire campus was on edge as chapel services and classes buzzed with things like "We need to pray for them" or "Our Christian values are under attack," and "This is spiritual warfare." School administrators and faculty warned us not to engage with any person from the LGBTQ+ rights group.

The entire campus' reaction to the LGBTQ+ group was both maddening and amusing. But whether it was outright homophobia or the more subtle "We need to pray for them," I questioned: If

God is love, then how could what these activists were asking for, equality and freedom to love, be so bad? I was "slipping away from the faith," as my church leaders would say. Yet in my reality, I was on that path toward true love—of myself, and my neighbor, regardless of what they look like, how they worship, where they're from, and who they love.

I wasn't quite ready to express this to anyone other than Hannah. Throughout that semester I had been contemplating my academic future, which was ancillary to my struggle with God and the worldview I was then living in. After some thinking, I had decided that I wanted to major in political science and attend the University of Southern Maine in Portland. It would cost less, since I would be attending an in-state college, and—the big bonus—it would give me more intellectual bandwidth and more freedom to explore the truth that I was struggling to come to grips with: my gayness.

I remember quite clearly the time in April when my church pastor's wife was visiting the college and we grabbed coffee to talk about how things had been going. I came right out and said that I was having a crisis of faith. She inquired as to what exactly was going on, but I couldn't muster up the strength to tell her the entire truth. All I said was that I was really struggling with God, and that I had already submitted an application to transfer to a college in Maine. At the end of our discussion, she offered to pray for me, and then we parted ways.

The transfer process involved filling out a lot of paperwork and going through the administrative processes at the Christian college. The final step was to have an interview with the director of student life, who was also in charge of students' spiritual life. When I sat down for that interview, I could feel that she was trying to uncover some other reason why I wanted to leave the college and if there was any way I would change my mind. She asked me if I was okay spiritually, which immediately made me feel defensive. I resisted giving firm answers to most of the questions she had about my experiences at Valley Forge. I simply told her that I wanted to study political science, which wasn't offered at the school. Finally, she gave up and said, "Well, let me pray for you."

By now, my parents already knew about my decision to transfer to USM, and that I was going to pursue a political science degree. They didn't seem too surprised, but just to assure them, I had indicated that I wanted to be housed on the substance-free floor on campus, which was in Gorham—about forty-five minutes from Naples. School was still a summer away, and I had just settled back in the Lakes Region, picking up summer shifts at the Bridgton Hannaford. (They had an academic leave policy, so I could take the school year off and work during breaks.) Everything seemed back to normal in some ways, except that internally, everything had changed.

Three people played key roles during that summer. One of my best friends from high school, B-Denny, had gotten home the same time I did, since we both went to Valley Forge. Home also was the group of "work friends" that I had made over the years. There was Catie, whose family was from Massachusetts and summered in Maine, near Shawnee Peak. She had two brothers, Nick and John, who also worked at the Bridgton Hannaford. And there was Kayla, whom I'd first met through B-Denny when he had brought her to youth group one time, when we were in high school.

I don't quite remember when I made up my mind to tell B-Denny I was gay; I think it was once we got home from school, in mid-May. We were hanging out at his house when I decided to drop the bomb. He was going to be the first (after Hannah) because I considered him to be the safest. Over the years, I'd picked up on some clues from his mom that all of them were okay with "the gays." For one, his mom was friends with a lesbian couple—so B-Denny had to be tolerant, I thought. At this point I felt a little more confident, after telling Hannah earlier that year.

I recall his reaction being a bit awkward, but there was definitely no hostility, despite both of us being quite involved with our church up until that summer. I breathed a great sigh of relief after telling him. It also felt a little ... anticlimactic. Here I was, kind of psyching myself up to make what I thought would be a big announcement, my adrenaline pumping as if I were getting ready for a fight. His awkward "Oh, cool!" kind of reaction took me off guard. In fact, after we continued with our day, watching dumb YouTube videos (B-Denny wanted to be a YouTube star at the time), I almost felt as if he was excited to have a gay friend.

This was going smoothly, I thought to myself. *Maybe everything is going to be okay.* My suspicions about him being okay with me being gay had been confirmed, which gave an extra jolt to my initial excitement. *Two down, the rest of the world to go*, I thought, as I gave myself a pat on the back.

In my head, everything was going according to plan. I would incrementally come out that summer, keeping most of the church community in the dark, and I'd be able to make a graceful exit with as little drama as possible.

I knew for sure that I didn't want my younger siblings to find out. I didn't want them to be discouraged or to see their big brother as a rebel and STD-ridden sexual deviant. I cared about my image when it came to them. I think I wanted to serve as proof that everything would turn out okay for all four of us, no matter the trials and tribulations we went through. I didn't want to hurt them with the news that their big brother was gay.

If I'm honest, I didn't want them to know because I was still deeply ashamed of who I was. I had not fully come to grips with the implications of my revelation, so it seemed selfish to ask them to.

I hatched what I thought was a carefully laid-out plan, telling people one by one in a kind of ladder system, which I felt would mitigate to the extent practicable any blowback I might receive from the broader church community.

But when does anything go according to plan?

The day after I told B-Denny, I walked into work, thinking it would be like any other day at Hannaford. Smile. Greet customers. Ring their items through. Bag them. Do carts. Just like clockwork. But I noticed right away that my co-workers were giving me curious looks. Then, someone came up to me and said they were happy that I had come out.

My physiological emergency evac protocol immediately kicked into gear. My heart rate peaked as I hit full-panic mode.

"Wait, who told you?" I asked.

"Oh, B-Denny did."

My face flushed with that bitter cocktail of embarrassment, shame, and outrage. I felt betrayed—by one of my best friends, of all people. *How could he do this to me?* I wondered over and over again as I raced to finish my shift.

My regular customers, excited to see me back home, noticed. One lady asked me if I was okay, commenting that I wasn't my usual perky self. Of course, I responded by briefly flashing a smile to try and ward off any more questions.

Deep inside, I was both smoldering and as cold as ice, on fire and shivering at the same time. I felt sick. Nauseated. I felt all eyes on me as if they were watching, waiting to see how I would react. I felt like my insides were crumbling, like a massive star had collapsed, leaving a giant black hole in its wake that was sucking the very life out of me. I felt weak and vulnerable, completely naked, as if I had been stripped and subjected to the kind of public shaming of old.

But most of all, I felt like I couldn't trust anyone—even my own best friend. I had taken a part of me that I had hidden for so long and shared it, in confidence, to be cared for and nurtured while I figured out how to go about this whole coming-out thing.

I felt that my ship, despite just having put out to sea, was already sinking, and I couldn't plug the holes fast enough as the weight of a watching and waiting world dragged me down toward the deepest depths of a sea of shame.

This, of course, was all in my head. Or, should I say, happening at my very core. The truth was that no one at work was exhibiting negative signs upon hearing the news. Perhaps mild surprise, and even a knowing smile, as if to congratulate me. I was feeling this sense of shame because my trust had been breached by my best friend, but I was also panicking at the thought of my family and my church community finding out before I was ready to tell them.

I guess the real question here is: Is anyone ever truly ready to take such a monumental and deeply existential step? Coming out is not only a revelation to the world, but a revolution of thought and being and existence. There are few phrases that encapsulate and so eloquently express deeply powerful feelings and emotions. We're all familiar with the impact of "I love you." But for so many like myself, uttering the three words "I am gay" typically comes after countless restless nights. Saying "I am gay" conveyed not only the truth that I had begun to accept about myself, but also the trust and confidence that I was placing in each person I told, and the expectation that this knowledge would be cherished and cared for.

The feeling of betrayal—whether it was warranted or not—was strong. But the greatest panic stemmed from the loss of control I had over the process of coming out. The loss of control of the narrative—who was told, when they were told, and where they were told. While telling my best friend that I was gay had gone perfectly, I had not anticipated that he would share what I'd told him in confidence with a co-worker in the deli department where he worked. I had not anticipated that the news would spread, as gossip often does within a workplace. Nothing was going according to plan. I was losing control of my own story, and I was angry, sad, and hurt, all at the same time.

When I finally punched out after my shift, I rushed through the door, barely holding back my panic and tears. I jumped in my car and started driving home, my mind racing. What would my family and church community do when they found out? What about my siblings? I had no doubt that my entire world would come crashing down.

It's a complete mystery how I drove the twenty or so minutes home without crashing my car.

I walked in the door of my home, my tears welling up and trying to break through. I was intent on not crying. I was so used to suppressing and holding back my tears that I was successful in doing so in that moment.

I paced around the kitchen, then I ran through the breezeway and up the stairs to the living room, where I paced around some more. Our pug Sadie had been snoring on the couch, and she woke up when I came in. She stared at me with her head tilted in her puggish way, like she knew there was something wrong.

That's when I hatched a plan to get ahead of the problem before my parents and siblings came home. I don't recall why I thought it was such a good plan, but I remember picking up my iPhone 4 and dialing my dad. His phone rang and rang as if it were going to ring for all of eternity. And with each ring, I was getting closer and closer to ending the call and going to hide in my room.

But I wanted to gain control of the situation, to take back some of the narrative—to get out ahead of the news that felt like it had been sent out via a million carrier pigeons to the entire world. My entire world. My church community, which was staunchly anti-gay and encouraged people to vote against same-sex marriage. The denomination that preached to me growing up that being gay was a sin. The very people who saw me as a young leader on a good path. The people who saw me as God-fearing. Devout. Passionate. Exemplary. Moral.

"Hey, bud, what's up?" My dad's voice crackled on the other end.

I could tell they were somewhere on the back roads of the Sebago Lakes Region, on their way home from family night or Bible study night.

"S-s-something happened," I stuttered. "Something bad."

"Are you okay? What happened?"

I paused, trying to explain to myself what exactly had happened that day, before saying, "I told B-Denny I was gay and he told people at work."

That's when I started sobbing uncontrollably. I hadn't cried that hard in such a long time. It was a bit of a surprise. Like many teenagers, I often came close to crying, like during those angry fits when I'd ask why I was being grounded and couldn't go to my friend's house, or why they wouldn't believe me when I said I wasn't rolling my eyes at the teacher earlier that day—it's just that my eyes were dry.

These tears were far different from those; they came in torrents, and I felt it deep down. These tears were mixed with shame, anger, and the strangely painful truths that often come with self-discovery.

"Everything's going to be okay, bud," Dad replied. "We're gonna be home soon."

That's when I sobbed a pathetic "Okay" before hanging up the phone. That's when it dawned on me that, yes, they were going to be home soon. And panic set in once again because I wasn't prepared to talk about what had happened at work that day, face-to-face.

Our Toyota Sienna pulled into the driveway, headlights cutting through the dimming light as if they were searching for me. As if those lights wanted to examine me under a microscope and reveal all my insides.

I could hear the voices of the kids as they clamored out of the car. I could hear door after door open as they entered the garage, then the breezeway, then the kitchen. Then I heard my mom and dad walking up the stairs to the living room, which was above the two-car garage, and I braced for the inevitable confrontation.

But it wasn't a confrontation. My mom and dad came in and hugged me. And that's when I spilled the entire story of how I'd told B-Denny I was gay, and how he'd then told everyone (an exaggeration) at work. It all just sort of tumbled out in a hot mess, which was what I felt like at the time.

My parents' response threw me off. They weren't mad. Hell, they looked downright sympathetic.

I soon understood why.

"Marpheen, we'll get through this," Dad said. "You're not gay."

"But—but—" I stammered. "I *am* gay."

"No, Marpheen," he replied. "You're not. You're just confused."

I don't know how you can be both shocked and not shocked at the same time, but that's what I felt. Both a sense of "Did they not hear a thing I said?" and "Why aren't they mad at me?" The simple truth, given the tense conversations and arguments we would have over the next few years, was that my parents truly believed I was merely confused. They sincerely believed that I "thought" I was gay, and that I had an unnatural, sexual attraction to other boys because I hadn't had a father figure growing up—because I'd had a dysfunctional childhood—or perhaps because I'd been molested or sexually abused at some point when I was a kid.

This is what the church had taught them. Beneath it all is the foundational belief in the nuclear family, which ironically is based more on mid-1900s nostalgia than it is grounded in Scripture. If you understand this much about the conservative evangelical movement, then you can see why their opposition to abortion and same-sex marriage, and their support of Christian "family values," is so fervent. Abortion, gay marriage, and sex out of wedlock all threaten the nuclear family, which they believe to be the ideal version of a family. I think this is because of its correlation to a time when America emerged on the world scene as a military and economic superpower, and experienced growth in other areas too. As David Brooks writes in *The Atlantic*:

> "Finally, conditions in the wider society were ideal for family stability. The postwar period was a high-water mark of church attendance, unionization, social trust, and mass prosperity—all things that correlate with family cohesion. A man could relatively easily find a job that would allow him to be the breadwinner for a single-income family. By 1961, the median American man age 25 to 29 was earning nearly 400 percent more than his father had earned at about the same age."

This period in which the nuclear family gained prominence is also when the evangelical movement as we know it today was born. It began with the founding of the National Association of Evangelicals in 1942, which by 1953 boasted ten million members. Moving from America's newfound prosperity and growth on the world stage in the 1950s to the sexual revolution and civil rights movement in the 1960s, we can observe evangelical Christians latching onto the idea of the nuclear family and the phrase "family values" that dominates American politics.

Seth Dowland writes about the importance of these values to the evangelical movement in his book *Family Values and the Rise of the Christian Right*, giving two reasons why:

> "First, evangelicals believed that gender was part of the created order, that men and women were created by God to fulfill different roles. In

traditional families, men provided and protected, while women bore, reared and nurtured children. Movements that viewed gender roles as the product of patriarchal social constructions—such as second-wave feminism—represented a denial of God's good creation, which spelled out biologically appropriate roles for men and women.

Second, evangelicals believed that God designed institutions like the family and the church to run under certain authority structures. While evangelicals voiced support for equal rights, they wanted to retain the authority structures that kept human sinfulness in check. Traditional families exemplified those godly authority structures: Husbands led their wives, and parents had authority over children. Promoting family values gave evangelicals a way to uphold their beliefs about gender and authority in the broader culture."

Gay marriage and the LGBTQ+ rights movement threatened the family values espoused by the church community we were a part of. Because they believed being gay was a choice—since God created everyone straight—then gay people are just confused! So I knew where my adoptive parents were coming from in their response to my news. I'd been taught the very same things. I knew the reason they weren't angry when I first told them was because they sincerely believed in the mantra, "Love the sinner but hate the sin."

In this instance, they hated the sin. They hated the idea of what I could possibly subject myself to. But in their minds they found a way to carve that into a wholly separate thing, an evil thing, with which I was afflicted. They saw it very much as a spiritual and moral disease:

Deep down I was a straight, heterosexual man who was confused and tempted to believe I was attracted to those of the same sex.

Too emotionally exhausted to argue, I resigned myself to going to my room, passing the kids along the way, who gave me hugs and told me they loved me. By the time I collapsed onto my bed, the crying had ended. What settled in next was a soft ache and a very small sense of relief—the kind that you feel when you think the worst has blown over.

But as if to get some lingering anger out of my system, I decided to go on Facebook and write a post about trust and disappointment. Facebook was relatively new at the time. Before the advent of its use for political and business advertising and spreading misinformation and conspiracy theories, it was more of a stripped-down public-diary version of what it is today. So for young people like me, who were first introduced to social media via Myspace and had migrated to Facebook in high school, it was the obvious place to air our grievances.

Before I could fall asleep that night, B-Denny's mom messaged me and gave me some real talk about my post, and how I shouldn't be so hard on B-Denny. And you know what, I shouldn't have. The guy was excited that one of his best friends was gay and he was one of the first to know. B-Denny's mom added the cherry on top by telling me that being gay is okay—that her good friends were a lesbian couple, and that her home would always be open to me. To this day, I thank B-Denny for, in a way, making it easier for me to come out. I don't know exactly how I'd planned to tell my parents, but I am sure it would've taken a lot longer than it did. And, really, it helped make that summer one of the most liberating I have ever had.

People at work were either glad or didn't give a damn. Generally, that's how it was in Maine. Rural Maine, to be exact. Your life was your business. Sure, there were the few men who huffed and puffed about it and said things like, "Well, don't get all gay over me." (I don't mean to be too harsh, but most of the guys who say things like this think a little too highly of themselves in terms of their attractiveness.) Generally, though, I feel most Mainers have a live-and-let-live attitude. That's part of the reason why Mainers approved same-sex marriage by citizens referendum in 2012, in my opinion.

As it turns out, I patched things up with B-Denny pretty quickly, and his house became my refuge from my own home, which grew increasingly tense as I argued with my family about whether or not I should go to church, and whether I'd been faking being a Christian the whole time.

I was also making up for my lack of teenage rebellion in my high school years. You see, after I came out, I began to blossom socially. I remember one co-worker was renting a camp on Highland Lake and invited me, B-Denny, Catie, and Kayla for a party out there. Up until that day, I had never touched alcohol, but when a co-worker asked me what I wanted to drink, I was drawn to the bottle of wine.

Next thing you know, I was feeling it. Especially when my friend Catie and I wandered down to the dock, where we both rolled around giggling about who knows what. The dock was only about four feet wide, so I am wondering how we didn't both fall into the water, given the state we were in. Despite being intoxicated, I remember that we talked about my sexuality.

That's when I got this strong—and drunken—impulse to grab my phone. Without going through the entire thought process, I seemed to have made a snap decision that I would not have made otherwise. I opened up my messages and started to type in "T-R-A-V-I-S," sending a message into the ether as I lay next to my friend Catie, staring up into the night sky. Travis replied with the usual *Hey, watsup*.

In one of the stupidest decisions I've ever made, I texted back, *Can I suck your d****? He immediately responded with shock, disbelief, and anger—replies that I wouldn't read until the following day. My mind in that moment, feeling for the first time the effects of too much wine, could not comprehend that I had just effed up in a monumental way.

Meanwhile, Catie and I had somehow climbed up the steep hill in the dark and made it back inside to hang with the rest of our work friends. As the night raged on, I felt, more than actually thought, that I was officially a part of this group of work friends, and not just someone gazing at them from afar, with judgment and secret envy.

The next morning, of course, I had a piercing hangover. The challenge for me was how to get home, walk into the house without stumbling, and comprehend anything that might be said to me. It was bad enough that my parents were growing increasingly aware that I was serious about this gay thing; now, to suddenly show up hungover, tipping them off to my new partying lifestyle? Fortunately, they weren't home when I made it back, and I was able to drag myself to my bedroom and collapse into bed.

That's when I picked up my phone and saw all the messages that Travis had sent me. I panicked. I shot off a flurry of texts, telling him that I was drunk, and that I was so very sorry.

After we'd exchanged a few more messages, he finally asked, "So does this mean you're gay?"

I thought about this one long and carefully. I had already jumped into deep, scalding hot water, telling my best friend of, by then, six years, that I wanted to have a taste of his man parts. I had to be strategic. I had to do this right. Once again, I needed to regain control of the narrative.

"I am bi," I replied.

In my head, I thought that this would be more palatable to him and other heterosexual people. Being gay was a complete no-no for the world, I thought. I thought being bisexual would be safer, because then at least people could feel some sort of hope—although hope of what, I didn't know. That I was still kind of straight and liked vaginas (even though I had never laid eyes on one, let alone come remotely close to touching one)?

"Dude, that's worse than being gay!" Travis texted back.

Does *nothing* ever go according to plan?

I was digging myself into a bigger and bigger hole with the half-truths and cover-ups that I kept piling on and on and on. And I was frustrated as hell that I couldn't get the people close to me to be okay with who I was—especially the guy I considered my closest friend and confidant. My crush. My actions that night and my ill-fated attempts to walk back my words made the situation worse. Travis and I had a falling-out, and for the next four or five years, we barely spoke or saw each other.

In those years apart, we both changed, as we all do. Later on I heard he had gotten married, and a part of me mourned again the loss of our friendship, and my absence from such an important time of his life. Years and years later, time worked its magic, and we both changed and matured for the better. While in law school, we reconnected when he reached out and asked me if I wanted to grab a beer with him and his wife and some of their friends.

I was elated, but I also felt a bit speechless and awkward when I met up with them at Pearl Tap House, a bar on Fore Street in Portland's Old Port. I think part of it was the very bro-like atmosphere in the air, weighing heavy with testosterone and college-age and mid-twenties guys, some of them cute and some of them not, on the hunt for a girl to bring home that night. But a lot of it was because of the four or five years that had passed without seeing or talking with each other.

I was kind to myself, though. I recognized that we had to break the ice that had frozen our friendship in time. It felt cathartic, too, which I'm sure he also felt. I think we both needed to be around each other but knew not to force it. Thankfully it was easy to strike up a conversation with his wife, whom I talked with for most of the evening. She caught me up on what their lives had been like since meeting in college and getting married, which I was immensely grateful for. By the end of the night, instead of just blank pages for the years we hadn't seen each other, we'd at least written in some mile markers.

Later that night after they'd dropped me off (his wife was the designated driver), he texted me as I was falling asleep.

Hey Marph (his childhood nickname for me), *I just want you to know, in case you thought it was my wife that got me to do this, that I really wanted to reconnect with you. My views have changed a lot and I wanted to reconnect with someone who I spent the better part of my high school years with.*

It was one hell of a way to end a good evening out with friends, both new and old. I slept like a baby that night.

Generally speaking, in the year after I came out, being more open with myself and others closed many doors, but it also opened up new opportunities. I stopped going to church completely, which was weird for me, since it had been such a ritual up until that point. I'd wake up on Sunday mornings and hear my entire family bustling around, getting ready for church, my dad doing his usual thing of going from room to room in an annoyingly cheerful mood, singing, "Good morning, good morning! Give God the glory, glory, glory!" Except now he'd skip my room because they all knew I wasn't budging; I most definitely wasn't going to church.

It was important to separate myself from the church in order to continue my journey of self-discovery, and it was also important for my mental health to not have to endure the stares, glares, and sad looks from the congregation that used to see me as a devout Christian man.

While that door was closed, a new window soon opened up. Instead of keeping my sexuality a secret and using religion to help mask it, I felt my guard drop and my heart open to people I wouldn't have otherwise considered my friends. I grew closer to Catie and Kayla;

those two and B-Denny truly helped to make that summer more than just the arguments and struggles I faced, coming out. In some ways, old habits never die. We drove around at night howling song lyrics and obnoxious noises at the top of our lungs, and B-Denny would have people over to roast marshmallows and bratwursts over a fire.

Our favorite thing to do that summer was to head over to a place we knew as Hiram Dam, about twenty minutes away from the Bridgton Hannaford. It felt like our secret hideaway from the world, but really, everyone in the Lakes Region knew about it, because they had all done the same thing we did at some point in time. On a Friday or Saturday night after we'd all get out of work, we'd usually drive there together. It seemed like we were driving to the middle of nowhere as we'd wind along the rural roads, until we'd spot the big boulder that marked the end of the dirt "parking area" up the bank from the dam. Once parked, we would walk the five or so minutes down the path until we could hear the running water. That's when the trail would empty us out onto this sandy peninsula-like bar that jutted out and curved into the reservoir, the body of water that pooled below the dam.

Other friends would already have been there for a few hours, and they'd have a bonfire blazing, tiki torches staked in the ground, and a few tents spread out. We would give a hoot and a holler to whoever was there and clamoring would ensue as everyone greeted each other. The variety of drinks usually included Budweiser, Coors, Corona, and Twisted Tea, things like that. Sometimes people brought a volleyball net and there would be a game going, but often we'd just settle in around the fire.

I remember that summer there was an enormous log with massive roots that looked like a crude crown. It was the perfect bench, and when things got rowdy, it became a stage on which we'd stand and sing or play king of the hill. Eventually we'd play a game of tag or cops and robbers, or maybe a Frisbee tournament. At some point, someone would have fallen—or run—into the water, which would prompt the rest of the crew to follow suit and jump in.

Eventually my dad confronted me on one of the mornings when I walked into the house at around nine or ten, hungover. It's funny hearing the stories from my friends or seeing the portrayals of rebellion on TV and in the movies, because parent–teenager confrontations all seem to echo the same clichés.

"Where have you been?" the adults would ask.

The answers would always be the same. "Nowhere!" or "At so-and-so's house, where else?"

"You'd better not be lying to me!"

"I'm not!"

"You are—I know you're lying. I know where you've been. You were at the dam, weren't you?"

I remember my dad saying this as he honed in like a hound on the hunt.

"So? It's my choice!" I remember replying.

"As long as you're living under my roof, you're going to live by my rules," Dad yelled. "That means no drinking and no partying."

I can't quite remember the conversation completely, but I know for a fact that, just like in the movies, I started to stomp off toward my room. An argument was the last thing my hangover needed; all I wanted to do was collapse into bed for a few hours.

These sorts of confrontations happened on and off as the summer progressed. At one point, after getting home the next morning after a fire at my friend B-Denny's, Dad again confronted me.

"I know you've been drinking at B-Denny's house," he said. "Next time, I'm going to call the cops on you."

Instinct told me that this was an empty threat. I knew he couldn't follow through with it because that would mean I'd get caught for underage drinking and have a criminal record. Talk about a life ruined before it's even begun! I think deep down Dad knew this, and that's why he never followed through. That, or maybe because I was spending less and less time at home.

Or maybe it was because there was something else we were also arguing about. You see, being a recently out and gay nineteen-year-old in the Sebago Lakes Region in 2010 wasn't as glamorous as it probably is for a lot of teenagers in Southern Maine nowadays. I imagine it's much the same for gay teens in Northern Maine, where populations are drastically smaller. I didn't know how to meet other gay guys in the area. Hell, I didn't even know if there *were* any other gay guys in the area. There was one who worked at Hannaford with me, but I wasn't particularly into him, maybe because he was a complainer. I was still in the early phases of coming out and still acted straight as a stick, and he was quite feminine for my taste at the time. (Now, I am proud to say, I have evolved quite a bit.)

It was really hard for me to find someone else like me in such a rural town, and prior to the passage of marriage equality via referendum in Maine in 2012. So I simply Googled "Where to meet other gay teens."

One of the first things that popped up was the now infamous Craigslist and the personal classifieds section. At first I was scared to look at the pages, and when I did, they all sounded pretty gross—until I learned how to filter my search results to put in age ranges. During that summer, I experienced everything except a face-to-face meeting. And by "everything," I mean the fakes and the perverts.

One scary memory is of a guy who found me on Facebook after I'd accidentally responded with my actual e-mail address. He wasn't too far away, somewhere in Raymond, which is about fifteen minutes from Naples. I blocked him as fast as I could (I still see him on my blocked list when I check to see if I need to unblock anyone).

Eventually I felt brave enough to post my own Craigslist ads. And, boy, were they cheesy. They went something along the lines of

"Hi! I am 19-years-old. Asian. I am LTR [long term relationship] oriented and I am looking for something serious with another young guy. I like music and driving around. I'd like to meet the love of my life." (If you thought that was bad, I can assure you that what I actually wrote was a hundred times cheesier; I'm happy to block out exactly what I used to write in those god-awful ads.)

Despite all the bad experiences, probability does work its magic sometimes, and I connected with a guy who was twenty, from Maine. He wrote a refreshingly deep e-mail about how his family was Catholic and they didn't really know he was gay yet. He was looking to find someone to spend time with. We exchanged e-mail after e-mail for a couple of weeks and then transitioned to AOL Instant Messenger (AIM).

After a lot of back-and-forth messaging, we exchanged numbers and talked on the phone a few times. But we had to end our conversations abruptly after he went on a trip to California to visit family and his younger brother caught him messing around with the guy from next door. It was a pretty sad parting. He had to delete his e-mails and messages and go completely dark to hide from his parents.

Even though we weren't dating, we had a connection as two boys from religious families who were still navigating the whole coming-out thing. A year or so later, I remember contacting him via e-mail and he e-mailed a photo of him and his boyfriend in Hawaii (where he had moved after coming out to his family, which I assume didn't go very well). He thanked me for being there for him during that time, and we continued to exchange e-mails every now and then before losing touch again.

Something else happened as a result of posting my love-letter-like Craigslist ads, something I never expected. An e-mail popped into my in-box that said something like "Hi, Marpheen. I came across your Craigslist ad and thought the description matched someone I knew from church, and I know for sure it's you. I am sad to see you posting here and engaging in this lifestyle, and I am going to tell your father." Now, I'm paraphrasing, as I don't have access to that e-mail anymore, but that was the gist. And boy, did it send me into a panic! For the next few days I tiptoed in and out of the house in an effort to avoid my parents.

A few days later, Dad stood strategically between where the phone was on the left wall and the fridge off to the right. In other words, right smack dab in the middle of the hallway, in front of the door that led down to my room in the basement.

"So, someone from church told me they saw you were posting on Craigslist," he said.

By now, I had my rhetorical defenses at the ready, and responded by saying, "Well, who was it? And why was someone from church searching the gay ads on Craigslist?"

"Don't make this about them," he replied, his voice raised. "This is about you."

"Well, how come you aren't wondering why they're looking at those ads!" I said, matching my voice level with his.

"Because you shouldn't be posting on that site looking for men to have sex with. You don't know these people!"

By that point, we were practically shouting at each other. I was so angry, and could feel the tears trying to burn their way out of my eye sockets. In my head, I was wondering how else I'd be able to meet other guys like me. Although I had started to come out, I still had no idea what to do with this part of me. How was I supposed to know I was really gay if I hadn't even dated a guy yet? How do I prove to the world that I am gay if I haven't even kissed a boy, let alone lost my virginity to him? I thought coming out was supposed to fix all of this for me.

Today, my views about my dad's response are different; more mature. Looking back, I am more understanding of why my dad responded that way. He was being a dad in the only way he knew how. He knew nothing about the new life I was embarking on, only what he'd been told by those in the church community. The sex, the drugs, the STDs, etc. What I saw then as judgment and bigotry I can see now as parental concern for my safety and well-being.

But the part of my teenage years that had been delayed—where teens test the boundaries, date, and experiment—was also making its appearance. And for my dad, whose two biological daughters had gotten pregnant out of wedlock, during high school—well, I could see how he felt like he was failing all over again. So while this was a very tough time in our relationship, the passage of time has allowed me to look back on it with grace and forgiveness, for both of us.

I wasn't old enough to go to gay bars and nightclubs. Portland was nearly an hour away, and gas was expensive. What was I supposed to do— go into a coffee shop and magically walk out with someone's phone number?

This was very much a delayed process for me, something most people got to experience starting in middle school. I felt like I needed to make up for lost time. There were so many frustrations and feelings all happening at once. Although I'd finally had a taste of freedom, what do you do with it when you've locked yourself away for so long? I didn't have any mentors who could help me navigate any of this.

That is, not until I got another e-mail in response to my Craigslist ad.

This time, the message went something like this: "You sound like a very sweet and kind young man, and I don't think this is the place for you to look for what you're looking for. I encourage you to try going to the group for queer youth called PRYSM. It's in Portland."

I ended up meeting this thoughtful man a few months later, and I thanked him for reaching out to me and referring me to the queer youth group. (We remain connected to this very day. He watches like a proud papa as I move and shake it through the community.)

Anyway, I looked up PRYSM (Proud Rainbow Youth of Southern Maine) and drove down for the next meeting, which was held at the time in a building on Forest Avenue. I walked through the door, glanced around the room, and spotted a woman with short black hair, her bangs slanted off to the side. I don't know what it was, but a little tingling in my brain seemed to come alive, producing something akin to a neon flashing sign that said "ALERT! LESBIAN! ALERT!" I was expanding my horizons. I was on a new, exciting journey!

She walked right up to me to introduce herself—her name was Sarah—and had me fill out some forms. She gave me a rundown of the agenda while I sheepishly looked around, feeling like I wasn't supposed to be there. As I was being introduced to people I kept glancing at the signs on the walls to avoid awkward and extended eye contact. That's when I spotted a poster that, in some way, reassured me that I was in the right place. A safe space. It was a variation of the famous "First They Came" quote by Martin Niemöller, and included the line:

"Then they came for the homosexuals
and I did not speak out
because I was not a homosexual."

Eventually, the time came for all of us to gather in a meeting room off to the side. Chairs were arranged in a circle and we all settled in. It was obvious the young people were looking around for new faces. In what became a common way of introduction in the ensuing years, Sarah asked the group to introduce themselves by including their sexual orientation and preferred pronouns. When it was my turn, I felt like my "I am gay" came out as a whisper, and I'm pretty sure I totally forgot about the pronouns.

Joining PRYSM, and later, starting my years at the University of Southern Maine, I became consumed with learning and experiencing as much as I could about this part of me that had been dormant and suppressed for so long. So much so that without really knowing it, I put other things about my identity on hold, especially being brown in a white world. Thinking back now, I think this was necessary to make up for lost time. In fact, the confidence and self-esteem I would gain through being involved in the LGBTQ+ community would ultimately give me the courage to explore my Cambodian identity and reconnect with my birth family.

There was a boy at the meeting who was Latino, and a bundle of flamboyant joy. We were going around swapping stories when he mentioned that he liked boys with big packages. Someone asked him how big he liked them, and he replied, enthusiastically, "Twenty-two!" Everyone gasped and giggled as we tried to imagine if such a thing existed. But he interrupted and clarified, "I meant twenty-two centimeters!" Everyone blurted out a collective "Ohhhh." Nonetheless, it was a humorous moment that broke the ice, especially for me.

Despite these new opportunities to be surrounded by other LGBTQ+ people, I still had much to discover and learn. I knew very little of this world other than the brief and stereotyped characters that happened to pop up in movies and TV shows that I would watch at home. During family movie nights I would seize up with nervousness when a gay character appeared. My gaydar would tingle a bit and I'd stop breathing, hoping my parents didn't notice that the character had piqued my interest. Sometimes I'd do a sneaky side-eye glance to see how they were reacting. I often got the sense that they, too, had noticed, but were keeping their feelings under wraps.

Now, I was finally in a room filled with queer people. I had never been in a space created solely to provide an open and accepting environment for people like me. Not only was I in a new environment, but I had yet to learn how to stop tiptoeing—how to shed my mask. It felt uncomfortable to be seen for who I really was. Indeed, all humans feel vulnerable when taking the risk to reveal themselves, their hopes and dreams, their fears and worries, their longings and desires. The act of letting someone in on what has been kept secret for so long still feels raw and new and cathartic even today.

When you have been inside your own prison for so long, living a lie according to the expectations of others—and, in my case, not knowing what *home* meant as a young child, and what it feels like to truly belong—you no longer know what it means to be yourself, because you haven't had the stable environment to explore "self" in relation to the world.

When you have a transient, unstable early childhood, you live day by day, week by week, month by month, barely grasping the concept of certainty. You have spent a great deal of time conforming, as well as code-switching, a term used to describe when people, especially people of color and other minorities, change their behavior, the way they talk, dress, and walk, depending on their circumstances and environment.

All humans naturally code-switch. You behave and act differently, say, when you are around family than you do when you're stopped on the side of the road, talking to a cop. We all do it naturally when we swear like sailors around friends, but when a child walks into the room we stop and tone down our words and talk in ways that a child would understand.

Except it's different for people of color. It's more about survival and avoiding confrontation, avoiding being seen as a stereotype or confirming what people may negatively assume or believe about certain people.

An obvious example of this is President Obama. People have a certain idea of what being presidential means. You talk, walk, dress, and behave differently. President Obama looked different from past presidents because of the color of his skin, so he had to overcome people's perceptions of him by code-switching, perhaps overcompensating, but saying precisely the right kinds of words, holding himself up and standing and walking in a way that people think is presidential. There's a video of President Obama at a diner saying to a Black cashier, when asked if he needs change, "Nah, we straight." Americans, including myself, wouldn't expect him to say that in front of a televised audience. For further reference, and a laugh, look up the YouTube video of President Obama's "anger translator" (Keegan-Michael Key) at the White House Correspondence Dinner.

When you've spent so long being something else, conforming and code-switching, it can get to a point where it's so deeply ingrained, it becomes a natural habit and instinct. Once you start to realize that you can relax and just be yourself—when you take that first breath of freedom—you've only just begun to learn what it means to be free. With that first breath of freedom and that first glimpse of a brighter future, questions and doubts begin to form like dense fog. The third law of motion says with every action, there is an equal and opposite reaction. The act of freeing yourself to be you will undoubtedly elicit an equal and opposite reaction—sometimes good, sometimes bad, and oftentimes a mixture of both. Setting yourself free will bring with it the uncertainty of what it actually *means* to be free, to live authentically as your true self.

In such instances, when anxiety and doubts about your future and your identity begin to cloud your mind, retreating back into the prison of conformity can drive you toward a dark abyss. It is vital to find people to trust and open up to—others who have gone through the same ordeal. Such people will help to renew the hope you felt in the beginning, burning off the fog of doubt and illuminating a clear path forward.

Coming out is not a one-and-done deal. We like to believe we are static beings impermeable to change, but science suggests otherwise. It is impossible not to change physically and emotionally. Time and space thrust each and every one of us on paths that bombard us with experiences that shape who we are. And for as long as we live, whatever happens to our consciousness after death, we are forever in a state of flux. Each collision, whether it's with others or with an event or experience, alters our path. As we grow, we learn to maneuver and adjust as transitions happen, gaining the skills and knowledge we need to overcome obstacles.

On that note, I do not believe in free will and the idea that we are free, in an absolute sense. I see free will more as a theoretical model to help us make sense of human behavior and its effects. Holding all else equal, we can theorize about how a person's actions will result in A, B, or C. But models are a means toward understanding. We can think of the will as an ever-progressing dialectic of action and reaction. When one wills an action, it is a reaction to some other action. That action then is met with a reaction, whether from oneself, from another, or from something other. Nothing is born out of nothing. An action is no exception.

This is why I say coming out is an evolution. We have to balance celebrating progress with not giving a false impression that things are all good now—that everything is all set for minorities and the marginalized. As same-sex relationships have become more mainstream, coming-out and coming-of-age stories have worked their way into pop films and pop culture, with music artists such as Sam Smith and Troye Sivan, and movies such as *Love, Simon*.

An album or a two-hour film gives but a glimpse into the experiences of LGBTQ+ youth and adults, all of which are often romanticized. In the age of social media, viral videos of people coming out to their parents or relatives portray pinnacle moments of the lived experiences of coming out. It is important for queer allies, especially, to know that an initial coming out (yes, there can be more than one) is the beginning of a new journey, as important and life-changing as announcing, say, a pregnancy or an engagement. People's perceptions of you change, almost instantly, as do their expectations and, sometimes, their behavior toward you. Based on their own lived experiences, this can be for the better, or, sadly, in some cases, for the worse.

When sharing their coming-out moments, some say that the people around them indicated they "always knew," or had a "sneaking suspicion." I was so good at hiding my sexuality that this never really happened to me while I was growing up. My fervor to be like my family and those in my church community—to survive, but also because I was sincerely in search of answers—fended off suspicion.

Some people come out around puberty, which, in my view, allows them to develop in conjunction with the sexual, physical, and emotional growth that accompanies that stage in life. These instances are becoming more common as LGBTQ+ people continue to become more mainstream.

Those of us who don't come out until after high school often find that our growth and development—connected to relationships, gender, beliefs, and sexuality—is delayed until we are able to live our truths openly.

Gorham, Maine, 2010–2012

● ◐ ◑ ○ ○

My transfer to the University of Southern Maine came through, and soon enough I was back in Maine full-time. The drive to Gorham was familiar. These were the same back roads I'd taken to spend weekends at the Cushmans'—the same roads my friends and I would take to go to the Maine Mall, down Route 114 through Sebago, Standish, and Gorham, to South Portland.

When I finally arrived on campus on moving day, the college streets and lawns were lined with cars, personal belongings, and luggage. Parents huddled together, barely making sense of the reality that was unraveling before them. I weaved my way through and found my way, with the help of a "Husky pack leader," to where I was to unload and move into my room in Anderson Hall, near the center of the Gorham campus. I picked this building specifically because it had a "substance-free floor," which I thought would assuage my parents' worries regarding my transfer to a public university (which they saw as a heathen party school).

I soon found out that this substance-free zone was on the fifth floor of the brick and cement building, one built hastily in the mid-twentieth century when colleges all across America were shepherding a host of veterans returning from war, aided by the GI Bill. There were no elevators, so I had to lug my belongings and books up five sets of stairs to the very top of the building. By the end I could barely move my arms, and I felt like my lungs were about to collapse.

Fortunately, I knew some of the people on my floor. Two of the guys were from the Lakes Region area and both had worked at the Bridgton Hannaford. My roommate, B-Denny, had long blond hair that gave off the vibe that he was either a gamer or into heavy metal—or both. Across the hall from me were two guys with similar hair who gave off the same vibe.

My first impressions turned out to be true as the semester progressed. The big gaming trend at the time was League of Legends, and come to find out, my entire floor and indeed a good number of people on campus played this MMO (massive multiplayer online) game. Before I knew it, I was sucked in as well, battling it out in Summoner's Rift. I was an okay player. The really good players were down the hall from me. They were gold or platinum, and really got into it. I could hear guys shrieking or shouting as they played, often through the night and into the wee hours of the morning, trying to climb higher in the ranks.

And, yes, despite the shared obsession with video gaming, we did have face time. We had all moved in on the weekend, and, of course, college parties were bound to happen. Despite being "substance-free," our floor was no exception to the college phenomenon of partying hard. Our first night was memorable in that I and some of the other new kids on the floor were led by one of the upperclassmen onto the trails behind the baseball fields. It was pitch dark, and we clung to each other in a line, weaving up and down and all around the dark, wooded hills. With our hearts pumping and under the influence of alcohol, the journey seemed to go on and on as we constantly tripped over logs and pits in the dark and had branches whack us in the face. We barely noticed, however, because we were headed to the Promised Land: an open field on the other side of the woods.

When we finally emerged from the woods, we saw before us a wide-open hayfield that sloped ever so slowly downward beneath the moonlight. Off in the distance was Route 25, car lights coming and going periodically. We sat together in this field, which had just recently been cut, and in my intoxicated state, I felt like the moonlight itself was magic dust powdering the scene before me.

The magic of the moment was interrupted when we—the new kids on the floor—noticed that our upperclassman guide had disappeared, leaving us there, in the middle of nowhere. We scrambled to the edge of the woods to see if he had wandered off to get some privacy. But he was nowhere in sight. Panic set in as we looked at each other and wondered what the hell was going on, followed soon after by a full-on race back in the general direction from which we had come.

All of a sudden, we found ourselves laughing. It was probably close to two a.m. by that time and the alcohol had begun to wear off. Whether the laughter was from the hilarity of falling for such a prank, or because our bodies were coursing with adrenaline, we tripped and fell and got mud all over ourselves as we ran back to campus. Amazingly, we did find our way back.

As I soon found out, however, when I started taking walks along those trails, the woods behind the baseball field were not that big. Easy to get lost in, depending on which direction you go, but the main path led directly to that field. I would later walk that path often, visiting the field to clear my head or to sit and ponder things.

Nature calls us, truly. It's a little voice, nagging you to return to your roots. A deep, physiological longing, perhaps driven by biological instincts, to find a respite from the artificial, less colorful environments we have erected around us. Nature, with all its green noise, reminding the restless soul of home and the caress of Mother.

College quite literally became my home for the ensuing years. I made new friends who became a part of my life, including Ethan, who I consider to be my first gay friend. The first time we met was when we were hanging out on the lawn just outside of Anderson Hall. We were lying down on the grass with another friend of ours, Kelly, who goes by the name Max now. There was also Cassandra and another freshman who was interested in her. It was late summer, perfect in the way that only Maine's summers can be.

As a recently out person, I was immediately drawn to Ethan. He was out and proud in the way he talked and dressed and wore his gauges. I believe, subconsciously, I knew I needed a friend like him. Both of us were Geminis, albeit at opposite ends of what I refer to as the twin spectrum. He was more orderly and liked to have a plan; I was more of an organized mess and preferred to fly by the seat of my pants. He called me out and challenged me— someone who was still emerging from my evangelical Christian upbringing—regularly.

Ethan had come out during high school in Lisbon. Our teenage years couldn't have been more different, but they were also the same in some ways. Both of us grew up in rural Maine. Both of us were gay. Both of us were outed by people we knew. Except that Ethan took hold of his identity and sexuality, unabashedly. He planted his flag and would not budge.

I suppose in many ways I envied him. I wished I had come out earlier. I wished I was as 110 percent sure about almost everything as he was. Some of our arguments while driving around or hanging out consisted of two stubborn boys who wanted to prove the other wrong. We didn't get into shouting matches, but our debates would often get intense.

Despite this, we stuck with each other: Gemini twins who seemed to sharpen each other. He was out and proud and loud about it in a positive way. If he felt discriminated against, he wouldn't hesitate to take a stand. It was only behind the scenes in our dorm rooms or private moments that he would let his guard down and express how much a particular instance had been hurtful. From him I learned how to take a stand for myself and the part of me that I was finally, slowly but surely, letting out into the world.

College was an easy place to do this. What college kid *isn't* discovering and reinventing themselves? It was acceptable to try new things and engage with new ideas and lifestyles. No one particularly cared who you were back home; campus was an alternative universe. At least for the first few semesters, it seemed. One of the most important aspects of college is that you find your people, the ones you click with, the ones you do everything with: parties, the cafeteria, intramurals, mall trips. Find the people who get you, and a few of them are bound to be your friends for life.

What became my source of community for the first few years was what we affectionately referred to as "The Gay," more officially known as the Center for Sexuality and Gender Diversity (CSGD), run by the same Sarah who coordinated the PRYSM meetings. It was in this safe space that I met other queer college kids of all backgrounds and identities. In between classes, we would pile into the tiny office and get comfortable, sometimes piling on top of each other on the one and only love seat. The only other furnishings in the office were some bookcases with queer literature and a desk for the work-study student who staffed the center.

The Gay was where our lives intersected. It was where we made new friends, found dates, broke up, made up, cried, laughed, and, yes, created drama. But it was *our* space. A space we created in our own image. It was messy at times, but it was also beautiful in its own way, reflecting the spectrum of colorful personalities that filled the small room with memories and a feeling of home away from home.

We all had our stories of how we'd gotten to this point, and through the years we welcomed many who had found their way there, whether by accident or by choice. Something bigger than ourselves—a common cause and a common hope—inspired us to put aside our differences and acknowledge that we exist together and thus we live and suffer together. This was made abundantly clear when we experienced both wins and losses in terms of LGBTQ+ equality in Maine.

Ironically, I had been on the other side of the fight up until the year before. I had yet to form the views I have today about being a bridge between the conservative and liberal worlds. It was important for me, as I was discovering, to separate myself from what I had believed previously.

It was becoming increasingly clear to me that the only party that supports gay rights was the Democratic Party, and that the only party that opposed them was the Republican Party, the one my parents and most of my family's church community belonged to. I felt that this was a line in the sand and I had to pick the side that supported me and who I was as a human being. Taking the polar opposite position, politically, from my family was another form of rebellion—of revolution.

Today, after many years of maturing into my identity and

becoming more secure about myself, I view things in less stark terms. The more secure in my identity that I have become, the less I see other views and identities as threatening to me. And in that, and in the acknowledgment of others' humanity, I find myself wanting to build more bridges rather than burning them down.

The following September, I found myself on the other side of the spectrum at Lady Gaga's rally in Portland's Deering Oaks park, calling for an end to Don't Ask, Don't Tell. This policy, put in place by the Clinton administration in the 1990s, allowed LGBTQ+ people to serve in the military as long as they didn't discuss their sexual orientation. Such a policy is considered to be anathema in today's world, similar to other "great compromises" in American history.

On the one hand, it did allow LGBTQ+ Americans to serve in the military, but not as their authentic selves. They were allowed to serve so long as they remained silent about their true identity and who they loved. Despite its good intentions, Don't Ask, Don't Tell was at its core dehumanizing and demoralizing. Enforcing this policy told these soldiers—who put their lives on the line for their comrades-in-arms and for those of us at home—that they were not equal. They were not the same. That somehow their "lifestyle" was a distraction to those on the front lines —that soldiers shouldn't have to worry about whether other soldiers found them attractive.

While we can't ignore how wrong the Don't Ask, Don't Tell policy was, we must also acknowledge the progress we have made along the way. Perched on our moral high ground today, it's easy to look down upon previous generations of American society who espoused ideas that, at the time, were deeply ingrained and embedded in the psyche of a nation. I often bring up this point when defining progress, but almost immediately my point is watered down to a jab: "That's just the way things were then." To understand the past is not to condone or excuse the ideas and actions of that era. Understanding the thinking of a bygone era is how we learn from history about how to move forward in the present day, making sure we don't get stuck in our own thinking.

The price of progress is necessarily paid with blood, sweat, tears, and, most importantly, time. But in a day and age of instant gratification, we have reduced progress and social change to actions that provide us with that temporary high of *having done something*. We apply our pop-up and pop-in mentality to movement building, but leave when the high has worn off or when the going gets tough.

Progress doesn't come cheap. Not only do we risk gaslighting ourselves when it comes to our history as a nation, and as a people, but we also risk romanticizing what it really takes for change and progress to happen. We risk obsessing over the glorified moments of great speeches and marches while forgetting the struggle. We forget the blood, sweat, and tears shed. We forget the toll that has been taken on mental and physical health.

When I look at Don't Ask, Don't Tell, I do more than just condemn it; I learn from it. It was a difficult time to be LGBTQ+. We were in the throes of a culture war that wanted nothing less than to keep LGBTQ+ people out of the mainstream, out of the public eye, and, thus, silent and invisible. As a nation, we had just emerged from the 1980s and the Reagan administration, which tried to ignore the AIDS crisis, and even referred to it as the "gay plague." But just before Reagan's election, another, more sinister phenomenon was quickly growing into a movement that has shaped American politics: the evangelical movement. The election of Ronald Reagan was the first in which evangelicals entered the political fray. Evangelical leader Jerry Falwell laid the foundations of this voting bloc with an organization called the Moral Majority, which caricatured abortion rights and homosexuality to grow a movement that wields tremendous power over the Republican Party today.

From the get-go, despite a fundamentalist moral message, the evangelical movement was already showing signs of an ends-justify-the-means strategy. Reagan, a twice-married man who rarely attended church, was elected with two-thirds of the evangelical vote. Fast-forward to when Donald Trump won 80 percent of the evangelical vote despite multiple marriages, numerous sexual scandals, and being a prolific liar. But few evangelical leaders seem to care—which is interesting, given that President Barack Obama, a self-avowed Christian and whose presidency was free of sexual or morally repugnant scandals, was considered anathema by the evangelical right.

It really boils down to two issues, which helped to bolster and grow Jerry Falwell's Moral Majority and the evangelical movement: LGBTQ+ rights and women's reproductive rights. President Obama, amid all the conspiracies regarding his faith and his citizenship, supported women's and LGBTQ+ rights and, eventually, came out in full-throttled support of same-sex marriage. President Trump's moral turpitude was overlooked because he was surrounded by evangelical and faith leaders who were advising his administration and driving policy that strips away hard-won rights for LGBTQ people and women, from the Department of Education's policies on whether transgender students can use the bathroom that aligns with their gender identity, to pushing through, with the help of then-Senate Majority Leader Mitch McConnell, three conservative Supreme Court nominations to lay the groundwork for state challenges that chip away at *Roe v. Wade*.

Back in 2011, I had a powerful sense of hope and optimism that fueled my self-discovery and my foray into organizing and activism. The sense of possibility was intoxicating. It seemed that the pulse of history was beating to the tune of our hearts, which hummed with hope and a longing that, one day in the near future, we could even see same-sex marriage legalized and our status as second-class citizens come to a resounding end.

My heart was filled with that sense that we were living in historic times. I felt an overwhelming and bountiful love and hope for humanity as a whole. For so long, growing up in the church, I had been taught that humanity was the problem—that humans were sinful creatures prone to evil and in need of God's saving grace. But in the months following the repeal of Don't Ask, Don't Tell, and that rally in Deering Oaks, my heart swelled with a new hope: Yes, humanity is capable of great evil, but humanity is also capable of goodness, compassion, and love, able to overcome our baser instincts and shed our tendency toward embracing the survival of the fittest.

I began to sense that perhaps the answers to the pervasive problems of the human condition are not to be found in the heavens or the hope of an afterlife; rather, the solutions are staring us in the face—in the moments when we feel that strong sense of belonging to the human race—when we believe that, together, we can overcome. That despite the various shapes and sizes, beliefs, cultures, and tribes that manifest in who we are individually, we share in our struggle against the frailty of the human condition. This is what should unite us and bring us together: to pursue the common good for all humankind.

I don't think I was the only one who felt this way. Other friends and acquaintances from The Gay realized that there was no student group focused on LGBTQ+ issues, so we rushed to our advisor and The Gay's coordinator to see how we could get one started. That's when I was introduced, albeit at a student level, to what is referred to as "process." There was a process for a student group to form and become formalized and thus eligible for use of the "Student Activity Fee" fund, paid for by every student enrolled at the university.

A smaller group of us got together and drafted a mission statement and vision, a constitution, and bylaws, and brought in Sarah as our advisor of the Queer Straight Alliance. We then had to get approval from the Board of Student Organizations and the Student Senate, at which point we were formalized. We held elections at our first meeting, where roughly a dozen other queer students gathered. What surprised me was that my name had been included in the nominations for president of the QSA, as it came to be known.

I don't quite remember what I was feeling in that moment. It was a mix, really. There I was, having just started coming out that previous summer. I was, in every sense of the phrase, a "baby gay." I still had a lot to learn, especially when it came to using the correct pronouns, or even confronting someone who had used a gay slur. I felt honored, but I also worried about whether I was the right one to lead this group of out-and-proud queers. At the same time, feelings of hope and possibility rang through the clouds of self-doubt and insecurity. I was still a bit of an introvert, but deep down, I knew that if I wanted to be a part of change, I had to step out of my comfort zone and do difficult things.

So when they held the vote for president and announced that I had received the most votes, I took a deep breath and prepared myself to dive in. Although still a bit unsure of what I'd signed up for, during that semester when I served as the QSA's first president, I grew and learned a lot about what it takes to be a good leader. I learned the importance of listening, empathy, and, at times, putting your own needs and desires aside for the common good. In many ways, I was good at what I did when it came to procedural stuff, like facilitating meetings and drafting agendas. I had also reached out to Equality Maine, which was looking for help on campus to gather signatures for the marriage equality referendum in 2012. I had a knack for this type of organizing. Where I failed was in not noticing, or turning a blind eye to, interpersonal conflict between members of the group, which spilled over into the group meetings.

The lesson I've learned from being a group leader is that you can't get a group or organization to focus on a common goal or purpose if interpersonal conflict and division is allowed to fester. Because I was so focused on what I thought I was good at—process and social action—I didn't take the time to be emotionally intelligent and attuned to the emotional well-being and engagement of each member. Being a leader is more than just making sure we stick to the agenda or attend required meetings or put on events. Being a leader means building relationships and being aware of group dynamics. It doesn't mean you are the one charging forward alone; often it means being the glue that keeps everyone sticking together.

Despite this, I received a certificate for my contribution to student life from the student government association, and I was proud of it. Even though it doesn't seem like much, it was proof to me at the time that someone had recognized I was stepping out of my comfort zone and trying to do good.

More importantly, it was something I could take home to show my parents. Granted, I didn't wave it in their faces; I just casually left it on the kitchen counter where my parents could see that I'd made "contributions to student life as president of the USM Queer Straight Alliance." For me, it was a way of telling them that even as a gay person, I could flourish—and that I *was* flourishing. That piece of paper, I felt, showed them that as a young gay man, I was considered a leader and a good person.

Over time this developed into a type of cold war over my sexuality. My parents would also leave things out for me to see, like things I had written, to casually remind me of the person I used to be—the super religious kid who led worship at youth group. They thought they were reminding me of who I was, but those things, when I spotted them, cut me to the quick, reminding me of who they *wanted* me to be, and indicating that they didn't accept that being gay *was* me being me.

During one visit home, I saw that my mom had left a book on the very same counter where I'd left my leadership certificate. It stung me so much that I still remember the title of the book: *Out of a Far Country: A Gay Son's Journey to God. A Broken Mother's Search for Hope*, written by Christopher Yuan, the son of Chinese immigrant, and co-authored by his mother Angela Yuan.

I didn't ignore it completely. Although I could guess what it was about, I turned it over to read the back cover, where, near the bottom, it read, "God calls all who are lost to come home to him. Casting a compelling vision for holy sexuality, *Out of a Far Country* speaks to prodigals, parents of prodigals, and those wanting to minister to the gay community." I was both saddened and angry inside, and my drive back to campus after this visit was a melancholy one.

When I came home that summer and settled into my old musty bedroom with blue walls and sports wallpaper running along the center, I noticed that my parents had done a little rummaging through my old things from high school. They'd left out some old photos from church, and a tape that I'd recorded of myself, singing a worship song. Little things like that.

The message was received, albeit not the one they thought they were sending. To me, these were relics of a past where I'd held back and kept a secret from my family and friends. They were relics of when I really did believe that the more I prayed and the more I devoted myself to God, that I would somehow be less gay, or that it would somehow disappear. It was a time of darkness—living in the closet, looking out at the world throw a barely cracked door.

That summer, I spent a lot of time outside of the house, either working at Hannaford or hanging out with my friends B-Denny, Catie, and Kayla. Like the previous summer, we drove around a lot, had bonfires, and went to the dam most weekends.

But being back in the Lakes Region felt different. At USM, I was surrounded by new friends, in a more open and accepting place. Back in small-town, rural Maine, I wasn't surrounded by LGBTQ+ friends or allies.

One incident darkened my summer—my first blatant encounter with homophobia. I had tagged along with a few friends to a bonfire and remember painfully trying to strike up conversations with people with whom I felt I shared no mutual interests. It was a mix of jocks and macho guys who were also home from school for the summer.

I felt like I was making a complete fool of myself, trying to connect with a group of guys who were talking about how many girls they'd had sex with, or singing along to some top billboard rap song while chugging PBRs.

I happened to glance up and saw one of the guys pointing to me and saying to the guys around him, "He's the president of the queers at USM." Sure, the way he said it was hurtful, but it was what happened as a result that shook me and my newfound confidence. All of a sudden it made sense why he'd been sitting there, stone-faced and glowering, when I was trying to strike up a conversation with him. Things became awkward after he made this comment to his friends. I felt walls go up and I felt my insides shrink and shrink and shrink. I felt small and insignificant and so very alone, even though I was surrounded by people.

That's when I went inside and sat on my friend's big love seat. I felt a mixture of sadness and anxiety. It seemed that all the growth I had experienced and pride in who I was had, with a few words, been reduced to ashes. Since coming out, I had experienced casual homophobia, but this was the first time I felt I had been singled out and made to feel like the "Other," without having any other brave queer or ally friends there with me.

I realized how much I missed being on campus, where, even though there was casual homophobia, I knew there were safe spaces, allies, and plenty of resources available. I also realized that out there in rural Maine in 2011, things were still not that great for LGBTQ+ people. Despite being just fifty or so minutes from Portland and the University of Southern Maine, the beliefs about LGBTQ+ equality and same-sex marriage leaned conservative—and still do, a decade later.

In rural Maine at this time, the stereotypes and stigmas about gay men in particular were prevalent in the way straight men would not-so-subtly say things like, "I am fine with gay people—just not when they hit on me," or the popular, "No homo!" Phrases like that paint being gay or queer as something strange or different or something akin to a bad habit or unhealthy choice. As if, like a bitter stout or a funky wine, being gay was an acquired taste.

If not through words, it was expressed through body language. Where once an acquaintance might have stood at arm's length, now it seemed they stood just out of reach. Where they once clasped hands or hugged, now they went in for an awkward shoulder pat at best, or a handshake, at worst. Humans are hardwired to notice these things, and to think otherwise is ignorant.

Those who are marginalized and discriminated against, especially after spending part of their lives in the closet, and victims of casual and/ or implicit bias are especially attuned to what others may be thinking or feeling—often in a negative sense. We learn to spot microaggressions even before we know what the word means. Like when I'm walking through Target or Walmart and another customer walks up to me, even though I don't have a red or blue uniform on, and asks me if I work there. People asking me "Where are you from?" and when I say I'm from Maine, they ask, "No, where are you *from*-from." And then following up with, "Oh, well, you speak very good English." Folks saying, "You're a very good driver," or asking me if I'm good at math. Or gay men saying, "You must be a bottom. Most Asians are very submissive and good bottoms."

It is a survival technique that triggers the fight-or-flight response. LGBTQ+ people and Black and brown people are constantly pounding on the panic button, whether it's because of an offhand remark or a joke told in passing, or body language and physical actions that trigger our defenses. Constantly having one hand near the panic button and only one hand on the wheel of life puts marginalized people at a disadvantage.

Meanwhile, those who do not live in fear of microaggressions, domestic violence, violence, racism, sexism, and bias, have both hands free and on the wheel. If one casts a wide net, everyone has some kind of privilege—for instance, if I have two legs, I have more advantages than a person with one; if I have one leg, I have more options than a person with none, and so on—so that word is overused and does not really point to the relative ease and comfort that each advantage brings. Those lucky enough to have the resources and advantages of wealth, power, acceptance, and position are able to enjoy the scenery of life a whole lot more. They have more control of the situations and circumstances of life. When life takes a wrong turn or there's a threat around the bend, they can control and more easily cope with the consequences. You can more easily make that sharp or unexpected turn when you have both hands on the wheel. But with one hand on the panic button, marginalized people either must slow down or find themselves in a life-and-death situation.

As I have experienced myself, being aware, consciously or subconsciously, that you are a target for microaggressions and bias, whether explicit or implicit, saps enjoyment out of life, family, work, and play. It creates a constant state of stress that has negative impacts on your ability to live your life to the fullest extent possible. When your default setting is always on defense mode, your biological hardware is put under tremendous strain. Stress and cortisol are evolutionary, biological responses to the occasional predator lurking about, and adrenaline provides a temporary boost in speed or power to help fight or outrun a threat. But prolonged exposure or living in a perpetual state of stress is not what the human body is built for, and can be linked to all sorts of negative physical and mental health outcomes. The kind of stress that places one's existence and identity under immense filial and/or societal pressure can be soul-shattering. It's the kind of emotional tension that can fray the human mind and tear at the seams of the human heart.

The negative impacts of this constant state of stress on LGBTQ+ people and Black and brown people are well documented. Study after study shows that there are dire health disparities, increased rates of suicide, mental health issues, and substance misuse disorders.

For instance, one study conducted by University of Southern California and University of California, Los Angeles scientists found that racism and experiencing racist incidents triggers an inflammatory reaction at the cellular level in Black Americans. Another interesting study published in the *American Journal of Public Health* found that even anticipating prejudice triggers both psychological and physical stress responses. These studies are among many that dig deep to get to the root of why marginalization and discrimination lead to health and achievement disparities. Similar studies conducted with LGBTQ+ participants show comparable results.

Harkening back to the earlier discussion about evangelical beliefs about homosexuality, this reality is twisted to create a circular argument too often employed by evangelicals: Homosexuality is an abomination and homosexuals do not have God in their lives; homosexuals are depressed, alcoholic, and disease-ridden because they don't have God in their lives. This conveniently allows an apologist to ignore that perhaps it is evangelicals' misguided beliefs, stereotypes, and stigmas about LGBTQ+ people, and their mission to turn society against us, that creates the epidemic of stress and the resultant physical and mental health issues among the LGBTQ+ community. Instead, they seek to establish a causal link between homosexuality and sin and negative physical and mental health issues.

I am proud to be an out gay man today who breaks down these stereotypes and proves that we are human. We cry, we get angry, we hurt, but we also find joy, meaning, and purpose in life. For me, fulfillment comes from helping to make the world a better place, by being involved in my community, giving back, and speaking up about the issues I care about. I have found happiness in channeling my optimism, along with the lessons I've learned as a Mainer from other Mainers—about grit and determination and community—to guide my work in activism, the nonprofit world, running for office, and being elected as an at-large charter commissioner for the City of Portland, Maine. While there is always work to do on many issues, Maine is the village that helped raise me.

Being home that first summer since I'd come out felt like I had taken a good few steps forward only to take a few steps backward and feel the closet door press up against me. Part of me wanted to crawl back into that closet, just for the summer—at least until I got back to school.

It was a weird period. At Hannaford, where I was once again working that summer, I'd see some of the guys from that party and I'd feel myself stiffen up every single time. As the summer progressed, I felt less and less safe at work—at being home in the Lakes Region, in general. I wasn't at college, where I felt safe with plenty of support and resources for LGBTQ+ students. I couldn't just walk down the dorm hall or across campus to see friends. In many ways, college for me felt like the Promised Land of safety and inclusion. Being home in the Lakes Region, especially after that party, shook my newfound confidence. I found that I was aching to head back to school.

At times, the anxiety was so strong that I felt nauseated and started to shake as I was ringing customers through or bagging their groceries. In fact, I preferred to go out and do carts and overexert myself physically, just to take my mind off the jitters I felt about being one of the two known gay men in a rural community. I felt myself closing off to the customers, whereas in prior years it had been a source of joy to try to make their day a little brighter. Some regular customers who always came through my line were visibly worried.

One woman in particular, probably in her mid-forties with shoulder-length salt-and-pepper hair, especially noticed.

"Hey, Marpheen, are you okay?" she asked one time.

I made awkward eye contact, faked a smile, and said, "Yeah, I am just tired."

"Well, you don't seem your usual self. I'm worried about you."

I widened my fake smile and gave her a nod of acknowledgment as I finished her order. I felt like she saw right through me, and I could see the sympathy in her eyes.

I would hole up inside my head and check the clock, playing those mind games about having only thirty minutes until my lunch, or just two more hours until I finished my shift. When I'd finally make it back to my car, I would feel exhausted, like I'd been holding my breath for seven or eight hours straight.

When I got home, I was too tired to talk to anyone. I'd go down to my room and watch a movie or listen to music. Later on in my college years, I would learn that I had been experiencing panic attacks. I also learned that some of my simple coping mechanisms at the time are actually backed by science. For instance, on my lunch breaks, I would grab some Greek yogurt (high in protein), some cherries, and some water or tea. That alone did wonders to ease the anxiety I felt. I also started jogging seriously around this time. Even though I had played soccer in high school, I had never committed to running like I did starting that summer, and I went from barely being able to do a mile to routinely doing four miles. These became my go-to strategies as I continued to struggle with anxiety throughout my college years.

When I returned to college that fall, I felt a whole heck of a lot better as I settled back in and started hanging out with my friends again. It felt like such a big sigh of relief—not only to be back with friends and on a more liberal campus, but also to be back in the classroom, as well. College was where my mind opened up and where I engaged with my professors and classmates on a wide range of topics.

I had declared my major in political science by that time, so many of my courses involved political theory. One class that was particularly fun was international relations. I remember learning about spheres of power and influence, hegemonies, and discussing things like Immanuel Kant's theory of perpetual peace.

One of the most enjoyable activities was a simulation where the class was divided into groups of four and five and assigned a fictitious nation with various advantages, disadvantages, and resources. Each country was engaged in secret diplomacy with other countries and had to meet certain criteria to win. I was especially proud of my contributions to the success of our group, which faced imminent war with a Spartan-like nation. Our country was saved when a rumor that the Spartan-like nation was planning an attack prompted me to negotiate a mutual defense treaty with another country. This saved both of us from the fake assault, and we emerged having met the criteria for winning.

I felt at my best when I was engaged in academic pursuits—or rather, I felt at home in the world of ideas and possibilities. I remember feeling a sense of hope about—and in—humanity as I read and explored the various ideas different political leaders and philosophers had expressed about achieving world peace or solving pressing issues. In this world of ideas, I dreamed of what would be possible if humanity only came together.

It reminded me of a passage in the Bible about the Tower of Babel, in which humanity felt as if anything was possible, and built a tower that would reach to the very Heavens. In response, God said, "If as one people speaking the same language they have begun to do this, then nothing they plan to do will be impossible for them. Come, let us go down and confuse their language so they will not understand each other" (*Genesis* 11:6–7).

I was amused by the idea that even God recognized the collective power of humanity and, in a way, feared it. God recognized that nothing would be impossible for humanity if we spoke a common tongue and set about toward a common purpose. But reading this also made me wonder if all the conflict in the world over borders, religion, culture, and misunderstanding was, according to the Bible, not the result of a sinful nature but rather an unintended (or perhaps intended) consequence of dividing humanity into tribes and nations that spoke different languages.

Then again, I would say that this is a version of God that was created. At the time, however, I didn't know the difference; I couldn't separate out that perhaps God exists separately from the narrative that humans have created. How I reacted to God, then, was a reflection of the church community I had grown up in and resented. This resembles the tried-and-true strategy of divide and conquer, used time and time again here in America by the likes of white supremacists and the patriarchy.

Just think about it: Humanity, with a common goal and purpose, had made so much progress that it alarmed God—so much so that He intervened. It mirrors in some ways the idea of the created rebelling against, or surpassing, the creator. Whether it be Frankenstein, robots, or artificial intelligence, humans have found ways to express the existential threat posed by the fruits of their own machinations and making. Perhaps, in a way, we fear ourselves and what we are capable of—and we have good reason, given our history of violence.

But this is the very thing about humanity that gives me hope. Our tenacity and grit. Our propensity to hope and improve and progress. Our natural instinct to evolve and our capacity for curiosity. We express all of these things in our big and small acts of kindness, love, and altruism. And while the current friction that exists between countries and peoples and entire continents has an equal and opposite reaction—in the form of xenophobia and war—I believe that connectivity, globalization, and the clash of civilizations and cultures will lead, in the long run, to a world in which we will pool our resources and aim for the Heavens once more.

As a sci-fi geek and voracious fan of *Star Trek* and *Star Wars*, I am waiting for the day when we squabble less among each other and take to the stars. I believe shows and movies like these capture quite well our imagination and hope that there is something out there yet to be discovered. Both of these shows envision not only humans coming together but entire worlds and alien civilizations cooperating, despite the myriad differences. But more importantly, it is the recognition that without everyone coming together, that dream is impossible. Again, this echoes our human tendency to point to something apart from us, whether it is to a deity, the Heavens and some mystery of the universe, or some great evil or threat, in order to unite and bring us together with one common purpose and goal.

I do believe we're in a period of paradigmatic shift wherein there are universal principles and rights that transcend borders, countries, cultures, and, yes, religions. Where once we looked to and created gods and demons and great beings to guide and channel human behavior toward cooperation and unity, we have begun to look within ourselves to find that common thread that ties us to each other and pulls us together. And from that deep wellspring of human longing for dignity and equality, we have established such things as the Universal Declaration of Human Rights, forums for diplomacy, and the social contract.

I would posit that instead of various deities creating us in their own image, we have created deities instead in our own image. Think back to the ancient Greek gods: Ares, the god of war; Aphrodite, the god of love; and Dionysius, the god of wine. The gods reflected back to us our hopes, our fears, our virtues, and our vices.

As our capacity for understanding and knowledge has evolved and expanded, we have begun to look less and less to the Heavens for hope, deliverance, justice, and retribution and have begun to peer into each other and ourselves to draw out such things as the rule of law and institutions that are created in our image, imbued with that sense of human hope and optimism. These things that we have built and our aspirational declarations serve as that constant reminder—a mirror, if you will—that reflects what it is that we long and hope for.

This is what drives me—this optimism for the future of humanity. My optimism, as well as my experiences growing up, my longing to understand the root causes of suffering and the human condition, have softened my heart and tempered my soul. And, thus, my bent is toward trying to listen to what people are saying, those moments when they open up about their upbringing, their families, and their lives, in an effort to understand their motives and their worldview.

Bringing people together requires humility, empathy, and a willingness to pay attention. When you get to the root of someone's worldview and belief systems, and the life circumstances and experiences that frame those things, you can better connect with that person. Keeping the peace and maintaining boundaries on how and what you talk about with others will also bear fruit.

I have found that it's only by being with others and showing them that I am human and no different from any other person, regardless of my sexuality or beliefs or lifestyle, that I can challenge the stereotypes and stigmas and beliefs they may have about LGBTQ+ people.

To steal some language I learned in the evangelical world, I have to be the light that shows them a different path, a different way of viewing the world and other people. As Katy Perry so poignantly put it, "Baby, you're a firework! Come on, show 'em what you're worth." Regardless of my sexual orientation, I am a human being deserving of basic dignity and respect.

Changing hearts and minds requires humility, empathy, and understanding. It requires that we maintain our optimism about other people and their ability to evolve and change. It means not giving up hope that they may one day have a change of heart. It means appealing to that deep human longing for dignity and equality that echoes in each of us—that childlike innocence, openness, and inclination to embrace the unknown.

This truth only grew stronger for me as I traveled back into the past. Not literally, mind you, but coming out led to a period of re-examining my roots and revisiting those who had come in and out of my life just as I had come in and out of theirs.

The University of Southern Maine was but a stone's throw away from the house I lived in as an eleven-year-old, with Sheila. For the longest time, I would drive back and forth without even thinking about it. But one fall day, I decided to stop by and reconnect. Not only because I felt a need for closure, but because I wanted to tell Sheila that all was forgiven—and I'd turned out okay.

The last time I had seen her was at my high school graduation. I remember her face was puffy and red, and her eyes were brimming with tears. I could tell it was a mix of pain, sadness, pride, and joy. Little did I know that my adoptive parents, who thought it was best that I didn't communicate with her after we'd moved in, had withheld Sheila's letters and birthday cards; whether this was to my benefit or detriment, I'll never know. But it fills me with sadness that my adoptive parents, no matter their intentions, put off the opportunity for both Sheila and I to find closure and to heal. My sister Tanya and I were the only two children to have lived in that big old empty house with her. We had filled voids in her life and probably helped ease some loneliness. Sure, there were challenges—she was a single foster mom—but she was dealing with children who had lived through some serious trauma and needed extra time, attention, and love to get through that.

I have always thought, in all my lived experiences and interactions with others, that the cruelest thing one can do is to deny someone closure. In doing so, you hold open the wound, letting the pain fester. You leave questions unanswered. Denying someone closure may give you a sense of power, but that power corrupts. It eats away at you on the inside.

In all those years that I'd lost contact with Sheila, I lost the chance to learn the value of forgiveness, mercy, and healing. Rather than allowing questions to remain unanswered, one must be prompted to have internal dialogue about one's self in relation to others. Now, of course this is more difficult in extreme cases of physical and sexual abuse; I will leave that to those who have experience working in those areas.

In my case, a lot of healing happened when I knocked on Sheila's door as a twenty-year-old. Even more so when we passed through the dining room where we'd struggled with my homework and I learned that I loved playing rummy, and when we sat in the same living room where I used to watch cartoons. We talked and talked, and I gave her the rundown of what had happened since we lost contact. Most importantly, we told each other that we were sorry.

Then she popped the question: "Are you happy?"

It wasn't just a simple question posed after having dinner or trying on new clothes. It was *the* question. The big one. The one about life and living. At that point in time, I was still coming to grips with my identity.

"I am okay," I replied hesitantly. "I came out as gay. Bob and Tracy aren't happy about it, but I am working through it all."

"I am happy for you," she said. "I am happy that you get to be yourself and discover who you are."

This was not the conversation I was expecting to have with Sheila. In all honesty, I didn't really think about what her position on my sexuality might be. But to hear her say these words meant a tremendous amount to me.

Overall, I left feeling as if both our wounds had begun to close. It felt cathartic. There was a feeling in my chest as if I had been holding my breath for far too long. During the next few days, I took walks in the woods surrounding the campus or went for nighttime strolls to reflect and process further.

The scars are still there, and they still throb with memories of the pain I experienced while living with Sheila those many years ago. But that's the difference: They're mere memories now, reminding me of how far I've come, and of the need for grace and sympathy—not only for my current self (and my younger self), but also for Sheila and the circumstances and challenges she was dealing with at the time. As the Buddha says, "Holding on to anger is like grasping a hot coal with the intent of throwing it at someone else; you are the one who gets burned."

Though Sheila was a source of great emotional and mental pain for me when I was living with her, holding on to that pain was like grasping a hot coal. The more I held on to it, without closure, the more it burned me. But when I allowed room for Sheila to explain things and apologize, and I allowed myself room to see things in a different light, the grace and empathy that was extended to Sheila was returned to me in kind—not necessarily through some cosmic rule of exchange, but simply by releasing my hold on that pain and allowing the wound to close.

After spending some time processing my reconnection with Sheila, I then set off to reconnect with relatives I hadn't seen since parting ways with them as a very young child, in San Diego.

Fort Worth, 2012

● ◗ ◖ ○ ○

I was browsing Facebook one day when a random idea popped into my head: *Let's see if my godparents are on Facebook.* That's when I hurriedly typed the name *Khandarith Hay* into the search function.

The first profile that popped up was an instant success. *It's him!* I thought as I saw the profile photo. It was unmistakably my godfather. He looked almost exactly the same as how I remembered him. I added him as a friend, and before long he added me back— and my godsisters Linda Hay and Sophos Hay added me, too.

I was squirming with joy, knowing that I had begun to

reconnect with relatives I hadn't seen since I was three or four. So many questions bubbled up as I went back and forth with my godsisters on Facebook Messenger. I began to ask them what I was like as a child and where we lived at the time and so on and so forth. They had been kids at the time, too, and didn't have the answers.

Around that time, I jumped onto a call with my godsisters and heard their voices for the first time in ages. Their voices had changed, obviously, but the voices of my godfather and godmother sounded almost exactly the same. Just hearing their voices made my heart swell; I didn't know what to feel, exactly, but I remember that I felt *all the feelings* at once.

The feelings inside grew more intense as I peppered my godfather with questions. He answered them slowly and softly, which was how I remembered him as a kid. But one answer in particular raised even more questions. They knew, through my birth mother, the situation that all four of us had been in. At one point they had explored the option of trying to get custody of me, but when they found out that we had all been placed with the Berrys and were doing well, they decided it was not in my best interest.

This created a little knot in my chest. It was a mix of anger and sadness—at no one in particular, but at the big unknowns raised by this revelation. It was a feeling of annoyance at the strange machinations of probability. A rush of hypotheticals about what life could have been like. I would have grown up bilingual, most likely, knowing both English and Khmer. I would have lived in just one household, going to schools in the same school district, maybe with a consistent circle of friends. I would have had lots and lots of Cambodian food. I would have received love and attention consistently from my godparents.

While I fantasized about this for months afterward, I also realized that I would have missed out on the foster parents, adoptive parents, friends, and neighbors I have met along the way to this point in my life. This, too, made my heart ache a bit, and also made me feel grateful for the life I have lived, even with all its twists and turns.

The little knot in my chest loosened when my godfather said something along the lines of, "You were like our son. You *were* our only son."

I felt a mixture of pride and pain hearing this. The pain was more for my godparents. They were older, and for them to be separated by thousands of miles and to lose contact with me no doubt caused them a lot of pain and anxiety, especially since they knew the situation I was in with my birth mom, who was struggling with trauma. Hearing that they considered me a son made my heart swell with pride—what can only be described as a warm sensation blossoming in my chest.

This feeling stayed with me during the months ahead as we made plans for me to fly to Fort Worth, Texas, where they now lived, to visit my godfamily, after which I would be flying to San Diego to reconnect with my biological mother, grandmother, and aunts and uncles. The added bonus of going to San Diego didn't even occur to me, it was actually my godfather's idea and he himself had paid for the plane tickets. Here was someone who still cared about me despite over two decades of separation and without hesitation booked me flights that would change my life and reconnect me with lost loved ones.

When the time came for me to fly to Fort Worth, I was home in Naples for the summer. Two or so years had passed since I'd come out and things had settled into a stalemate of sorts. My mom at one point confessed, "College has been good for you." I was just happy that we could agree to disagree, and that we'd found a way to coexist.

My adoptive parents were happy when they heard I was going to reconnect with my godparents and my birth family. They drove me to the airport, along with my sister Tanya. At the small but well-laid-out Portland International Jetport, we embraced and took pictures before I went through the TSA line on the third floor and disappeared beyond the security gate.

My connecting flight was in Newark, New Jersey, which I believe is everyone's least favorite airport—that, or O'Hare in Chicago. It was vastly larger than Portland's airport and bustling with people of all different shapes, sizes, colors, and attire.

In Portland back then, I mostly saw white people—men in business suits, or families sporting cargo shorts, capris, and Crocs. It's a little more diverse these days, with travelers arriving from all over the country, and the world, to tour Portland's restaurants and craft breweries. I'm sure some rent a car and drive up US-95 or Route 1 to Bar Harbor and Acadia National Park, or even Katahdin, while others head south to beaches like Old Orchard or Ogunquit.

Compared to Portland, the airport in Newark was a hot mess. I remember having to jump on a shuttle that went to a different part of the airport, and from there, pressing on through mobs of confused travelers to finally make it to the correct gate for my flight to Dallas.

When I landed in Dallas, my godparents, Khandarith and Leap Hay, were waiting for me. Tears were welling up in their eyes as they saw me walking toward them. They knew what I looked like because of my Facebook profile, but also, I didn't see any other Cambodian or Asian people around me as I entered the welcome area. I suppose that's one of the perks of having brown skin—I stick out!

We exchanged hugs, my godfather grabbed my suitcase, and we walked off toward where they had parked. They kept stealing glances my way. Despite all the years, I felt like it was a homecoming of sorts. I felt a growing anticipation as more and more questions bubbled up inside of me as we drove the thirty or so minutes to Fort Worth.

When we arrived, I was greeted by a number of Cambodian "relatives." In our community, almost anyone who has some sort of familial connection, no matter how distant, is considered close family. This is quite different from my white, evangelical upbringing in rural Maine, where the emphasis is placed on the nuclear family—dad, mom, and kids. In Cambodian culture, and many others around the world, views of family are more expansive, similar to how Americans viewed family before the Industrial Revolution and two world wars.

This more expansive view of family is reflected in the expectation that younger Cambodians are to take care of their older parents by having them live with them. That's why so many Cambodian families here in Maine are multigenerational households. This flexible view about relatives also works its way into the Khmer language. You always refer to elderly men as *ta* (grandfather), elderly women as *yeay* (grandmother), men older than you as *pou* (uncle), and women older than you as *ming* (aunt). You refer to men the same age as you as *bong* (brother), and women around the same age as *bong srey* (sister). In Cambodian culture, the entire family, including aunts and uncles and other relatives, is involved in raising children. Quite literally, the entire village raises the children together, which differs from the nuclear family approach where the father and mother are seen as the main caretakers of the children.

From left and right I heard memories and stories from when I was a little kid. All of this was happening as piles and piles of food were laid out before us. I was a little embarrassed and speechless—it was a little too much attention for my introverted side to handle—but I plastered on a smile and powered through, aided by the delicious smells and tastes of my childhood, which brought back memories and a small sense of belonging. At the same time I felt uneasy, because over the years I had lost much of my

Cambodian heritage, customs, and language. My godfamily felt simultaneously like family and strangers to me. I could only half understand what they were saying through the broken English and Cambodian phrases that swirled around. And to see that they had a pretty typical life in America, I wondered, as I have mentioned before, what life would have been like had I moved to Texas with them as a four- or five-year-old.

My godfamily owned a small two-bedroom house in a historic district. It had beige vinyl siding and reddish-brown roof shingles. The porch had reddish-brown brick columns and white-painted railings between them. The interior had old laminate paneling and carpets that looked like they were from the 1960s. My godparents had bought the house for somewhere around $30,000 in cash in the late 1990s. They weren't rich—very working-class—but like other Cambodian families, they saved a lot and borrowed very, very little.

It was a strange feeling—to feel at home yet still like a stranger—brought on by memories of what used to be, and thoughts of what could have been, and actually was. It was a perfect storm, a mix of joy and belonging with uneasiness and an unsettling disconnect, realizing I didn't get the chance to see everyone around me as they grew up, or changed with age.

When I borrowed my godparents' car and drove around Fort Worth, visiting the mall and running errands, I wondered what life would have been like had I grown up and gone to school there. Life would have been very different, of that I am sure. There was more diversity here. Larger Hispanic and Black communities and, of course, a good mixture of Vietnamese and Cambodian people.

I even pondered the difference in climate. It was summertime, so it was often hot and sticky. Not that Maine wasn't like that in the summer, but in Texas, it seemed even more ... punitive? And I have always loved thunderstorms. Maine thunderstorms, that is. The one thunderstorm I remember while visiting my godparents in Texas was on a whole new level. I remember going for a jog once when menacing blue clouds rolled in above the city. I had just made it to the elementary school nearby when the first crack of thunder signaled the impending downpour. The thunder sounded louder than it did in Maine; whether it was actually reverberating through the air or whether I was shaking in fear, I can't recall. But in today's parlance, I was *shook*.

I jogged back home as fast as I could, but not before a thick column of lightning flashed down not too far away and cracked like a giant whip. I panicked, having never seen anything like this before. My running shorts and shirt were soaked, and I was desperately trying to protect my phone from getting water-damaged. Fortunately, the worst of the thunder was over by the time I made it back to my godparents' house, but the rain was still pouring down like cats and dogs—or, should I say, since I was in Texas, like cattle.

Once I'd made it inside and showered, I plopped on top of my bed and listened to the rain and rumbles of thunder, slipping into that space between conscious thought and dreams. Thunder and rain have always seemed to provide the perfect echo chamber for contemplation. These are the moments when I've always refocused and processed memories and recent experiences, moments that stilled my soul and filled me with a gentle peace, often rocking me to sleep.

Over the course of the two weeks I stayed with my godparents, they shared photos and stories with me from when I was very little. I would talk to them about what I was like then. It was important to me, as the person I was at the time, as it still is today.

One story in particular sticks out. We were talking about what I was studying in college and what I wanted to be. They were a little surprised, I suppose, that I was studying politics and was, at that time, considering going to law school.

"We always thought you were going to be a doctor," my godmother said.

My eyebrows scrunched up ever so slightly. *A doctor?* I thought. *You need to know a lot of math and science for that, my weakest subjects.*

"When your godfather was very sick one time," my godmother said, interrupting my train of thought, "you kept watch over him and did everything you could to take care of him. So we thought that one day you would be a doctor, because you liked to help people."

This story shattered the narrative I had told myself of how I was as a kid. My experience in foster care—the anger, the feelings of separation and abandonment and such—had warped my view of myself. My experience, for instance, with the judge and the owner of the junkyard in Riverton had somehow made me see myself as an angry kid, a thug, someone who bullied. As I jumped from home to home, I could see the fear in the eyes of my foster mother and adoptive parents when I would explode in anger and yell. The look in their eyes made me feel like I was a monster, full of rage and sadness, so I suppose this seeped into my view of what I was like before the age of nine. I also struggled in school, which made me think I was a bad student, but later conversations with Portland teachers I reconnected with told a different story.

Sure, I was dealing with a lot of anger, sadness, and feelings of loss, but those feelings didn't define me entirely. My godparents and elementary school teachers and education techs all described me as a kid I barely remembered: bright, inquisitive, curious, creative, and always willing to lend a helping hand. These were traits that I'd lost in the narrative I had created about myself, as someone who was not only afraid and defensive, but also a person who instilled fear in the eyes of those whose job it was to make me feel safe. This story fit into my status as an "other," an outsider—someone who hated the fact that I didn't fit in with those around me, that I looked different, and that I felt different.

It shook me, hearing about how my godparents thought I would grow up to be a doctor because of how caring and helpful

I was as a young child. It reflected a side of myself I'd forgotten. It felt foreign to me. Distant. Remote. It created a dissonance in my head and in the core of my being.

You mean I wasn't just a messed-up kid with a messed-up life? I thought to myself. *I cared? I helped? I was kind?*

I knew those things about myself as I sat there with them in their Texas home, but it began to dawn on me that perhaps this had always been me at my very core, from the time when I was a young child. Despite the shifting sands of time and the storms roiling inside me, there were parts of me that, although buried at times, shone through all of that.

My godparents told story after story about what life was like back then. My godmother told me stories of bath time, rubber duckies, and the time I got soap in my eye. My godfather told me about his time in the Cambodian church and how I would run around during Sunday school and the worship service. Even though I was only their godson, they painted a very vivid picture of presenting me to the world as if I were their very own. Their faces beamed with pride and joy.

"You were our son, Marpheen," my godfather said. "Our only son. And we loved you, and we love you still. We still consider you our son."

I fought back the tears that were welling up inside. This was part of the journey of finding my place in the world and understanding where I fit in the grand scheme of things. Knowing that I was a part of their lives and that I held a special place in their hearts confirmed that I mattered, that I was loved, and that I had made a difference in their lives, as they had in mine.

But being called their son raised other questions for me.

Being considered a son carries with it not only a sense of pride but also a weight of duty. As I felt my roster of parent figures expand, that responsibility seemed to multiply. I wondered whether this feeling of duty to parents was cultural, or if it had to do with being the oldest sibling, and filling in, as much as I could, when my birth mother was absent, or in need of emotional and personal support.

It wasn't until I stumbled on some research about intergenerational transmission of trauma that I began to piece some of this together.

My birth family, including my godfamily, were refugees who escaped genocide and experienced the trauma of seeing their loved ones, friends, and neighbors massacred. I have personally witnessed many of them trying to cope with this trauma by drinking too much or working too much. The ungodly hours and number of jobs my elders worked couldn't be explained by simply saying they were hardworking immigrants taking full advantage of newfound opportunities.

For the generation of us born in the United States after our refugee parents landed on these shores, the trauma was passed down to us secondhand. In the least extreme cases, survivors spoke very little about their life during the era of the Khmer Rouge, as if it were a deep, dark secret they wanted to forget. In many cases, it came down to parenting styles, whether the parent-survivor was clingy or overprotective. At its most extreme, it resulted in broken homes, whether from neglect, substance use, domestic violence, or, in my case, being placed in foster care and adopted.

Scholars and global institutions like the United Nations have taken up the study of intergenerational transmission of trauma, especially trauma caused by genocides such as the Cambodian genocide and the Holocaust. A common theme emerging from this growing body of research suggests that, while not totally indicative of outcomes for children of survivors, intergenerational trauma may be transmitted most recognizably in the way we metabolize stress, and in a greater risk for post-traumatic stress disorder.

Much of the work around intergenerational trauma and its

intersection with epigenetics is thanks in large part to researchers who studied Holocaust survivors and their offspring. Dr. Yael Danieli, a clinical psychologist, spearheaded the creation of an Inventory for Multigenerational Legacies of Trauma and a body of reference work. I had a chance to meet her while participating on a panel on generational trauma at USM. Dr. Rachel Yehuda, director of the Traumatic Stress Studies Division at the Mount Sinai School of Medicine, has done a tremendous amount of work tracking PTSD and heritability on a molecular level. Over the past decade or so, more work has been poured into studying intergenerational trauma in Indigenous peoples and descendants of slaves.

Not as much research has been conducted into Cambodian survivors and their descendants. It could be cultural, as suggested by *The New Republic* writer Judith Shulevitz in her article, "The Science of Suffering," which discusses the growing field of transgenerational trauma research and the Cambodian community. In this article, Shulevitz discusses how cognitive behavioral therapy, with its roots in Western and Jewish traditions around confession and memory, is not necessarily the way Cambodian genocide survivors—much less Asian cultures in general—deal with trauma. As noted in the article, bringing up memories associated with trauma can have the exact opposite effect, and can lead to retraumatization of the survivor. What has worked better is a more culturally responsive approach, taken by the Cambodian Advocacy Collaborative in Southern California:

> The program has four prongs: outreach and engagement to reduce the stigma of mental health issues in the Cambodian community; workshops to educate community members about topics like mental and physical wellness, signs of mental illness and how to cope with stress; case management to provide referrals needed for health and social

services; and social support activities, such as Cambodian New Year celebrations, temple visits, water blessings for healing and positive energy, and potlucks.

Preliminary data show that 57.7 percent of participants reported reductions in the effects of past trauma on their current well-being, while 69.3 percent of those with depression-related symptoms at the beginning of the program reported reductions in symptoms.

In diving into the direct research done on the Cambodian population in America, I found a scientific explanation for the sense of duty and responsibility that I mentioned earlier. In my case, I experienced role-reversal parenting, in which the parent-survivor turns to the child to have their emotional and personal needs met. As one group of researchers found, there is a strong correlation between parent-survivors who show trauma-related symptoms, role-reversal, and an increase in likelihood and levels of anxiety and depression among their children.

Having to provide emotional and personal support to my birth mother at a very young age, as well as caring for (to the extent possible) my younger siblings helped to shape who I am today. This added a layer on top of the Cambodian cultural values around collectivism and family, and an extra layer on top of my personal instincts and inclinations, as described to me by those who knew me in my early childhood.

My response to being considered my godparents' son was, again, a mixture of pride and worry. In my heart of hearts, I truly want to give back to those who have had a profound influence and involvement in my life. The questions in my mind were not if I had to or whether I should, but rather how. How do I become successful, and how do I bring the ones I care about along with me? How do I pave the way forward and make it easier for my younger siblings? How can I help them succeed as well?

For me that doesn't necessarily translate into love and affection, *per se*, but it almost always takes the form of providing advice and guidance in figuring out how to navigate systems, processes, and life in general. It's important for me, as someone who taught myself how to navigate college applications, financial aid, housing, and so forth, to make it easier for my siblings to do the same. The inclination to want to make things easier for those close to me and to help them navigate the world comes naturally to me.

My idea of achieving success is not just for me, but for my family, and to fulfill my dream of making a difference in the lives of those around me. Success, the way I envision it, is finding a way to truly make a difference, and attacking problems at their very root. In doing so, I will be able to improve the lives of others, including my family.

Aspiring to this kind of success often takes the form of being able to navigate a particular system. As a kid, this was evident in my playtime, which probably informs my belief that playtime and boredom are vital for a child's development. For instance, growing up, I loved LEGOs, but I don't recall ever looking at the manual and following the instructions step by step. Instead, I would look at the image on the front and the pieces laid out before me and try to construct it from just the image. Building a LEGO set in that way took longer, for sure, but it solidified in my memory what went where, and I could deconstruct and reconstruct the set from memory, without referencing the manual.

It was very much the same with learning the piano. I resisted reading the music; instead, I listened to the music and tried to match it with the images of the notes, rather than actively reading and playing the notes themselves. The creative in me would much rather visualize something or feel it and learn it, hands on.

This must have something to do with me being a second-generation Cambodian American, in the sense that I was an intermediary between two worlds. I had a Cambodian ethnicity and background, but I was born in the United States and for part of my life, raised by white families, living in white, rural communities.

These two worlds didn't always coexist peacefully. As a brown child living in a world dominated by white people, I had to learn how to code-switch. In the early years, I spoke Cambodian at home and with family friends; at school, I learned that this was not acceptable. Cambodian get-togethers were more on the feisty side, but with white people, I learned to be polite. When I transitioned to foster care and eventually to adoption, and was no longer being thrust back and forth between a Cambodian world and a white world, code-switching was what I felt was needed to survive and fit in.

When I started reconnecting with my Cambodian relatives, it was as if the switch was stuck toward the white side of talking, dressing, and behaving, as if I was permanently stuck in white mode. I couldn't code-switch back because I no longer knew Cambodian, and I hadn't seen my biological Cambodian family in a decade. When I was younger, after Tanya and I would see our birth family, we would be in a funk for a couple of days. This led the Berrys to conclude that the visits were most likely causing us to relive some of the trauma of separation, and that it would be better for the visits to end.

Code-switching and learning how to navigate systems and processes of, by, and for white people takes a tremendous amount of work, and, much like being multilingual, makes us not only street-smart but also society-smart. However, it comes at a cost. Juggling two worlds is exhausting—mentally, physically, and spiritually. Especially if you're also juggling code-switching as a gay man of color. There are just multiple layers and intersections that make it even more complicated.

Being an alien from two worlds, so to speak, also creates a tug-of-war between two sets of cultural values. Cambodian elders, for instance, complain about how the young people are giving up on Cambodian culture and values and becoming "too American." One of the main ways this manifests is in how we balance two countervailing values: American individualism and Asian collectivism. This clash can be observed in interactions between older generations of Cambodians and Asian immigrants and Cambodian and Asian Americans, or those who came here at a very young age and those who were born and grew up in the United States. (As an example of this, observe the conflict between the lead character and her fiancé's mother in the 2018 film *Crazy Rich Asians*.)

For me, individualism was vital to my coming out. I had to realize that I am who I am, and that part of one's happiness comes from being true to one's self. But even through all of my years living in white communities, collectivist values instilled in me by my Cambodian heritage and childhood still found ways to come to the surface. I think this is another key reason why, when considering success and career, I also think in terms of my family and carrying them with me. While individualism proved useful in figuring out my identity—and I have plenty of posts about John Stuart Mills from my short stint as a Libertarian to prove it—my journey toward embracing a fusion of individualism and collectivism has informed both my personal sense of identity in terms of my politics, beliefs, and values, as well as my role in the grander scheme of things.

This isn't to say that I had it all figured out by the time my two weeks with my godfamily came to a close. Although I felt like a weight had been lifted off my chest, in that many questions about my early childhood had been answered, as we drove to the Dallas/Fort Worth airport, I wrestled with new questions.

How did my godfamily fit into the picture? I already had an adoptive family, and a foster family that I held dear. Now I had my godfamily; although we had been separated for nearly twenty years, I cared for these people deeply. I loved them. How was I going to help care for them in the future, as I would my adoptive family?

What does it mean to belong? To be home? To be family?

These questions echoed in the chambers of my heart and mind as I walked through the airport in search of the gate for my flight to San Diego, where I would reconnect with my birth mother, grandmother, and aunts and uncles.

San Diego, California, 2012

There's nothing quite like a California golden hour.

I had landed in San Diego International Airport late in the afternoon and had just gotten off the phone with Uncle Sambo, who was pulling up to the terminal.

When Sambo hopped out of the car to greet me, he didn't look like he'd changed much except that he was taller, and bald. He was wearing his John Deere work clothes in the same way he had worn his oversized T-shirts and jeans back in Maine—with a sense of cool style. In many ways, it was fitting that he would be the one to pick me up. Second to my grandmother, he was next in line in terms of the one who held a steady presence in my life and my mom's life. When he was sixteen or so, he had spent a good portion of one of his years in high school living with us in Riverton Park. My mom was having some extra trouble back then, and my guess is that my grandmother sent Sambo to keep an eye on us, even though she was only a few miles away, on Front Street.

We drove along North Harbor Drive. Across the harbor, speckled with sailboats and yachts, was a blur of high-rises. The scenery changed as we took a turn and headed up hills covered in those iconic California homes that look like they are clinging to the landscape for dear life. It was a constant stop and go, stop and go, until we finally hit the Martin Luther King Jr. Freeway, which I remember because of the name, and likely because we used it often during my stay. As we headed over to Fairmount and the City Heights area, the dusty hills and canyons and the tightly packed houses with their plaster walls brought a faint feeling of familiarity, blurry in my mind, as if I could grasp the memories if I just focused a little harder.

Our conversation sputtered. I had so many questions, and my mind was overloaded with the sights and sounds of a place that had once been home, with people who were once my family. Sambo's mannerisms and phrases exuded an intimidating smoothness, while my side of the conversation was peppered with *wickeds* and *geezums*. In my Abercrombie T-shirt—the sleeves tight on my biceps—and American Eagle khakis, I looked and sounded every bit the part of a preppy white gay college kid. I had lost touch with my roots.

My unexpected lifeline in the conversation was John Deere, which happened to be Uncle Sambo's employer. What rural Mainer can't talk tractors?

Our final turn was onto a dirt road that dipped into Manzanita Canyon. Just after the turn, we parked behind a house tucked into the side of the hill. Uncle Salut—the one who is six months younger than me—ran out of the house, and we hugged before he launched into his characteristic half-snicker, half-joking mode of making conversation.

"Daaaamn, Marpheen," he said as he took a step back and looked me up and down. "Look how big and tall you got. Must be all that American food, man."

I thought of how much milk I drank, growing up in white households.

We walked onto a shady cement patio and came into a small kitchen with a laminate floor, a white fridge, and a gas stove.

"Ma, look who's here!" Salut said in Cambodian, and my grandmother, who was busy cooking, turned around.

She was a tiny lady, and I stood about half a foot taller than her as I hugged her. She said something in Cambodian as her eyes brimmed with tears. I was smiling and nodding and trying to process everything that was coming at me. Culture shock is what it was. The smells, the sounds, and the sight of a kitchen and home with all brown people felt like water trapped deep below the ground. I knew it was all there—the heritage, the culture, and, yes, the language— but I couldn't quite tap into it; it was as if I was hearing muffled noises on the other side of a wall.

Salut translated, back and forth, between me and my grand-mother, until she remembered that she was in the middle of cooking. As she cooked, she'd turn around every now and then and look at me with eyes squinted, scrunchy cheeks, and a wide, cheeky smile with some missing teeth. She would make a noise, something like *ehhhyah*, and mutter something to Salut or Aunt Saly—who was a year and a half younger than me, but fluent in Cambodian—before turning back around and continuing her cooking.

Food was another language that my grandmother spoke— and this one I could understand. She fed me. I ate. And if my plate was empty of jasmine rice, she'd pile on another plate's worth, as if to declare the abundance of her love. Her cooking spoke to me of home and belonging.

She served us *prahok ktis*, a common Cambodian dish with mashed and salty fermented fish, minced pork, palm sugar, and coconut cream, served with slices of cucumber, raw Thai eggplant, green beans or long beans, and rice. The first bite I took brought me back to a simpler time. It was pungent. Salty. Tart on the tip of your tongue. A hint of spice from the chili peppers. A perfect pairing with some greens and rice.

After we'd made short work of that dish, we went out onto the patio and feasted on *lok lak* and rice—slices of beef marinated in a combination of oyster sauce, fish sauce, soy sauce, and sugar, and other ingredients that elude me—stir-fried and served on a bed of romaine lettuce and tomato, with hard-boiled eggs.

After dinner, I hung out with Saly and Salut in Salut's room, and just like that, we were those same kids back in Portland who had played with matches and tried to sneak into my uncles' rooms. But more than fifteen years had passed, and our paths had diverged. In some ways, parts of who we were then, aspects of our personalities and our temperaments, had survived all those years. In other ways, we had outgrown and shed some of them. Saly was working two serving jobs and saving, while Salut was working on a physics degree at the University of San Diego. Physics—how it straddled the line between hard science, theory, and mystery—intrigued me, and gave us something to talk about.

Hanging out like we used to for the first time in over a decade seemed like the right moment to tell them, "Hey Salut and Saly, I'm gay."

"No way, nuh-uh," I can remember vividly Salut replying in disbelief. "You? I couldn't even tell!"

Saly had a different reaction similar to an *I told you so* or *Ha! I knew it.*

Together, we strategized about how to tell the rest of the family. There was no trepidation or worry about any adverse reactions from the rest of the family. In a very different manner than my experience with B-Denny and my Hannaford co-workers, they wanted to protect me and give me some control over the process. So we decided that Saly would be the right one to tell my maternal grandmother, our matriarch. She didn't exactly clue us in on when, but when I was helping my grandmother grind peanuts with a mortar and pestle, I saw her look at me with a mischievous grin, I knew it was happening and I was ready.

Saly looked at my grandmother with a glint in her eye and spoke to her in Khmer, saying something along the lines of "Ma! You know Marpheen likes …" as she formed an "O" with one hand and proceeded to put her pointer finger through multiple times. My grandmother looked at Saly, then at me and smiled and gestured for me to continue. Saly later told me that my grandmother had said that all that matters to her is that I am happy. When we told my birth mother, she could've cared less as long as she still could have grandchildren.

At some point later that night, I had the bright idea to Skype my siblings back home so that my grandmother could talk to them. My two younger siblings barely knew or recognized their aunt, uncles, or grandmother, but our grandmother certainly recognized them! Watching her eyes well up with tears as she looked at the faces of her grandchildren whom she hadn't seen in roughly fifteen years—or ten years, in Tanya's case—was both painful and cathartic.

I knew how it felt to be separated from my birth family and then to be reunited; I was living it at that very moment. But for my grandmother, it must have been on an entirely different level. She had seen many of her relatives and countrymen slaughtered. She had come to America seeking refuge and safety for herself and her children and future grandchildren. It makes me sad to imagine how hurt my grandmother must have felt to see her family ripped apart *again*. To lose her grandchildren—to be told she wasn't allowed to see us because it was traumatizing for us, was, for her, a new trauma. Watching her touch the screen and cry and speak in Cambodian tore me apart, and I was barely able to hold back my tears.

Toward the end of the call, she defaulted to the English words she knew.

"I love you … *yeay* loves you." By this time she was smiling, her cheeks bunched up and her eyes wet with tears.

It was a lot for all of us to process. In a way, we all relived some trauma that evening, both individual and collective. But we did it with the benefit of knowing that we were all okay, and many of us were together. That we'd all survived—perhaps a bit broken, bruised, and scarred, but still clinging to our family connection, and the hope that, someday perhaps, we could all be together again, in the same place.

The next day, after a light meal of a salty sardine sauce with sides of veggies and rice, I helped my grandmother run errands, getting some firsthand experience driving around the city.

San Diego is laid out in grid fashion, rather than the mishmash of streets intersecting at a million different angles and tightly packed, as if we were still riding around in a horse and buggy, like we find in Maine. San Diego also had a visibly superior bus system, for obvious reasons, being a bigger and more public transit-dependent city. I mused on this while listening to my grandmother babble away in Cambodian. I liked listening to the modulations of her voice even if I didn't understand what she was saying.

We stopped to fill a five-gallon tank with water and grab some ingredients at the Cambodian grocer. But the major stop was the Cambodian temple. Besides the kitchen, I could tell this was one of my grandmother's happy places.

The temple is a focal point for the Cambodian community, heavily frequented by the elderly to fill not only their spiritual needs but also their social needs—which is the case with churches, too. Religion provides community, a sense of belonging, a sense of home away from home—and a place to show off your long-lost grandson. Even if I did greet the first elder I met with a handshake rather than clasping my hands and giving a slight bow.

As my grandmother picked up some food at an open market at the temple, her friends tried to feed me. I fumbled greetings, blushed like a five-year-old, smiled, nodded, and laughed my way through conversations as my grandmother continued to introduce me and the elderly ladies smiled and spoke to me in Cambodian. Even though I didn't know what they were saying, I always had a knack for listening. And so I listened, intently, to inflections in their voices and changes in tone. I found myself nodding and smiling at various points as if I did understand. I think they must have noticed, because they continued to speak Cambodian to me as if they were willing it back into my conscious mind.

I liken it to something like phantom pain, but instead of feeling pain in toes that I no longer have, I have an inkling of understanding a language that now eludes me. Language is all around us, and we take it for granted. It is passed on to us. It evolves. It grows with us. It becomes an extension of us, the expression of our identity. Many kids like me who grew up in a bilingual or multilingual home understand this. The pressure from the dominant culture to speak only English, despite an increasingly interconnected world and a smorgasbord of languages, has the power to sever the extensions and expressions of ourselves through the language of our immigrant parents and grandparents. Although I have picked up a few more phrases here and there since this visit, it remains merely an echo of what it used to be.

In the two weeks that I was with my Cambodian family in California, we visited beaches, piers, and parks and did a lot of fishing—which, if you're familiar with Cambodian culture, is a hobby that seems to be akin to a cultural tradition.

One evening Salut and Saly and their friends asked me if I wanted to go fishing during the "grunion runs." I had no clue what a grunion run was, but pieced it together when they described it as a seasonal event when these silver fish ride the waves to shore to reproduce.

We went at night when the tides were highest. Armed with buckets, we scoured the beach for signs of the fish. At first, there were only a few here and there, but as the tide came in, swarms of silver fish flooded the beach. It was one of the most fun experiences I'd ever had, running beneath the moon and trying to catch the flashes of silver in my hands. With a little practice, I soon settled on a method, impressing Uncle Salut, who characteristically said, "Daaaaamn, Marpheen. You're good at this, huh?"

After we had a good amount of fish in our buckets, we rode home to show off our evening catch to my grandmother. She smiled and inspected the fish as we plopped the buckets down in the tiny kitchen. She knew just what dishes she could use them in.

For the Fourth of July, we headed to Mission Bay, where we had a barbecue, played games, and, as night fell, settled on the shore to watch the SeaWorld fireworks from across the bay. From our little patch of beach, I heard a mix of Cambodian and English. On one side of us, I heard Spanish. On the other side, Vietnamese. The clusters of people around us had packed different foods and played different games and different music while celebrating one America—a multicultural America.

Back home in Maine, every Fourth of July celebration I'd been to had involved mostly white people. But here, I was celebrating the holiday with people who looked like me. It gave a whole new meaning to what Independence Day actually represented—not America's past, but America's future. I felt the sense of America becoming something different, something more.

In that moment, America was the land that my refugee family had dreamed of as they fled the Khmer Rouge. Some Americans say that immigrants and refugees don't "share our values." They couldn't be more wrong. It is this mixing of languages, traditions, faiths, and foods, all in the name of liberty, freedom, and the American dream, that makes America worth fighting for and protecting.

People who uproot their lives to flee persecution based on their religion or political views are exactly the people who share the American values we hold so dear. They know the yearning and longing to breathe free. They understand equality and fair treatment. They, who fled tyrannical governments, despotism, corruption, and disorder, understand the importance of the rule of law. If there is any group of people who America should look to in reinvigorating our commitment to democracy, freedom, and equality, it is those who come to America in search of those very same things.

A true democracy doesn't exist in a static state. It is a necessary thing for a democracy by, for, and of the people to change with the people who constitute and participate in it. A truly healthy democracy exists in a state of progress and change. Given that the majority of students in US public schools today are from minority backgrounds, the multiracial democracy rising up could break new ground as a democracy that is bolstered by a diverse people with diverse religions, beliefs, cultures, and traditions. It will not come without bumps in the road, but if we each commit to guiding America along its path toward a multiracial democracy, while addressing our past sins and transgressions, it is exactly the America that our families dreamed of when they made the choice to leave their home countries.

That said, nefarious forces are at work that worry me. With every action there is an opposite, equal reaction. I see the rise of an emboldened white supremacist movement that endangers the progress we have made in the past century and a half. As we can observe from such horrific events as the Holocaust and the Khmer Rouge regime, it does not take a majority to capture the imaginations of a people and to lead them to commit genocide and crimes against humanity. The Nazis, for instance, won only roughly one-third of the popular vote in the 1933 elections in the Weimar Republic. By exploiting a fragile and chaotic government that had endured hyperinflation and took the global Great Depression especially hard, the Nazis, with the silence of a great number of Germans, moved to exterminate the Jews and other minorities.

Pol Pot and the Khmer Rouge did much the same in taking advantage of the chaos of postcolonial Cambodia, albeit with great help from the public relations opportunity that arose from American bombs along the Cambodian–Vietnam border. It is during our most absurd times, in the face of great adversity and calamity, that our baser instincts toward our own survival and the survival of those who are most like us take precedence above all else. Those dangerous beliefs arise in times of uncertainty and fear with promises that ultimately hinge on the death of hundreds, thousands, and millions of people.

What we have learned from the atrocities endured by our ancestors is that it is hopelessness that breeds hate and inhumanity. It's that feeling of powerlessness that leads us down the path toward apathy and acquiescence, giving silent consent—and thereby lending power—to the charlatans and soothsayers who promise the world but deliver only death.

PART FIVE

Mother

●◗◐○○

Reconnecting with my birth mother and father has been one of the most difficult things for me to think about and process.

I have had many fathers and mothers throughout my life. Many grandmothers and grandfathers, aunts and uncles, sisters and brothers. I am grateful for each one of them, and my love for them is not in question. In fact, if the opportunity arose where I would have to exchange my life for theirs, I can say without a doubt that I would rise to the occasion.

The very American idea of a nuclear family seems distant to me. I can understand the familial bond and attachment, but I also understand that this kind of bond is typically nurtured, nearly unbroken for years, without family separation and estrangement. It has taken a lot of time and emotional processing for me to arrive at and accept the fact that I simply don't have that bond with my own birth parents—or with my foster and adoptive parents.

When I arrived in San Diego, I was ready to reunite with my grandparents, uncles and aunts. But I was still very unsure of how reuniting with my birth mom would go.

I know some of you may be wishing for a happy reunion

scene, with tears shed and smiles throughout. But this isn't an episode of *Dr. Phil*. This is real life.

When Uncle Salut mentioned one day that my birth mom was going to stop by to see me, I felt a mix of emotions. I wasn't sure what to expect, what to do, how to proceed. Sure, I knew about the broad, popularized instructions—to hug and cry and talk it through and then forgive and forget. But when she walked in and saw me, and I saw her, I still wasn't quite sure what to feel. I had yet to process all of my emotions and thoughts about the past month I'd spent, reuniting with family members. All these years later, I'm still working on it.

So when my mother walked in, I resorted to the strong and silent mode that I had known and lived for much of my life—partly to guard my feelings, but also to show her that I was still the strong, protective son that she'd known all those years ago. The son who would try to fight with her abusive partners. The son she taught to make eggs and rice so that I could help feed my siblings. The son who endured her anger, her sadness, her absences. The son who tried his best to smile through it all. Strong and silent. Resilient and enduring.

Unlike long-lost family reunions the likes of which are shown on *Dr. Phil*, there was no crying and talking it through. Not only had about ten years passed, but we also had a language barrier. We couldn't communicate enough to even begin to fill in the divide that had grown between us, let alone build up the kind of bond that goes beyond blood and takes years and decades to nurture and grow.

If that seems sad, well … it is. Does it mean I love her any less? Not at all. She is my mother. I am her son. She gave me life and she tried her damn hardest. It hurt a lot to realize this at that moment, just as it was painful to learn how to accept the circumstances and conditions of life that had brought both of us to this point.

In many ways, the pain was born of guilt. Guilt that I couldn't turn back time and fix everything. That I hadn't done better to try to stay connected with my birth mom. The guilt that I just let life push me around and sweep me away. The guilt that I didn't fight harder. So many sources of guilt that poked like a thousand needles.

Part of healing means confronting these very difficult feelings and emotions. For years, I wrestled with this guilt and I was angry at times for being so fixated on it. But over the years following these reunions with family members, I learned to accept and learn from the circumstances and conditions of life that had brought me to this point. Anger, pain, and guilt turned to acceptance, which then gave rise to agency.

Yes, there are circumstances and conditions that affect how we live and love. But the beauty in life is that, no matter what, we have the power to act. The power to change the circumstances and conditions not only of ourselves, but of those around us, and those around them. That has been the healing part—the recognition of my own inherent power to chart and change the course of my own life, and to help chart and change the lives of others in a positive way. In essence, my struggle with time—with the past—is that it flows into the future. While it has its currents, and it ebbs and flows, we still have agency to chart our own course.

My birth mom and I didn't cry or have a deep conversation, but we did spend some time together eating, shopping, and going about our daily tasks. She would converse in broken English every now and then before switching back to Cambodian. A common theme that came up, as it had during our sporadic phone calls in past years, was that she was looking forward to the day when I would be able to buy a big house and have a good-paying job. She was looking forward to moving in with me and helping around the house, helping to care for my kids.

I realized this was culturally Cambodian. Households are often multigenerational, especially in America, where the two parents often work double shifts and overtime while the children are at home with the grandparents.

As I have alluded to in my writing about my godparents, I understood this and embraced it as a part of myself. This sense of duty to my family, to care for them, despite losing my connection to them for years. Somehow, I always felt like this was what was *supposed* to happen. But deep down, I also felt that my mom, of all people, deserved it the most, because of the hell she'd lived through.

This was also why I worked especially hard to not be angry or deeply sad around her. Sure, I would be annoyed sometimes by how clingy she could be, but I'd just gently remind her that I needed some space. At my core, this wasn't just a cultural thing or a Buddhist thing; for me, it was also recognizing the deep suffering and the soul wound she carries around with her.

I, too, carry deep suffering and a wounded soul, but it is of a different kind. While I have also lost loved ones, unlike my mother, I've been able to reconnect and reunite with many of them. She is not able to reunite with those she lost in the Cambodian genocide. She is unable to erase the violence and abuse carried against her, against her body, and against her family, friends, and fellow Cambodians.

Understanding these things about my mom was a huge step toward beginning the healing process within myself. The next step was recognizing that it wasn't my fault—that I was a kid, and I couldn't fix her—or anything about my situation growing up. The final step in my healing process was realizing that in my current-day life as a grown man, I have agency. I have the power to change the course of my future—not necessarily with one swift and single action, but with a series of actions and decisions, habits, and practices.

One thing I contemplate every now and then is how I can provide some peace to my mom, a survivor of the Cambodian genocide. She has already expressed what would make her happy, something that I have also struggled to find during my time growing up: a home. She has said that she wants to be a part of my life and the lives of my future kids. Beyond the cultural aspects of that request, I personally am willing to work toward providing this for her in the future, simply because I hope it will give her peace and make her no longer reliant on abusive, exploitative men.

This idea clashes in some ways with the white culture I grew up with in my adolescence. I am not saying that Americans absolutely don't let their retired parents move in and help with the grandkids, but I don't feel the same *expectation* is there; and in many ways, American seniors don't want to burden their kids by moving in. What I've often seen in America are seniors holding on for as long as they can to their homes until either the upkeep or their health demands a change. Then, most often, they transition into a nursing home or senior care facility. I think America makes it convenient, or tries to, for seniors and retirees to not be a burden to their kids. And culturally, I think this has become ingrained in our expectations and living habits.

I had a conversation with my adoptive mom upon returning to Maine, and told her that my birth mom had mentioned living with me in the future. My adoptive mom seemed surprised and said something along the lines of, "Oh, that must be hard on you," as if it was something I didn't want, while in fact it was something I'd thought about a lot and in many ways wanted. Assuming that I wouldn't want my birth mom to live with me felt like an attack on my birth family's culture. Like when I was in my teens and my adoptive, evangelical parents had made comments about how un-Christian the Chinese were, aborting babies with their one-child policy. I am not saying that the one-child policy isn't wrong, but rather that I felt annoyed because they seemed to be putting down Asians.

Reuniting with my birth mom after so many years didn't answer all of my questions or heal all of my wounds. Reunions like this are hard, especially when a language or cultural barrier exists. You can't make up for a decade in an hour, a day, a week, or even a year. This was the hard reality, knowing it would take a lifetime to answer the questions I had left. The most important thing was that I'd taken the first two steps in the healing process: understanding the pain and suffering my mother had endured, while also recognizing my powerlessness as a child, and that it wasn't my fault.

The task now is to fully realize my own agency and the power in my choices, and how it affects not only my life but the lives of those around me. I don't believe in complete free will, but I believe that each choice we make and action we take is a ripple in the great ocean of our existence. Some actions and choices send out ripples that turn into waves, while some simply fade away. Some may collide with others or get lost in the larger currents of time and being. Nevertheless, there is power in our choices, and collectively we can turn the tide of history, either for good or for bad.

This is the healing truth that I have come to know, and it applies to my relationship with my birth mother. Unlike during my childhood—when I was faced with life-changing choices like whether to leave or stay with my mother—I now have some degree of agency and a little more clarity. I didn't have to face a grave illness or be on the brink of death to realize that what I do with the time I have remaining on this Earth is precious. Those years of pain and heartache taught me that the past is permanent, but the future is not. And there is power in that knowledge.

All this is to say that despite being separated from my birth mother and my birth family during my childhood, it is now my choice to invest time in those relationships—to explore the part of me that is Cambodian, a survivor, and the son of survivors.

Father

● ◑ ◐ ○ ○

It is harder to wrap my head around my birth father, who has largely been out of the picture since I was born, except for a few visits while I was living with my godparents in San Diego in the early 1990s.

To be honest, I've never felt it normal to know where one's father is. The men I knew in my early childhood came and went. It was the women who raised us.

My first foster father, as I have mentioned, was for me the model father. Both sensitive and strong at the same time, without all the trappings of toxic masculinity. He is who I measure all men by.

I think it's the American idea of a nuclear family that drives the narrative that every child needs their father. Growing up in an evangelical family and going to a private Christian school, the message was that the nuclear family is God's ideal, the natural order of things. One man and one woman, together in holy matrimony, procreate and populate the Earth. In this model, the father is the king of his castle, and conservative values regarding privacy and gun rights come from this. We were taught that society's greatest ills have been born of the absence of family structure and a model father to provide order and stability for the family.

Of course, these ideals of the nuclear family, patriarchy, paternalism, and masculinity conveniently suppress the rights of women, slaves, immigrants, LGBTQ+ people, and other minorities. As a teenager, I soaked up these conservative values, and as I hid in the closet, they made me feel abnormal. I heard them loud and clear: I was gay because I was either sexually abused as a child or because I didn't have a father figure. It was an easy stereotype and generalization to make, because I *didn't* have a father figure in my early childhood. But gay kids come out to their fathers and mothers in "normal" households, just as they do when they have a single mom, a single dad, two moms, or two dads.

All of that aside, I was curious to know who my father was and what he was like. The chance came one afternoon when I was visiting my birth family during my 2012 trip.

I wasn't prepared for it at all. Uncle Salut simply said that my dad was coming over that afternoon to see me. My mind kind of went blank. I didn't know what to say or what to do to prepare.

When the moment finally came, it was something quite extraordinary, really.

My father walked in and said in broken English, "Hi. I am your dad."

He held a strange-looking stringed instrument, a Cambodian tro. Unlike a violin or a fiddle, it consists of a cylinder-shaped sound box at the bottom, with the open ends covered in snake skin or leather. A tall stick runs from this cylinder to the top, forming a handle where pegs are placed. Either one or two strings then run the length from these pegs to the sound box.

After looking me up and down (he is about six inches shorter than me), he sat down, picked up his bow, and began to play. And in that moment, he began to weep.

The rest of us stood or sat around in silence, drinking in the moment.

I was speechless. I didn't know what to say. Again, we faced the language barrier, but somehow, my father chose to speak in a language that we both understand: music. The music he played conveyed his emotions and more than twenty years of lost time in a way that words could not. I still struggle to describe it with words. What it was, was magic.

Although I harbored no resentment toward my birth father for not raising me, I had felt a certain amount of trepidation when it came to meeting him. And now that he was here, I didn't know what to feel. As soon as he started playing, all of my apprehension was washed away, replaced with a sense of peace—that everything was whole and good and forgiven.

My birth father had expressed his sincerest and deepest apology in the only way he knew how, and that was enough for me.

In return, I smiled. I hoped that was enough for him.

Epilogue
● ◗ ◖ ○ ○

You may feel unsatisfied with this ending, and if you do, I understand.

As I boarded the plane to fly back to Maine, some of my questions had been answered, but I found I still had many old— and some new—questions that remained. About family. About life. About what home means, and time and space. Questions about faith, humanity, and existence. But these are the questions each of us struggle with in our own ways as we live our lives.

Like the moon, with each phase, we are becoming more and more our full selves. And each time the cycle begins again, we are becoming fuller yet.

My winding road of self-discovery has opened my eyes and my heart in ways I could not have imagined had I remained stuck in the soul-starving dissonance of striving to be someone I was not, trying to feel things I didn't feel. My experience of reinventing myself anew, again and again, gave me a window into the lives of others: eyes to see their struggles, to read their emotions, and to try to understand and feel empathy and compassion.

One of the many gifts parents give their children are their names. My birth mother gave me the middle name *Sotear*, which means "compassion" in Khmer. My parents also gave me the name Chann, which means "moon." While I'm not one to put too much stock in fate, something as small as a name can have an impact on a life—on my life, and what I choose to do with the time I have here on Earth.

My devotion to justice and equality. My commitment to inclusion and equity. My deep desire to improve the human condition. These beliefs drive me to be a part of change, working on LGBTQ+ and immigrants' rights, and seeking knowledge and education in politics, law, and urban planning. I have helped to found and lead various LGBTQ+ and immigrant organizations, and I'm currently one of the leaders of the Cambodian Community Association of Maine—not only to serve my fellow Cambodians, but also in an effort to further reconnect with my heritage and learn the language, culture, and traditions of the family I was born into.

I have learned to not judge a book by its cover. To listen and learn with empathy. To treat others as I want to be treated.

When I sit across from my adoptive parents, who believe that being gay is a sin, I remind myself of the choice they made when they decided to reunite me and my younger siblings. That their faith helped lead them to that decision. And though their faith teaches them to view homosexuality as an abomination, and their faith community looks down on the gay community, I teach them nothing if I choose to cancel them and remove myself entirely from their lives. Instead I have chosen to be my full, authentic self, joining them at Thanksgiving and Christmas dinners and summer barbecues, giving them what might be their only opportunity to see a gay person living, loving, and breaking down the stereotypes and stigmas that help to reinforce negative beliefs about gay people.

When I grab a drink and talk with my high school friend Travis, I remember that there are more ways to love than just one. As boys who have become men, we've outgrown our childhoods and who we were back then. Despite falling out and going years without seeing or talking to each other, there is still hope that we can rekindle our friendship. Though it may never be the same, it will be something new. Something that takes work, cultivating, and care.

When I visit my Cambodian family, my birth parents, my *yeay*, and my other relatives, I recognize the turmoil, heartbreak, and trauma they've lived through. Despite it all, they persevere. They cling to family and to each other, no matter how broken they may be.

They have shown me how to do the same, to forgive, to live with grace and empathy. To reconnect with my Buddhist roots and to see that it is my duty and calling to help ease the pain and suffering in the world. Whether it's through my work as an elected official, activist, and leader in the Cambodian and immigrant community, helping a neighbor, or simply stopping long enough to listen to a stranger and hear their story, to understand and empathize with them, I feel I'm doing my part for the greater good of humanity.

All the people I know and love have taught me this. Living and growing up in Maine, in its cities and small towns, among its rivers and lakes, has taught me this much. And I have so much more of life to live, so much more love to give, and many more lessons to learn.

ACKNOWLEDGMENTS

●◗◗○○

In 2014, I stood before a crowd numbering in the hundreds. Folks from all different backgrounds and cultures, who spoke different languages, all were gathered and holding up signs that said #WeAreMaine. As I shared my story and how general assistance and other social safety net programs kept my childhood situation from deteriorating further, I felt heard and I felt that my story was making an impact as the crowd cheered and applauded.

Writing that speech was the first time I ever pieced my story together from start to finish, albeit from a 30,000-foot view to fit within the five minutes I had. In that moment and in the following days and weeks, my eyes were open to the idea that my story, all the twists and turns and intersections, could speak to people and make a difference.

Since then, I spent years writing, taking a step back and processing, reflecting, researching, corroborating stories, and reconnecting with the folks mentioned in my book. It took me years and years to keep coming back and revisiting my story, to keep adding to it, because part of this process was revisiting and digging up old traumas in a way that wouldn't open up old wounds that had healed over. But that very same process, as exhausting and emotionally draining as it was at times, helped to deepen my relationships and to deal with trauma that I didn't even know was there.

As I wrote earlier in this book, memory is a fickle thing. And when memory and time walk into a bar, things get fuzzy.

So first and foremost, I would like to thank my birth mother and grandmother, who endured and witnessed the Cambodian genocide firsthand. I thank my uncle Pheakdey Chum, who never failed to respond to my hundreds of inquiries, text and Facebook messages about this story or that one, or whether it was true that something had happened. I would also like to thank my first foster family, Mark and Debi Rix, for reliving both the moments of joy and sorrow that we shared together.

I am thankful for my adoptive parents, Bob and Tracy Berry, for reuniting me and my three younger siblings and taking that leap of faith. We have our disagreements, but what family doesn't? I would also like to thank Papa (Peter Berry) and Grammy Anita for being pillars of warmth and kindness.

And while there are too many friends, colleagues, acquaintances, and fellow community members to name, I would like to thank my village who believed in and encouraged me along the way: Sarah Holmes, Christopher O'Connor, Kelsea Dunham, Erin Swanson, Rachel Talbot Ross, Reza Jalali, Mary Allen Lindemann, Tae Chong, Carol Wishcamper, Daphne Felten-Green, Mary Bonauto and Jenny Wriggins, Amy Paradysz (who helped me edit and submit my manuscript), and Genevieve Morgan, all of those at Islandport Press, and so many more!

ABOUT THE AUTHOR

● ◗ ◗ ○ ○

Marpheen Chann, a second-generation Asian American, is a civil rights advocate, writer, speaker, and gay man. In 2014, Chann was the first of his biological and adoptive families to graduate college. He studied political science, philosophy, and economics at the University of Southern Maine, where he helped start the Queer Straight Alliance. He also co-founded the Cambodian Community Association of Maine, and still serves as its president. Chann has devoted his career to civil rights
and advancing diversity, inclusion, and acceptance in education, politics, and municipal government. He is a popular speaker and uses a mix of humor and storytelling to help others view topics such as racism, xenophobia, and homophobia through an intersectional lens. His service to Portland and the Cambodian community is a way of giving back and connecting to his ancestral roots. Chann lives in Portland and hopes to someday foster and adopt his own children. Until then, he's content being an uncle to upwards of ten nieces and nephews (including dogs and cats). *Moon in Full* is his first book.

@marpheenchann on Instagram, Twitter, and Facebook